EUROPE IN
THE NEW CENTURY

A **EUROPE** Magazine *Publication*

EUROPE IN THE NEW CENTURY

Visions of an Emerging Superpower

edited by
Robert J. Guttman

LYNNE
RIENNER
PUBLISHERS

BOULDER
LONDON

Published in the United States of America in 2001 by
Lynne Rienner Publishers, Inc.
1800 30th Street, Boulder, Colorado 80301
www.rienner.com

and in the United Kingdom by
Lynne Rienner Publishers, Inc.
3 Henrietta Street, Covent Garden, London WC2E 8LU

Library of Congress Cataloging-in-Publication Data
Europe in the new century / edited by Robert J. Guttman.
    p.   cm.
    Includes bibliographical references and index.
    ISBN 1-55587-852-0 (pbk. : alk. paper)
    1. Europe—Foreign relations—1989– 2. Europe—Economic conditions—
1945– 3. Europe—Politics and government—1989– 4. Twenty-first century—
Forecasts. 5. European Economic Community. I. Guttman, Robert J.
D2003.E95   2000
940.56—dc21   00-042554

British Cataloguing in Publication Data
A Cataloguing in Publication record for this book
is available from the British Library.

Printed and bound in the United States of America

        The paper used in this publication meets the requirements
⊗   of the American National Standard for Permanence of
        Paper for Printed Library Materials Z39.48-1984.

    5 4 3 2

For my daughter Margaret

Contents

Foreword

ROMANO PRODI

As the twenty-first century begins, the European Union (EU) is facing two unprecedented challenges: to redefine its own borders and to develop new methods of governance. Enlargement will increase Europe's weight in world affairs. First, however, we must get our internal structures right to prevent them from becoming overstretched, and we must carry out a thorough review of our policies, evaluating their impact and relevance.

The question of how much political integration is necessary for an enlarged Europe depends, of course, on what kind of Union we actually want. Is a market Europe with a common currency enough? Should the EU become a new superpower rivaling U.S. leadership? Or should we limit ourselves to being a civilian power that leads by good example? The EU has to develop a sense of its own identity, a vision of its place in the world, and this should be done before enlargement and before the task becomes even more difficult. Of course, applicant countries should be closely associated with this process.

To cope with the political and economic challenges of globalization, we will need a substantial amount of political integration at the EU level. At the same time, to facilitate the emergence of a better global governance system, strong regional entities similar to the EU will have to be created elsewhere. A strong, multilateral system of global governance is not only in our vital European interest: it is also crucial to peacefully solving the world's upcoming conflicts over climate change, migration, nuclear proliferation, and resource scarcities.

To exert true global leadership, the EU must speak in a coordinated way. Only then will its leadership be both credible and effective. To that end, however, the member states of an enlarged Union must settle their internal differences, develop a common identity, and actually get down to joint action. We certainly need strong institutions at the EU level, but we also need member states prepared to think and act for the Union as a whole. All levels of government—from "Brussels" to national governments, local authorities, and civil society—must be involved in shaping, evaluating, implementing, and monitoring our policies in the new century. *Europe in the New Century: Visions of an Emerging Superpower* provides a balanced look at the new Europe and the European Union.

—Romano Prodi,
President,
European Commission

Acknowledgments

This book is the result of the combined effort of many individuals. I am especially grateful to Søren Søndergaard, former acting director of press and public affairs at the Delegation of the European Commission in Washington, who had a vision for the book and promoted the idea to the European Union, which provided the funding.

Thanks to Sue Burdin, my assistant, for the excellent work she did in organizing everyone involved in the book and for preparing the manuscript for publication. Angeliki Papantoniou from Greece and Terhi Kiviranta from Finland also provided valuable assistance conducting research.

The cooperation of the European Commission's Washington delegation is greatly appreciated. Special thanks to the delegation's former ambassador, Hugo Paemen, and to Willy Hélin, director of press and public affairs, for their support.

Many thanks to Chris Patten, European commissioner for external affairs, Etienne Reuter, head of the European Commission's Hong Kong delegation, and Ove Juul Jørgensen, head of the EC's Tokyo delegation for their invaluable contributions.

I am very grateful to all the writers who contributed and to the journalists who conducted the interviews. A special thanks to Massimo Capuano, Robin Cook, Elisabeth Guigou, Jean-Claude Juncker, Anna Lindh, Emma Marcegaglia, Peter Mitterbauer, George Papandreou, Mary Robinson, Stefan Röver, and Peter Sutherland, who agreed to be interviewed for the book; and to Europe's visionaries of tomorrow—

the young people from each of the fifteen European Union countries who spoke out on what it means to be European in the new century.

We also would like to acknowledge Lynne Rienner, Sally Glover, and Lesli Athanasoulis at Lynne Rienner Publishers.

— Robert J. Guttman

Introduction

Robert J. Guttman

Europe in the New Century: Visions of an Emerging Superpower looks at the twenty-first century. Unlike the majority of books published on Europe that concentrate on the past, especially on the wars of the twentieth century, *Europe in the New Century* looks ahead to present a view of what Europe might look like in the next twenty years.

We certainly do not have a crystal ball or any other great psychic powers, but we have assembled the best journalists working in Europe today and asked them to look ahead in their respective areas of expertise to forecast what Europe might look like down the not-too-distant road.

The key "visions" of the book come from the young people of Europe today, who will become the leaders of a more united Europe in the new century. We have asked a person from each of the fifteen European Union nations to write about being European at the start of the twenty-first century. From students to schoolteachers to computer consultants to journalists, each of our "typical" Europeans presents an episode from his or her life that captures one way of being European.

The final chapter contains exclusive interviews with the leaders of Europe today, who present their "visions" for the Europe of tomorrow. Ranging from heads of state to government ministers to corporate CEOs to entrepreneurs, today's leaders envision the Europe of tomorrow—the Europe of the new century.

Lionel Barber, the news editor of London's *Financial Times* and its former Washington bureau chief, starts off the first part of the book, "Politics," with a witty and humorous look at Europe in the year 2020.

1

We see a Europe confronting some of the same problems of today, but with new answers.

Solange Villes, a journalist from Paris, sets the tone of the book in Chapter 2 with a background on the history of the European Union from its beginnings in the 1950s until today. She profiles the European Commission, the European Parliament, and the Council of Ministers.

Europe is definitely not yet of one mind politically, culturally, or otherwise at the start of the new century. In Chapter 3, Reginald Dale, columnist for the *International Herald Tribune,* analyzes the multitude of beliefs, ideas, and philosophies that make up Europe today. Leif Beck Fallesen, editor in chief of the Danish business daily *Borsen,* looks at the future of the nation-state in Chapter 4.

Martin Walker, a former European correspondent for *The Guardian* and author of numerous books, sketches the outline of an enlarged Europe in Chapter 5. In the new century, more and more countries will be applying to join the European Union. From Poland to Malta to Estonia, the new Europe will be growing rapidly.

Part 2 of the book concerns foreign policy, and Martin Walker leads off the section in Chapter 6 with a forward look at Europe's future foreign policies. Christopher Patten, the European commissioner for external relations and former governor of Hong Kong, presents an overview of the European Union's foreign relations for the first few years of the new century in Chapter 7. Circling the globe, Patten moves from Europe's relations with the United States to its interactions with the smallest African countries.

In Chapter 8 Lionel Barber lays out the New Transatlantic Agenda of the European Union and the United States. Despite the newspaper and television headlines that make much of the trade disputes between the EU and the United States, the transatlantic relationship is one of the most durable and profitable in the world.

Many European and Asian nations have been meeting regularly since 1996 in an association called the Asia-Europe Meeting (ASEM) to coordinate their political and economic agendas. In Chapter 9 I discuss ASEM and, more specifically, the European Union's policies with regard to China, Hong Kong, and Japan.

David Lennon, formerly a bureau chief in Cairo and Jerusalem for the *Financial Times,* writes in Chapter 10 about Europe's growing relations with the Middle East and how Europe complements the United States in the Middle East peace talks.

In Chapter 11 Martin Walker analyzes European Union and Russian relations in the new century and finds that Russia's internal economic problems cast a shadow over its foreign policies. Walker also provides an overview of related security issues, including Bosnia and Kosovo, North Atlantic Treaty Organization (NATO) enlargement, and a new defense structure for the European Union.

The European Union has become the leading provider of humanitarian assistance in the world. David Lennon concludes Part 2 of the book by commenting on the EU's various development assistance programs and whether they are achieving their goals.

Turning to the euro in Part 3, "The European Marketplace," Lionel Barber, one of the world's leading experts on Europe's new single currency, explains exactly what will happen in the next few years as the euro replaces other currencies. The introduction of the euro has been one of the most significant events in Europe's economic history. Barber shows why it is succeeding and why the euro is already the second-most-used currency in the world behind the dollar.

Europe is fast becoming a leader in a number of high-tech industries. In Chapter 15 Bruce Barnard, a journalist based in London and former European correspondent for the *Journal of Commerce,* profiles the new businesses and technologies of Europe, from Nokia in Finland to SAP in Germany. Barnard also informs us in Chapter 14 about the success of the single market and what final steps will be taken in the twenty-first century to complete this ambitious project.

Susan Ladika, a reporter based in Vienna, talks in Chapter 16 about how Europe is creating jobs and new employment in the new century. Using Ireland as one of several business case studies, she shows how a nation once considered to be on the fringes of Europe can now draw on new technologies and a young, educated workforce to compete with the biggest nations around the world.

Europe in the New Century: Visions of an Emerging Superpower provides an intriguing vision of what a superpower will look like in the next twenty years, one that is quite different from the views held in the mid-twentieth century. In the future, the term *superpower* will have meanings in addition to "military power." In the new century *superpower* will refer to groups like the European Union, which will have strong market economies; young, highly educated workers who are savvy in high technology; and a global vision. The young Europeans speaking out in Chapter 17 flesh out this new definition of *superpower.*

The European Union is bringing together a diverse group of countries, yet each nation is definitely keeping its individual identity. European countries are combining their resources in many areas in order to be more competitive in the ever-increasing global marketplace. Although the Europe of tomorrow may be more unified in many areas of commerce, economics, and politics, cultural differences will still exist.

We are on uncharted ground as we explore the new century. It will be vastly different because of technological breakthroughs but also quite similar, in many respects, to the Europe of today. People will still consider themselves Irish, French, German, Italian, or Spanish, but more and more they will begin to feel a common European identity in addition to their national citizenship.

In the last section, our visionaries' predictions and thoughts on the new century provide the theme for a unique book, one that indicates a fascinating, prosperous, and, we hope, very peaceful twenty-first century.

Part 1

POLITICS

I

Europe in the New Century: A Scenario

Lionel Barber

In the autumn of 2020, the heads of government of thirty European countries gathered in Berlin to sign the treaty founding the Confederation of the United States of Europe. The ceremony in the Reichstag opened to a swirling rendition of Beethoven's "Ode to Joy" and continued with a keynote address by Tony Blair, elder statesman. As delegates raised their glasses of pink champagne, Blair posed an uncomfortable question: Would the new confederacy be capable of wielding the political power commensurate with its economic weight?

This same question had plagued Europe ever since Jean Monnet, Robert Schuman, Paul-Henri Spaak, and the other founding fathers had launched the process of European unification after the end of World War II—a political experiment without precedent that sought once and for all to end the nationalist rivalries that had plagued the continent for centuries.

In many respects, "Europe" had been a spectacular success—reconciliation between France and Germany, the launch of the single European market, and the introduction of the euro in 1999. Together, these achievements had helped to build a new European polity that rivaled China, Japan, and the United States in terms of economic power.

Yet national pride, a laborious decisionmaking process in Brussels, and a painful inferiority complex in the face of U.S. military and technological prowess had combined to prevent the European Union from living up to its name and realizing its true potential on the international stage.

The EU had also been hampered by the separate challenge of absorbing new members from the former Soviet bloc. This historic process had been gradual, starting with the Czech Republic, Poland, and Hungary in 2005. Slovenia, Malta, and the divided island of Cyprus followed in 2008. The Baltic states, Slovakia, and Switzerland followed in 2010. In 2015, Bulgaria and Romania entered the EU. Three years later, the admission of Croatia brought the total membership of the EU to thirty countries.

The entry of Croatia was a defining moment. Not only had the EU doubled its size in twenty years, but also it had extended its geopolitical reach into the Balkans, a regional powder keg that had exploded with the breakup of Yugoslavia in 1991. (The traditionalists argued that Slovenian entry was hardly a precedent since Slovenia was little more than an annex of Austria.) The admission of Croatia (as well as Bulgaria, once an outpost of the Ottoman Empire) raised a host of difficult questions.

First, there was the issue of where Europe's boundaries really lay. Was it conceivable that the European Union should seek to admit other members of the former Yugoslav federation, including former war-torn Bosnia-Herzegovina and newly democratic Serbia? Was Albania, a bandit statelet still recovering from the excesses of fifty years of Stalinist rule, a credible future member of the Union? And what about the perennial question of Turkey's relationship with the Union, a matter even more pressing since its formal alliance with the Turkic-speaking Central Asian states?

Second, the governance of the Union had become even more complicated with enlargement, despite regular efforts by the member states to address these matters through piecemeal reforms agreed at so-called intergovernmental conferences (IGCs). These issues included the size of the European Commission, the right of member states to their own individual commissioner, the balance of power between small and large states in the decisionmaking Council of Ministers, and the size and precise role of the European Parliament.

Third, there was a broader political dilemma at the heart of the EU. Governments had ceded wide-ranging powers to EU institutions without ever trusting them to use these powers. The traditional European method had been to promote economic integration in order to obtain political objectives that had remained deliberately obscure. The elites orchestrating this process argued that the method was justified because no one had an interest in frightening electorates; but the critics countered that the approach was an affront to the principles of accountability, democracy, and popular legitimacy.

Economic and monetary union (EMU) was the last hurrah for the Monnet method for building Europe by stealth. Surrendering control over the money supply and interest rate policy was a breathtaking concession for the nation-states of Western Europe. From January 1, 1999, decisions in this area lay in the preserve of the European Central Bank (ECB) in Frankfurt. Despite several hiccups—notably the dollar-euro crisis of 2005, which led to a reconfiguration of the international financial system and the brief suspension of Italian membership in the euro zone in 2010—EMU had been a success measured in terms of economic growth in the euro zone and the use of the euro as a reserve currency.

By 2015, however, the need to define the EU's goals and establish clearer boundaries between the supranational institutions (European Commission, European Court, and ECB) had become more acute than ever. At this point, Tony Blair, acting in concert with the leaders of France, Germany, Poland, and Spain, called for a new constitutional settlement in Europe. It was time, he declared, for a constitutional convention along the lines of the historic gathering in Philadelphia that produced the Constitution of the United States of America.

Blair was better placed than most of his fellow European leaders to put the case. He was Europe's longest-serving prime minister, a man of ceaseless energy who had worked with single-minded determination to end his country's age-old ambivalence toward the continent. At home, he could also point to his own constitutional settlement in Britain, which had produced a peaceful and prosperous federation of England, Wales, Northern Ireland, and a Scotland that was independent in everything but name.

Blair offered his own contribution to the debate in the Euro "Federalist Papers" circulating at the time, through an essay entitled "EUrope: My Way Forward." His blueprint borrowed heavily from Franco-German thinking in the early 1990s. In crude terms, Blair declared that the challenge was how to reconcile the EU's commitment to a "wider Europe" through expansion to the east with a "deeper Europe" that had inevitably resulted from the launch of the single currency.

This tension between the "wider Europe" and the "deeper Europe" had become obvious in the early years of the twenty-first century. After the entry of Britain, Denmark, and Sweden in 2002–2003, the euro zone comprised all fifteen members of the Union. The advantage was that divisions between the original eleven-strong euro club built around France and Germany and the four outsiders no longer existed; but the disadvantage was that EMU raised the prospect of a new "Velvet Curtain" dividing prosperous western and poorer eastern members.

The gulf between east and west had become apparent in the wake of the agreement in 2005 on the terms of the first EU enlargement to the east, encompassing the Czech Republic, Hungary, and Poland. Thanks to strong pressure from the Mediterranean countries led by France, Spain, and Portugal, the fifteen heads of government had insisted on lengthy transition periods to institute the Common Agricultural Policy (CAP) and allow for free circulation of farm products. This delay was designed partly to protect higher-cost producers in the west, but it would also spread out the exorbitant cost of extending the generous CAP price supports to Poland, where one-quarter of the working population derived their income from the land.

Other lengthy transition periods specified in this agreement covered environmental policy—where the eastern Europeans were still struggling to clean up the pollution of the communist era—and the free movement of labor. Here those countries bordering the former Soviet bloc—notably Austria and Germany—had shown themselves to be ultra-orthodox. They insisted that controls should remain in place for ten years in order to guard against the influx of cheap labor, especially in the professional sector. Their arguments were infinitely strengthened by the provisions of the Schengen Treaty, which allowed free circulation of people among signatory countries but created a uniformly strict control on entrants from outside this new zone of "freedom, security, and justice."

Blair had always been a fervent advocate of eastern enlargement, but he was well aware that British motives in this area were invariably suspect. Memories of Margaret Thatcher were still strong, and many thought that Blair, a self-confessed admirer of the Iron Lady, was still intent on using enlargement to dilute broader political integration and turn Europe into little more than a free trade zone. Blair was determined to lay this particular ghost to rest as part of a wider constitutional settlement between Britain and Europe and within Europe itself.

His first premise was that a "core" Europe existed between members of the euro zone: that is, the fifteen member states of the EU plus Switzerland and Norway. For more than fifteen years, most of these countries had developed a fairly sophisticated macroeconomic policy, in which the independent professionals running the European Central Bank cooperated with the elected politicians meeting in the Council of Economic and Financial Ministers (ECOFIN) forum. The biggest institutional step came when member states agreed to allow one political representative to sit alongside the president of the ECB and speak for the euro zone in a new G5 forum that also included the United States, Japan, China, and Russia. For Britain, France, Germany, and Italy, participants in the old G7 arrangement, this concession signaled the birth of a genuine "monetary Europe."

Blair's second premise was that the new, wider Europe had to become more flexible. This would require the imposition of minimum obligations on members in key areas to preserve the coherence of the Union, such as competition policy, external trade, the single market, and the signatory of treaties with other countries. But it would also require a continuation of the policy of "subsidiarity"—the devolution of decisionmaking to the lowest appropriate level—which had contained irredentist tendencies in northern Italy, Catalonia, Corsica, and Scotland. In Blair's view, indefinite subsidiarity would require signatories to the constitutional convention to enumerate the powers that the states would delegate to the Union, buttressed by a Bill of Rights.

His third premise was that the Union had to turn the much-vaunted Common Foreign and Security Policy into a credible instrument of power projection. For years, the Europeans had ducked this challenge by pursuing their own narrow interests and relying on the U.S. military presence as an insurance policy in times of crisis. But after the bloody intervention in the former Serbian province of Kosovo by the North Atlantic Treaty Organization (NATO) and a less than impressive European response to the Iraqi-inspired collapse of the Saudi Arabian kingdom in 2005, the U.S. Congress insisted on a substantial reduction in U.S. troops in Europe and a more active European role in shouldering the security burden. The advances in electronic and satellite warfare made it even easier to argue in favor of a sharp reduction in U.S. troop levels, which had fallen to 25,000 by 2010.

These views found widespread support among European leaders. Jean-Marie Colbert, the French president, was a firm advocate of a European "defense identity" that would harness European technological prowess to a grander goal of a "political Europe," thus helping France defend its traditional interests in stabilizing its southern flank against an inflow of immigrants from North Africa while containing the power of a united Germany and its economic surrogates in the east.

Edmund Stoiber, the aging German chancellor, was a reluctant convert to the vision of a "political Europe." Long a *bête noir* among Europe's political elite because of his aggressive defense of his native Bavaria against the intrusive power of Brussels, Stoiber had mellowed in his later years, especially after his upset election victory in 2006. But he was unwilling to be constrained by an exclusive Franco-German alliance and keen to develop closer relations with Britain, whose economic success he envied. In the end, his own fear of repeating the mistakes of the twentieth century—when a revanchist Germany found itself caught between France and Russia—proved too strong to resist, and he went along with Blair.

For Italy and Spain, the appeal of "political Europe" was as strong as ever. Fifty years before, successive Christian Democratic governments in Italy had used the then European Community to provide political cover for the economic reforms necessary to break the gridlock caused by the standoff between the communists and the right. Spain, too, had invoked the perspective of European Union membership to assist in the transition to democracy after the Franco regime. So it was hardly surprising that these two medium-sized powers were ready to join in a British initiative aimed at producing a lasting constitutional settlement.

The decisive argument, however, was that individual member states needed to cooperate more closely in order to exercise influence in a world dominated by regional groupings. These included the United States and its North American Free Trade Area, which encompassed most of Latin America; the awesome power of China; a resurgent Japan supported by its links with the Southeast Asian prosperity zone; a shrunken but still powerful Russia; and greater Turkey (which included most of the Central Asian states that were formerly members of the Soviet Union).

The question was: How do leaders reconcile their inchoate desire for a "political Europe" with the public's lingering attachment to the nation-state? Stoiber argued that people had to think in terms of a multiple identity for the ordinary citizen, which would encompass regional, national, and European characteristics. Thus, a Bavarian attending the World Cup would wear his short leather trousers and feather cap and would cheer for the German football team inside the stadium, but, of course, he would pay for his match ticket in euros.

From Blair's vantage point, Europe would divide into concentric circles. The first circle would embrace the members of the euro zone, with their high degree of macroeconomic policy coordination; the second circle would include the members of the Union waiting to join EMU but already part of the core in terms of their adherence to the single market and to the *acquis communautaire* (the rules and obligations of membership); and the third circle would embrace those countries willing but unable to join the Union.

The next step was to reorganize the Council of Ministers so that the Union was not held hostage by the national veto, especially by so-called microstates such as Malta or filibustering states such as Greece. In essence, this involved trading the national veto for a generous voting allowance in the Council of Ministers, which would maintain the delicate balance of power between small and large countries, and offering the small states a reasonable chance of having proper representation in the European Commission (now reduced to fifteen commissioners).

By far the most difficult task was to reach agreement on a new European constitution. Many predicted it would be an impossible task to reconcile the interests of countries with different languages, cultures, and traditions. Indeed, it took two years of debate among the finest minds on the continent to agree on an acceptable definition of *federalism*. The Bill of Rights was no less contentious, though Blair's argument that delegates should draw inspiration from the Declaration of Independence struck a powerful chord.

The final document was mercifully short and readable. Instead of the impenetrable Maastricht and Amsterdam treaties, the public was offered a document that approximated plain English (and French, German, Italian). It gave some hope to those in favor of a more centralized approach to decisionmaking, but it came down broadly in favor of "nation-states' rights."

The new Confederation of the United States of Europe was the successor to the European Union. But there were many who said it resembled the Holy Roman Empire, and they comforted themselves in the knowledge that, though far from perfect, this arrangement lasted longer than most.

2

The Path to Unity

SOLANGE VILLES

The European Union is the most unusual international organization of modern times. The uniqueness of European integration is that sovereign nations delegate their sovereignty and exercise it jointly. In the early 1950s, the delegation of sovereignty—by the original six founding member states, Belgium, France, Germany, Italy, Luxembourg, and the Netherlands—was confined to coal and steel. Today, this "shared sovereignty" encompasses all sectors of economic activity in fifteen EU nations in a single market with 370 million citizens.

The European institutions—mainly the European Commission, the Council of Ministers, and the European Parliament—have been created to foster the goals of European integration (see Appendix at end of chapter). The smaller countries, not surprisingly, have traditionally been at the vanguard of European integration because it empowered them to decide together with the bigger nations.

The European Union is not yet the United States of Europe, and the crucial question for all politicians is: Will it ever be and does it have to be? Neither is it a federation or a confederation of states. It has no military power and no president or government as such. The Union has a very limited budget, which barely exceeds 1 percent of the joint gross domestic product of its present fifteen member states.

Its "constitution" comprises several treaties that have confirmed and consolidated its progress toward economic and political integration. At the same time, the EU is much more than a vast free trade zone. The European Union has supranational institutions that take decisions that are legally binding for its member states.

Now that the single currency, the euro, is a fact, European leaders face both the greatest challenge and the greatest opportunity of their lives: to achieve in the earliest stages of the twenty-first century the political unification of Europe. These leaders are closer than ever to fashioning a political Europe that would fulfill its responsibilities in defense and security, that would be embodied by a president, and that would be able to translate its economic clout into a real political power on the world stage.

On May 9, 1950, Robert Schuman, minister of foreign affairs of France, formally launched a proposal to combine coal and steel production between Germany and France. Schuman claimed that his plan would "lay the first concrete foundations of the European federation which is indispensable to the maintenance of peace." "Europe," he added, "will not be built at once, or as a single whole: it will be built by concrete achievements which first create de facto solidarity."[1]

On April 18, 1951, France, Germany, Italy, Belgium, the Netherlands, and Luxembourg signed the treaty in Paris creating the European Coal and Steel Community (ECSC). This first truly European institution was focused on a "narrow front"—coal and steel, the two vectors of industrial power that had been at the heart of the casus belli between France and Germany. The UK declined to join, refusing to give up any bit of sovereignty to a supranational organization. At the same time, the ECSC provided for a quantum leap in terms of European integration because coal and steel were going to be managed on a day-to-day basis by a "high authority," the first really "supranational" European institution. Its decisions were legally binding for all partners, and last but not least, it secured its financial independence with a budget financed through a levy on the steel and coal produced by each member country.

The idea for the ECSC originally came from an extraordinary Frenchman named Jean Monnet. Monnet, often called the "Father of Europe," believed that controlling the raw materials of war (coal and steel) was key to a successful reconciliation in Europe. In 1952, the ECSC was established with Monnet as its first president. His genius was to combine imaginative and almost utopian ideas with highly calibrated blueprints for institutions that would tackle the several practical problems facing Western European governments. Monnet, who was unique in that he became a major political force without ever running for elective office, served for only three years, after which he resigned to campaign for further exercises in integration.

The six founding countries of the ECSC also worked on a far more ambitious project—taking responsibility for their own security. By the summer of 1954, five out of six member states of the ECSC had ratified the European Defense Community. On August 30 of that same year, a rare coalition of Gaullists, communists, and half the radicals and so-cialists in the French Assembly definitively buried the project.

THE TREATY OF ROME: THE COMMON MARKET IS BORN

The six founding countries continued to move toward economic inte-gration. In 1957 they decided to create a single market and to manage in common the nascent peaceful use of nuclear energy. Two treaties were signed on March 27, 1957, in Rome, one creating the European Eco-nomic Community and the other launching the European Atomic En-ergy Community (EURATOM). Common policies were established in the fields of agriculture, transportation, and antitrust policies; customs duties began to be dismantled; and the four fundamental freedoms were guaranteed: free movement of persons, goods, capital, and services.

In its preamble, the Treaty of Rome recalls the necessity to create "an ever closer union among the people of Europe." Fifteen years later, as Denmark, the United Kingdom, and Ireland were about to join the original six founding members of the Community in Paris at the end of 1972, the six reiterated their wish "to transform before the end of the present decade and fully respecting the previously signed treaties the entire relationship between the member states into a Eu-ropean Union." At the time, the Europeans had elaborated their first concrete and sophisticated project of economic and monetary union (EMU) in the so-called Werner Report, named after the finance min-ister of Luxembourg.

Portugal and Spain formally requested accession to the Community in 1977. And in June 1979, European citizens for the first time directly elected their representatives to the European Parliament. The Commu-nity remained attractive to nonmembers, and in the 1980s the European Economic Community continued to grow as Greece, emerging from years of a military regime, joined the EC as its tenth member state on January 1, 1981, and Spain and Portugal finally joined in 1986.

In the mid-1980s—helped by a spectacular drop in oil prices—the European engine moved toward integration. Jacques Delors, the new president of the European Commission, offered a "new solidarity deal" to the twelve European Community members. Delors set a major goal: create a single market without internal borders by January 1, 1993. In addition, he offered to help less developed European regions (Ireland, Spain, Portugal, and Greece) to catch up with the others through an unprecedented financial support program destined to achieve European solidarity between "rich and poor."

For the first time in the history of the European Community, the Treaty of Rome (the European Constitution of sorts) was being given a new impetus. The Single European Act, signed on February 17, 1986, improved the decisionmaking process of the Community by extending the use of majority voting among its members. It had also, modestly, extended the power of the European Parliament.

The new treaty also gave a push to political integration: political cooperation that had developed between the member states in a pragmatic way became one of the prerogatives of an emerging political Europe. Taking advantage of the new momentum created by the single market, Jacques Delors convinced German chancellor Helmut Kohl and French president François Mitterrand that a single market without a single currency would be like an acrobat without a safety net.

Germany was ready to "sacrifice" its strong deutsche mark on the altar of a single European currency. In exchange for this concession, however, Kohl needed and wanted a quid pro quo: a federal model for Europe supported by political integration. The now twelve member states of the European Community agreed to revise the treaty again, which culminated in a marathon final meeting in the little town of Maastricht, Holland, in December 1991.

In the meantime, history had taken unforeseen leaps: the Berlin Wall was splintered into tiny pieces, and the Soviet Union was in shambles. Some partners in Europe feared that Germany might favor the geographic eastern European hinterland and loosen its ties with the rest of the community.

FROM MAASTRICHT TO AMSTERDAM: THREE STEPS FORWARD, TWO STEPS BACK

The Maastricht Treaty officially entered into force on November 1, 1993: the European Union was officially born. The treaty did provide for a series of steps forward, the most obvious being the single currency that saw the light of day on January 1, 1999. The Maastricht Treaty also paved the way for a Common Foreign and Security Policy as well as a common policy in the field of immigration and asylum. It broadly sketched the contours of a European defense policy, provided for cooperation among member states' justice and police forces, and created a European citizenship: nationals of member states are allowed to vote or to be elected in the country where they live for both the European Parliament and local elections.

But there is a flip side to the coin. Transfer of sovereignty in the "new" sectors of foreign and security policy, as well as in home affairs, is very limited. Europe's national leaders did not accept the idea that European institutions were entitled to interfere in such sensitive sectors of national sovereignty. And member states may well have a point: in their present format, European institutions—the European Commission and the Council of Ministers—do not qualify, both in terms of staff and logistics, for such missions.

At closer range, however, a more thorough scrutiny revealed another valid explanation, namely a clash between France and the United Kingdom about Europe's role in defense matters. Former French president François Mitterrand was in favor of a broader autonomy for Europe both inside NATO, through the establishment of a European defense pillar, and in the framework of the European Union, through its merger with the Western European Union (WEU), as a forerunner to a future "military arm" of Europe. Yet the UK, a stalwart supporter of the Atlantic partnership in these matters, would never have accepted any European military intervention outside the "American umbrella."

THE DANISH HICCUP: THE WAY TO MULTISPEED EUROPE

Beyond the feuds among politicians, the Maastricht Treaty's honest attempt to modernize the Rome Treaty was received in a very lukewarm fashion by the European public.

The treaty also highlighted the widening gap between citizens and the political class in Europe. The Danes contested European integration in the clearest way: on June 2, 1992, they refused the Maastricht Treaty in a popular referendum. The vote sent shock waves through the political establishment across Europe. Every European leader held his or her breath because the vox populi in France, later in the year, also had to decide on Maastricht. On September 20, the "ayes" made it, but only by a very narrow margin.

The Danish hiccup had an aftermath. On October 16, that same year, the European summit adopted a separate statement about a Europe closer to its citizens, followed in December by a decision that granted Denmark a series of derogations. In May 1993, the Danish people said "yes" to Maastricht.

Clearly, the Maastricht Treaty enshrined, for the first time in the history of the European institutions, that in spite of their being full members of the European Union, some countries could rather easily get a rain check on certain issues. In this way the multispeed Europe was born. Hence, only eleven countries—also known as Euroland—initially joined the single currency. Although Greece did not initially qualify on the basis of its overall poorer economic performance, the United

Kingdom, Sweden, and Denmark have decided to temporarily stay outside the monetary union, mainly because their citizens are not ready to abandon their national currency.

In a way, the 1990s reminded the elders of the 1950s, as the need for updating European institutions sped up the sequence of successive "reform bills." The leaders postponed a long-awaited debate on the most crucial dilemma facing European institutions: how to reform them so as to be prepared for the entry of new member countries.

The latest enlargement of the European Union took place on January 1, 1995, when three neutral countries—Austria, Sweden, and Finland—joined the European Union. By the late 1990s, time for debate was running out: more than a dozen countries were knocking at the door of the European Union, a majority of which belonged to the former communist bloc. Successively, Poland, Hungary, the Czech Republic, Slovakia, Estonia, Lithuania, Latvia, Romania, Bulgaria, Cyprus, Malta, Slovenia, and Turkey said they wanted to become members.

As a result of this pressure, the now fifteen-countries-strong European Union signed the new Amsterdam Treaty in October 1997. It did clarify the functioning of the EU institutions: rules became more democratic; the role and the legitimacy of the president of the European Commission was enhanced; procedures governing common foreign policy issues were simplified; policies developed outside the European treaties, such as the rules governing the abolition of physical borders inside the EU—known as the Schengen agreements—were included in the EU; a clause regarding human rights was introduced to set a clear benchmark for candidate countries; decisions by the Council of Ministers would be taken on qualified majority more often than before; more recent EU policies, such as consumer policy, were strengthened; and a multispeed Europe was no longer taboo, provided those members that wished to move toward economic and political integration could not be prevented from doing so by the others. Still, once more the main issue at stake—reforming the institution so as to welcome future members—had not been addressed. The most obvious explanation of that failure lies in the relative weakness of the Franco-German relationship.

History shows that Europe was built on the foundation of a strong relationship between France and Germany. In spite of his global reluctance regarding supranational institutions, Charles De Gaulle had developed a good partnership with Chancellor Konrad Adenauer, and later on, the European engine was regularly fueled by the pairing of Valéry Giscard d'Estaing and Helmut Schmidt. That European integration came as far as it has depended greatly on the close relationship between the French Socialist François Mitterrand and the German Christian Democrat Helmut Kohl.

EUROPE'S INSTITUTIONS IN THE TWENTY-FIRST CENTURY: THE DANGERS OF DILUTION

The next enlargement of the European Union, which no sensible expert on Europe would envision before the years 2005–2006, will be the last opportunity for the European leaders to rejuvenate the European Union's institutional maze. They will not start from scratch. Today a broad consensus has emerged that the European institutions born in the early 1950s are not fit to cope with a European Union enlarged to twenty member states or more.

Making any prognosis about the future outlook of the European Union's institutional framework, quite honestly, is comparable to looking into a crystal ball. The questions are numerous, the answers vague. What will be the shape of an enlarged Europe? Will the twenty-first century witness the birth of the United States of Europe? What will be its borders? Will the European Union remain an economic giant with no political influence? Can the European Commission be transformed into a genuine European government headed by an elected president? Will the European Union set up a bicameral system, with the European Parliament as a House of Representatives and the Council of Ministers reshaped into a European Senate? Although crucial, the answers to these questions are not easy.

"In an enlarged European Union of, say thirty member countries, it will simply not be possible to maintain ambitious goals such as set out in the present treaties," warns Jacques Delors, former president of the EU Commission and current head of the think tank Notre Europe. "The consequences of such a situation should be clearly drawn and one ought to reflect upon the co-existence of two 'circles'—a first, wider, circle stressing positive management of a large single market and economic interdependence to the benefit of all its members; and a second, narrower, circle—of course open to the others—including those countries that want to sail into the direction of a political union."[2]

Delors still believes in "a truly federal approach which will clearly define 'who does what' and where exclusive competence of nations lies. . . . I would call this a concept of federation of nation-states which implies merging all 'pillars' created by the Maastricht Treaty, a total integration of monetary and economic policy into this framework and its ultimate embodiment through the election of a president by the European Council."³

The Amsterdam Treaty, the latest version of the European "constitution," entered into force on May 1, 1999. During the first two years of the new millennium, a new intergovernmental conference will convene to prepare the most crucial reform of the European institutions. The road to the next round of negotiations will be more than bumpy, and passions will flare. The most predictable scenario is a tough battle between bigger and smaller EU countries: the debate leading up to the Amsterdam Treaty foreshadowed that family feud.

Three main issues emerge: the size and the functioning of the European Commission (the executive body of the EU), the relative weight of voting power of each country in the Council of Ministers, and a further reduction of each country's right to veto measures in the Council. There is a general view in European capitals that the number of members of the European Commission cannot and should not increase indefinitely, no matter how many new members are added.

The European Commission might well be the principal victim of the next debate about the future outlook of the European institutions. Over the years, and more precisely during the 1990s, its influence has been declining. This institution, which has been the real engine of European economic integration—with its unique and exclusive power of initiative—has been criticized as an unaccountable bureaucracy. Those critics ignore the reality of the distribution of powers in Europe: the European Commission is accountable for its acts to the European Parliament. By resigning en masse in March 1999, under pressure from the Parliament, those who sat on the European Commission paid the highest price.

The EU's political authority has repeatedly been challenged at its borders by a succession of crises and wars in the Balkans. From a purely institutional point of view, the unprecedented resignation en masse of the European Commission cast doubt in citizens' minds toward the EU institutions. "In the past we had to face several crises," former European commissioner Karel van Miert recalls, "but they were salutary in that Europe each time managed to get its act together and take its responsibilities. Now, paradoxically since the advent of the euro, it is as though we cannot focus any more: we are going in circles and confronted with Europe's future, politicians have lost the basic sense of necessity and responsibility."⁴

Large EU countries argue that the lack of reform of European institutions has reduced their influence and that the arrival of new "small" countries, with the exception of Poland, will worsen this situation. The larger countries claim they could do with one commissioner less—presently each "big" country (France, Germany, Italy, the United Kingdom, and Spain) is entitled to two portfolios in the European Commission—provided the distribution of votes in the Council of Ministers is adjusted in their favor. At the end side of the spectrum, the smaller countries are not prepared to accept any change in the weighing of votes in the Council of Ministers unless their bigger partners give up more national sovereignty in a clearly identifiable extension of qualified majority decisionmaking. Discussions about national sovereignty have definitely entered the "red zone" in that they touch upon issues in which larger member states are jealously coveting their prerogatives: foreign and security policies, taxation, reform of the treaties themselves, and financing of the EU are among the most crucial.

The future outlook of these negotiations, however, is not hopeless: since the debate over the Amsterdam Treaty, a "pink" wave—as some journalists described it—has swept across European politics. At the turn of the twenty-first century, eleven governments (among others, those of France, Germany, the UK, and Italy) share common social democratic values. After the Thatcher and John Major "euroskeptic" years, current UK leader Tony Blair seems to be more of a Europhile. Not only has he pledged the entry of the pound into the euro if the right economic conditions are met, but he firmly pleaded in favor of a European integrated defense system at a so-called Franco-British summit in St. Mâlo in 1998.

Of course, the proof of the pudding will be in the eating. The British prime minister might well possess the key to Europe's future institutional outlook. If British goodwill materializes and Britain joins the single European currency, then a more ambitious political Europe may be seriously contemplated.

European leaders must also be careful about public opinion as was demonstrated in the fall of 2000 when the Danes voted in a referendum against adopting the euro. The citizens of the European Union, although generally reluctant about changes, have asked for more transparency. They also want symbols to identify with a broader "country" called Europe: in that perspective, the euro, which will be jingling in citizens' pockets in January 2002, has been a major achievement in terms of European visibility.

If the economic integration of Europe has gone widely unnoticed by its citizens—who benefit from the huge continental market in their daily life—the political integration and the institutional reshuffle that inevitably goes with it will have to be clearly explained to them. Or as Jacques Delors stated around the end of the twentieth century: "If Europe is only about a single currency, we'll have an Adam Smith–type hyper–free trade economy and a Metternich-type rule of the strongest in political terms."[5]

During the first half of the year 2000, several European politicians—notably Joschka Fischer, the German foreign affairs minister, and Jacques Chirac, the French president—came up with new ideas that could fundamentally reshape the architecture of Europe's institutions. Their speeches sparked an intense debate over Europe's future. The debate, which will continue, reminds one of Delors's views on the same idea: to survive, Europe must be more than a mere trade zone.

APPENDIX: THE EU INSTITUTIONS[6]

The European Union is governed by five institutions: the Parliament, Council of Ministers, Commission, Court of Justice, and Court of Auditors. In addition, the heads of state and government and the Commission president meet at least twice a year in European Council summits to provide overall strategy and political direction. The European Central Bank is responsible for monetary policy and managing the euro in the economic and monetary union, which now comprises eleven states.

The EU governing system differs from all previous national and international models. Unlike the United States, the European Union is founded on international treaties among sovereign nations rather than a constitution. The power to enact laws that are directly binding on all EU citizens throughout the EU territory also distinguishes the European Union from international organizations.

The European Union has been described as a supranational entity because its member states have relinquished part of their national sovereignty to EU institutions. The member states work together, in their collective interest, through the joint administration of their sovereign powers. The EU also operates according to the principle of subsidiarity, which characterizes most federal systems. Under this principle, the EU is granted jurisdiction only for those policies that cannot be handled effectively at lower levels of government, that is, national, regional, or local.

The EU system is inherently evolutionary. It was designed to allow for the gradual development of European unification and has not yet achieved its final form.

EUROPEAN PARLIAMENT

The European Parliament comprises 626 members, directly elected in EU-wide elections for five-year terms. The president of the Parliament is elected for a two-and-a-half-year term. Members of the European Parliament (MEPs) form political rather than national groups.

The European Parliament cannot enact laws like national parliaments. However, its legislative role has been strengthened over the years. The Maastricht Treaty provides for a co-decision procedure that empowers Parliament to veto legislation in certain policy areas and to confer with the Council in a "conciliation committee" to iron out differences in their respective drafts of legislation. The Amsterdam Treaty extends the number of policy areas in which Parliament can exercise these powers. Earlier, the Single European Act gave Parliament the right to amend proposals for legislation (cooperation procedure) and gave it veto power over the accession of new member states and the conclusion of association agreements with third countries (assent procedure).

The European Parliament acts as the EU's public forum. It can question the Commission and the Council, amend or reject the EU budget, and dismiss the entire Commission through a vote of censure. Since Maastricht, Parliament has an appointed ombudsman to address allegations of misadministration in EU institutions and agencies. It has the power to self-initiate investigations into malpractices in the implementation of Community law by setting up temporary inquiry committees (e.g., as in the recent "mad cow" crisis).

The European Parliament holds plenary sessions in Strasbourg and Brussels. Its twenty committees, which prepare the work for plenary meetings, and its political groups normally meet in Brussels.

EUROPEAN COUNCIL

The European Council brings together heads of state and government and the president of the Commission. It meets at least twice a year, at the end of each EU member state's six-month presidency. The Single

European Act formalized the European Council, which was not fore-seen in the original EC treaties.

COUNCIL OF THE EUROPEAN UNION

The Council of Ministers enacts EU laws, acting on proposals submitted by the Commission. Since the implementation of the Maastricht Treaty, its official name is the Council of the European Union.

Comprising ministers from each member state, the Council strikes a balance between national and EU interests. Different ministers participate in the Council according to the subject under discussion. Agricultural ministers, for instance, discuss farm prices in the Agriculture Council, and economic and finance ministers discuss monetary affairs in the Council of Economic and Financial Ministers (ECOFIN). The ministers for foreign affairs provide overall coordination in the General Affairs Council. They are also responsible for foreign policy in the framework of the Common Foreign and Security Policy. Each government acts as president of the Council for six months in rotation. The Council is assisted by a Committee of Permanent Representatives (COREPER), comprising member state officials holding ambassadorial rank, and a secretariat with a staff of about 2,000 people.

EUROPEAN COMMISSION

The Commission is the policy engine of the EU. It proposes legislation, is responsible for administration, and ensures that the provisions of the treaties and the decisions of the institutions are properly implemented. It has investigative powers and can take legal action against persons, companies, or member states that violate EU rules. It manages the budget and represents the European Union in international trade negotiations.

The commissioners—two each from France, Germany, Italy, Spain, and the United Kingdom, and one from each of the other member states—are appointed for five-year terms by common agreement between governments and the president of the Commission. The European Parliament approves the appointment of the Commission as a body. The Commission president is appointed by agreement among the member governments in consultation with the European Parliament for a term of five years. Up to two vice presidents are appointed from among the commissioners.

The commissioners act in the European Union's interest, independently of the national governments that nominated them. Each is assigned one or more policy areas and is assisted by a small cabinet or team of aides. The Commission's administrative staff, based mainly in Brussels, numbers about 15,000, divided among more than thirty directorates-general and other administrative services. Since the EU has eleven official languages, about 20 percent of the Commission staff are translators and interpreters.

EUROPEAN COURT OF JUSTICE

The Court of Justice, sitting in Luxembourg, is the Union's "Supreme Court." It ensures that the treaties are interpreted and applied correctly by other EU institutions and by the member states. The Court of Justice comprises fifteen judges, one from each member state, appointed for renewable terms of six years. Judgments of the Court in the field of EU law are binding on EU institutions, member states, national courts, companies, and private citizens and overrule those of national courts.

Since 1988 a Court of First Instance, consisting of fifteen members, has assisted the Court of Justice. This court has power to hear actions brought by EU officials, competition and coal and steel cases, and actions for damages. Its decisions are subject to appeal to the Court of Justice on points of law only.

EUROPEAN COURT OF AUDITORS

The Court of Auditors, based in Luxembourg, has extensive powers to examine the legality of receipts and expenditures and the sound financial management of the EU budget.

3

Differing Views on a United Europe

REGINALD DALE

The quest for European unity has been going on for almost as long as there has been a place called Europe, which, according to how it is calculated, is between 2,000 and 3,000 years. Arguments over what form that unity should take have been going on for almost as long. For most of Europe's existence, of course, attempts to unite the continent have been by force of arms, undertaken in order to ensure the dominance of a single power. Those efforts have usually met ferocious resistance, plunging the continent into endless wars. But even now that unification is a peaceful process, differences over how Europe should be united remain wide and often fierce. As it attempts a further burst of integration for the new millennium—with a fledgling single currency and heightened efforts to achieve political integration—Europe still speaks with a myriad of different voices.

Those voices express widely divergent views over such basic questions as how far Europe should unite politically and inside what kind of constitutional or institutional framework, what policies a united Europe should pursue, how far nation-states should retain control over their own destinies, and even over where Europe ends: Is Turkey European? Should Ukraine be a member of the European Union one day? What about Russia?

The varying views reflect deep differences in national cultures and experiences, as well as differences in geography, religion, language, and philosophy. The differences are not just among countries, but within countries. They reflect contrasting political viewpoints and sociological and educational backgrounds, as well as generational differences.

But some clear trends emerge from surveys carried out by the European Commission and other organizations in recent years. The polls consistently show that the better educated, the young, and at least until recently, men, are more inclined to favor European integration. The less well educated, older people, and women were less likely to be favorable and often less likely to have an opinion. Those trends were confirmed in a Eurobarometer opinion survey released by the European Commission in March 1999, which also showed that men, the young, and the better educated were more likely than the other groups to believe that European integration has been successful over the past fifty years. Recently, however, there has been a slight tendency for women to become more favorable to European construction—perhaps because they are catching up with men in other aspects of modern life, such as education and jobs. Overall, 54 percent of citizens in the fifteen member countries of the European Union said they believed that "a great deal" or "a fair amount" had been achieved in terms of European integration in the past half century, whereas 34 percent felt that very little or nothing had been achieved.

But there were big variations among the member countries. In Luxembourg, the small grand duchy at the heart of Europe that is home to some of the EU's central institutions, 75 percent believed that a good deal of integration had been achieved—versus 11 percent who said little or none. In Italy, at the other extreme, 48 percent said little or nothing had been achieved, and only 41 percent believed a lot had been accomplished. Given that Italians have traditionally been among the most enthusiastic supporters of European integration, the poll takers were forced to conclude that this was the Italians' way of saying that not enough had been achieved during these past fifty years.

After half a century of integration, it is true that a "European identity" has been slow to emerge. Very few people told the Eurobarometer pollsters that they felt "only European"—with Luxembourg, at 13 percent, the only country in double figures. Other responses ranged from 7 percent in France to a bare 1 percent in Ireland, Greece, and Finland. Those who felt that they owed their identity exclusively to their own nationality were far more numerous, with the British predictably the most nationalistic. Sixty-two percent of Britons said they felt "only British" and not European at all, closely followed by the 60 percent of Swedes who felt the same way. But the figure dropped to 46 percent in Germany and, perhaps surprisingly, only 35 percent in France, which is often considered the most chauvinist nation in Europe. Reassuringly to believers in the European cause, across the fifteen EU nations as a whole, 54 percent said they felt both that they were European and that they belonged to their own nationality.

Clearly, according to these results, feeling European is not inconsistent with pride in one's own nationality—just as in the United States people can be proud to be, say, both Texan and American. And despite fears in many quarters that economic and political integration will lead to a dilution of national identities, there is little evidence that this is happening. On the contrary, there is plenty of reason to suppose that national characteristics honed through centuries of often violent history will be hard to eradicate.

Europe's history still defines its present in ways unimaginable in the United States. When the Emperor Charlemagne introduced a single currency throughout his territories around the year 800 A.D., two countries bordering his lands resisted the new coinage. They were England and Denmark—the very same two countries that 1,200 years later insisted on the official right to opt out of Europe's new single currency, the euro. Despite all that happened in between, English and Danish attitudes toward the euro are still more like those of their ancient ancestors than those of their modern continental neighbors.

But the attitudes of many of today's Europeans can be traced even further back. Two thousand years after its heyday, the map of Europe still bears the imprint of the Roman Empire, the border of which still roughly divides the continent into "barbarians" outside the empire in the north and "Latins" inside the empire to the south. In Germany, people who come from the small section of the country that was inside the "limes," the Latin word for the empire's frontier, are thought to have a different character from other Germans. Very broadly speaking, the northerners have historically tended to be Protestant, individualistic, more committed to free trade, and more attached to the kind of democracy that stems from the grass roots upward. Southerners have tended to be Catholic, more attached to ties of family and community, more inclined toward state intervention and protectionism, and more likely to be governed by rule from the top downward.

Those historical differences are still reflected in modern-day arguments over issues like how open the EU should be to trade with the outside world—the so-called issue of fortress Europe—and how transparent and democratically accountable its institutions should be. Northerners, particularly the new Scandinavian member states—Sweden and Finland, who joined the EU in 1995—are more inclined to press for transparency and open democratic procedures, whereas Latins are more inclined to believe in the value of personal relationships and the effectiveness of private contacts.

Some scholars also see another modern inheritance from Charlemagne's empire or at least from the three smaller empires into which it broke up in the ninth century A.D. They say the great architects of

European integration—people like Konrad Adenauer of Germany, Paul-Henri Spaak of Belgium, and Robert Schuman of France, who have often been called the fathers of Europe—have always tended to come from the middle of the three empires, the Lotharingian, which was wedged between the two competing empires that ultimately evolved into today's France and Germany. "Lotharingians," who include people from the border areas of France and Germany, have always had the greatest interest in a peacefully united Europe that stops the two big traditional enemies from trampling over them.

It is certainly true today that the EU's institutions—in Brussels, Luxembourg, and Strasbourg—are spread through the middle empire along the line that divides France and Germany, which also roughly represents the frontier of the Roman Empire. And it is also true that the smaller countries in between France and Germany—Belgium, the Netherlands, and Luxembourg—have always been among the staunchest advocates of strong central European institutions to keep the bigger countries in check.

Unlike in the United States, where ethnic stereotyping is taboo, it is alive and well in Europe. Although the stereotypes are frequently exaggerations, they also often contain kernels of truth derived from long experience that help Europeans to understand and deal with their neighbors. For although the United States is a nation of immigrants, many of whom sought to shed their previous national allegiances, European nation-states were formed by peoples who are still largely in the same place that they have been for hundreds of years, still speak the same language, and are proud of their ancestral cultures. Thus in matters of European diplomacy, it can be helpful to know that national characteristics—French pride, English and Danish stubbornness, Dutch mercantilism, and the Italian tendency to leave practical arrangements to the last minute—will often shape a country's attitudes and negotiating positions.

It is certainly a mistake to overlook the manifold cultural differences and habits that separate even the closest of European neighbors. When Sweden was negotiating its entry into the EU in the early 1990s, one of the biggest sticking points was over a special kind of snuff beloved by Swedes but unknown in other countries. When Britain negotiated the terms of its membership nearly thirty years ago, there were bitter battles over regulations governing such items as the British sausage, which is made with less meat than its continental equivalent. There have been similar disputes over British ice cream, made with less cream than on the continent, if any at all. Although powerful commercial interests were at stake in these disputes, few continentals, and certainly not the French, could understand why the British were so attached to such delicacies.

But cultural differences often run much deeper. In 1992, when Denmark was about to vote in its first referendum on the Maastricht Treaty—providing for economic and monetary union and a single currency—someone in Brussels thought it would be a good idea if Jacques Delors, then president of the European Commission, got involved on the side of the "yes" campaign. But as one of Denmark's leading newspapers, *Politiken*, wrote at the time, "Delors' direct intervention in the referendum was a disaster. The victory of the 'no' campaign [later reversed in a second referendum], was due to some degree to Delors' 'meddling,'" the paper wrote.[1]

Part of the reason was Delors's unconvincing denials that the EU's smaller countries would see their influence reduced and his warnings that member countries should prepare themselves for an "intellectual and institutional shock" during discussions of the EU's further expansion in the months ahead. But the main reasons were cultural and psychological. In many ways Delors incarnated all that Danes dislike about European integration. "The little Frenchman," as *Politiken* described him, was seen as arrogant, bureaucratic, patronizing, and out of tune with Danish public opinion and its concerns.

Delors had much the same effect on the British, who have always shared many of the Danes' feelings about Europe. For Prime Minister Margaret Thatcher, always hostile to strong central EU institutions, Delors had three strikes against him—he was Catholic, he was a Socialist, and he was French. Her antipathy to Delors was shared, enthusiastically, by much of the rabidly anti-European British popular press—as exemplified by the notorious banner headline "Up Yours, Delors" that appeared on the front page of a mass-circulation tabloid when the Frenchman had caused some trivial offense, now long since forgotten.

But to many people elsewhere in the Union and particularly to the most ardent devotees of the kind of European integration envisaged by the EU's founding fathers, Delors was a hero whose name will be forever enshrined in the European pantheon. Delors presided over one of the most active periods of European integration, including the move to the single market, and was instrumental in the construction of economic and monetary union—alongside French president François Mitterrand and German chancellor Helmut Kohl. All three leaders believed that big steps forward to European unity should accompany German unification so as to bind a greater Germany more tightly into the European family.

Kohl was undoubtedly the greatest force for European integration of the 1980s and the 1990s. His emotional commitment to anchoring

Germany inside a united Europe—forged by his childhood memories of World War II and its aftermath—was a beacon to many, to others a source of derision. Euroskeptics and even some less passionate pro-Europeans scoffed at his famous comment that economic and monetary union was an issue of war and peace in the twenty-first century. And yet to anyone interested in European history, it was clear what Kohl was talking about. Many of today's Europeans may have been lulled into a sense of security by the half-century of peace since World War II—the longest period of peace since the Roman Empire.

In the words of Simon Serfaty of the Center for Strategic and International Studies in Washington, D.C., "Amid the ruins of many past decades of wars and civil conflicts stands a Europe that has never been as economically affluent, as politically stable, as widely united and as deeply peaceful as it is today."[2] Even the war in Kosovo has not altered that fundamental truth—in a way, it has confirmed it. In the area covered by European integration, war is unthinkable. War is now only conceivable in areas like Yugoslavia that have not felt the benefits of integration and the stability brought by the prosperity and democracy that are among integration's most essential features.

For more than 2,000 years, however, attempts to unify the continent—whether by the Romans, Charlemagne, Napoleon Bonaparte, or Adolf Hitler—have always had much more to do with war than with peace. And those conflicts still shape Europe today, in much the same way as do the ghostly borders of Europe's former empires. Deep-lying memories of tyrants like Napoleon and Hitler, who sought to take over the continent by force and caused immense suffering and destruction, still shape Europe's collective consciousness. They help to explain why so many Europeans, particularly in Britain, are still fiercely resistant to a centralized European government. Even at a more parochial level, the city of Brussels long resisted closer coordination between its nineteen communes because such links might recall "Greater Brussels," the single central administration forced on the city by Belgium's Nazi conquerors in World War II. And many Britons for years opposed the construction of the Channel Tunnel because the idea was first hatched by Napoleon as a means of invading Britain.

Yet if warlike attempts to unite Europe have dominated the continent's history at least until the second half of the twentieth century, they have also often been accompanied by a more peaceful and idealistic way of looking at Europe's ultimate unification. As long ago as the first century, the Greek philosopher Strabo said that the two instincts in human beings, the peaceable and the warlike, live side by side in Europe and "the one that is peace-loving is more numerous and thus keeps control over the whole body. . . . Europe," he continued, "is both varied in form and admirably adapted by nature for the development of excellence in men and governments."[3] And although the Romans generally expanded their empire through the might of the legions and their technological and organizational superiority, they liked to think they were ensuring peace and making the world more civilized (which in most ways they were). Just as the latest drive to unity arose from the ashes of World War II, so many of the earlier peaceful visions followed periods of conflict. Clearly, extreme British opponents of integration who attribute the origins of the European idea to Hitler could not be more wrong.

In the seventeenth century, after the destructive Thirty Years War, the rise of the nation-state was accompanied by visionary but unrealistic schemes for what was known as "Universal Monarchy." All those projects "argued that if Christendom was to be made safe the princes of Europe had to abandon the pursuit of their individual interests to make way for a single world monarchy," according to *Early Modern Europe: An Oxford History*.[4] The problem with these schemes, apart from their lack of reality, was that they all involved the triumph of one European state, first Spain and then France, over everyone else.

Just as is the case today, many of the early proposals for European unity were inspired by the French. In 1620, the Duc de Sully, the former first minister of King Henry IV, proposed a "Grand Design" that would have meant altering the boundaries of Europe to create fifteen national states ruled collectively by a senate composed of sixty members (four from each state), with seats in Nantes, Metz, and Cologne. This Europe would have had a standing army and a fleet—a degree of unification that has not even been achieved today. By the 1840s, people had already begun talking of a "United States of Europe," and by the mid-nineteenth century French economists were proposing something quite similar to today's economic and monetary union—an economic union with a single central bank.

When the latest drive to integrate Europe began after World War II, the idea of a United States of Europe had been adopted by Britain's famous wartime leader, Winston Churchill (although he did not mean Britain to be included) and by Jean Monnet, the Frenchman often seen as the prime intellectual architect of today's European Union. Monnet was the principal author of the theories of economic and political integration that the EU has pursued for the past half century.

Today, with memories of war receding, the immediate postwar visions of a United States of Europe have waned somewhat, though not as much as their opponents often think, and the approach to the European ideal still varies widely between different countries. According to a French opinion poll cited by the *Economist* in June 1999, only 8 percent of people in Denmark, 27 percent in Britain, and 37 percent in Germany said they wanted a single European government. But the numbers were much higher in France (53 percent) and in Italy (71 percent).

In a more skeptical age, if they want to gain support for European integration, today's political leaders often have to disclaim that it will lead to a "United States of Europe" or, more ominously, a "European super state." That is particularly true in the less integration-minded countries. It is noticeable that support for a more integrated Europe still seems stronger in the six founding countries of the European Community than it is among the later arrivals. That may reflect their longer experience of membership and its benefits. But it is also true that, virtually by definition, the six founding members were also more attached to the idea of integration in the first place.

Jose Maria Aznar, the prime minister of Spain, is a good European and the leader of a country that is highly supportive of European integration. Spain joined the European Community in 1986. Yet Aznar says categorically, "Europe is never going to be the United States—never. The United States of Europe will never exist like the United States of America. Historically, it is impossible."[5] Most Europeans would agree that whatever final form it takes, a united Europe will be sui generis, not identical to any other federal or confederal structure. But many are not inclined to state so definitively as Aznar that something similar to the United States is "never" going to be possible. Here is the opinion of a Spanish participant in a focus group organized by the U.S. Information Agency: "For Europe to get united, each one looks after his own interests, so to become 'one' it is going to take many, many years." A German focus group participant had this to say: "How long did America need in order to grow together to this unity? There was a Civil War. It took longer until there was a consensus and they had somewhat written off their own [regional] interests. In Europe, it won't be a ten-year thing either. The problem is that there are countries which used to be large powers and also still have such thoughts."[6]

The German put his finger on one of the main fault lines dividing European opinion. Proud big countries with long and glorious histories like Britain and France are more inclined to want arrangements that maintain national sovereignty. A Europe of nation-states, rather than one integrated under supranational institutions, was the aim of two of the most dominant national leaders of the postwar era—President Charles de Gaulle in France and Thatcher in Britain. And although their successors have not taken such an assertive line, their policies have often reflected those basic convictions. Thus the late French president Mitterrand proposed a European confederation, not a federation, and British politicians—and public opinion—remain resolutely opposed to a "federal" Europe.

But the concept of a "federal" Europe is a good example of how European voices can speak at cross purposes. For the British, a "federal" Europe means one that is highly centralized and in which supranational institutions exert control over national governments. For the Germans, who have lived happily in a federal republic since 1950, a "federal Europe" means just the opposite—one in which a great deal of authority is delegated from the center to the national or regional level, just as national power is delegated to the *länder,* or states, in modern Germany.

In fact, member countries are often attached to ideas of a European government that reflect the way their own countries are run. The Dutch want a strong and open European Parliament, reflecting their own long tradition of strong and open parliamentary democracy. France has sought, in many ways successfully, to model the Brussels bureaucracy on its own powerful, elite corps of civil servants that still largely runs France in the centralized tradition inherited from the time of Louis XIV. Britain, at least until recent moves to "devolve" political authority away from Westminster, has also been one of Europe's most centralized countries, with a powerful London-based bureaucratic elite.

But there is a big difference between French and British attitudes toward European government. Britain has always tried to slow down the construction of a centralized Europe, dragging its feet before each new step to unity, whereas France has favored integration as a vehicle for asserting French leadership. In the run-up to the single currency, France saw economic and monetary union as a means of regaining a degree of French sovereignty over its economic decisionmaking. The thinking was that instead of simply having to follow interest rates set by the German Bundesbank, as in the period before the single currency, France would have greater influence in an economic and monetary union because it would have its own representatives in the European Central Bank.

That scenario may not turn out to be quite correct. Today's French central bankers, whether in Paris or Frankfurt, are much less inclined than in the past to turn to the Paris government for advice or instruction. But the French attitude was remarkable for the contrast with that of Britain, which has always tended to see economic and monetary union as a threat to national sovereignty, not a means of extending it.

Smaller countries, like the Netherlands, Belgium, Luxembourg, and Ireland, who have suffered historically at the hands of bigger powers, have traditionally been most enthusiastic about the pooling of sovereignty—as a means of keeping controls on the larger countries. As a result, they have often sought to strengthen the more supranational central institutions, notably the Commission and the European Parliament, at the expense of the intergovernmental Council of Ministers—although few even of the smaller countries want the Council to lose its role as the Union's main decisionmaking body.

Some believe that that traditional support has wavered recently, not least because the influence of the smaller countries in the central institutions seems bound to decline as the institutions are reformed to prepare for the EU's next wave of enlargement, which will see the entry of former communist countries in central and eastern Europe. But it is not just the smaller countries that want closer economic and political union. Germany under Chancellor Kohl was especially keen that economic and monetary union should quickly lead to political union, partly to ensure that Germany's historical demons would never be able to reappear.

Kohl's electoral defeat in the autumn of 1998 has removed some of his brand of pro-European emotionalism from German politics. Gerhard Schröder, who succeeded Kohl as chancellor, had this to say in a BBC interview in March 1998, five months before his election victory: "Helmut Kohl's generation thinks Germans must be part of Europe to prevent Europe from being frightened by Germany in the future. . . . My generation believes that Germans don't have to be part of Europe, but we want to be."[7]

Two generations after World War II, it is certainly true that an increasing number of Germans do not feel the need to be shackled by guilt for deeds for which they were not personally responsible. But it is also true that most younger German opinion leaders, whether in diplomacy, politics, academia, or the media, remain extremely pro-European. Even if they lack the emotional commitment of Kohl, their views still tend to be close to those of the traditional supporters of Jean Monnet–style integration. The views of most educated Germans lack the nationalistic undertones that can often be detected among the "chattering classes" of France or Britain.

The same can be said of most educated Italians, who have always been among the most enthusiastic supporters of the European idea. Among the reasons for that are Italy's short history as a nation-state, its defeat in World War II, its tendency to distrust its own government in Rome, and a pleasing lack of national arrogance in its dealings with its European partners.

Spain, Portugal, and Greece, which joined the EU as countries emerging from dictatorships, have their own special reasons for enthusiasm about the European vision. All three countries, but especially Spain and Portugal, which had been dictatorships for much longer, saw membership in the European institutions as the symbol of their final acceptance in the club of civilized Western nations.

It is perhaps understandable that Britain has found it hardest of all the major European powers to show enthusiasm for the cause of unity. Britain emerged as a victor of World War II with many Britons still believing that much of their empire would last for a long time. Britain was the only European country that participated in the war and was not occupied by enemy forces or defeated or both. As the British author Hugo Young has pointed out, for the continental nations, European integration after World War II was a kind of victory, the construction of something positive from the rubble of death and destruction. For Britain, it was a defeat, an arrangement reluctantly accepted, which codified the loss of Britain's traditional independence from the continent, its empire, and its role as a top world power.[8]

Britain has long been good friends with the likeminded people who surround the North Sea—the Dutch, Danes, and Norwegians. But its main natural affinity is not with France, Germany, or Italy but with its kith and kin in the English-speaking nations across the seas—in the United States, Canada, Australia, and New Zealand. And it is in their attitudes toward those "Anglo-Saxon" nations, and especially the United States, that the cacophonous voices of Europe are often at their loudest—especially on either side of the English Channel. For although many in France—and particularly French intellectuals—have long believed that Europe should be constructed in opposition to the United States, most Britons (as well as most Germans, Dutch, and Scandinavians) believe it should be built in partnership with the United States.

France is now modifying those views. French leaders still sometimes express resentment at the existence of a single "hyperpower" and advocate so-called multipolar policies to balance U.S. domination—to the fury of many Americans. But French foreign minister Hubert Vedrine has made a point of trying to persuade his countrymen to be realistic about U.S. power and not always automatically oppose U.S. ideas. French analysts say that the virulent strain of anti-Americanism that has long marked most French intellectual movements is on the wane. It is certainly true that France is much more tolerant of Anglo-Saxon culture and the English language than it was twenty years ago.

Despite its long history of trying to distance itself from the United States in the North Atlantic alliance, France was a model ally in the North Atlantic Treaty Organization's (NATO's) military campaign against Kosovo in the spring of 1999. "We are always there [alongside the Americans] when it really counts," says a senior French diplomat.[9]

But France in many ways remains the odd man out in the Atlantic alliance. According to an opinion poll published in April 1999, when the bombing of Kosovo was in full swing, 68 percent of French people were worried about the United States being the sole superpower, and 61 percent said U.S. cultural influence was too great. There were similar levels of disapproval of U.S. economic and military power. Asked whether there should be a new European force to replace NATO altogether, 57 percent of the French respondents said yes, against an average of only 36 percent in all NATO countries.

Such attitudes inevitably color the whole question of what kind of Europe people want. Most French people say they don't want Europe to become an "Anglo-Saxon" market economy—an opinion that has in some ways become more pronounced since the Socialist-led government of Lionel Jospin took office in 1998. Jospin says yes to the market economy, but no to a market society. But although Jospin's leftist coalition is just one of a number of center-left governments that now dominate the EU politically, few of the others would agree with him.

In Britain, "New Labor" prime minister Tony Blair is only too happy to have inherited the pro-market reforms pushed through—in the teeth of Old Labor opposition—by Conservative governments in the 1980s and early 1990s. He is actively looking to the United States for new economic ideas to copy, for example, in the field of welfare reform, and would like the whole of continental Europe to follow in Britain's footsteps.

In Germany, Chancellor Schröder would certainly like to do so. But he is finding it hard. He still has to persuade his Social Democratic Party to accept the kind of economic and political reforms that Blair successfully imposed on the Labor Party before his election victory.

It is not only in France that open markets can still be controversial—particularly when debate turns to measures to curb unemployment, the continent's biggest economic and social problem. Continental countries with long traditions of state intervention are still much more likely to look to government action to help create jobs. Thus a recent discussion document adopted by a number of center-left governments, entitled "The New European Way," placed greater emphasis on the need to create jobs through taxation and other public policies. The aim, it said, should be to shift the burden of taxes from labor to capital.[10]

In his inaugural speech to Parliament in November 1999, Schröder said his government will "seize the unique opportunity that the new [political] constellation in Europe presents" and seek a coordinated European policy in creating jobs. Others, however, are concerned that such ideas could undo Europe's closer embrace of market policies. Carlo Azeglio Ciampi, the former Italian treasury minister and now his country's president, insists that lower taxes remain the main prerequisite for higher growth and job creation. The EU member states should commit themselves to a path of equal and simultaneous reduction in taxation and current government expenditure.[11] Romano Prodi, president of the Commission, has also warned against excessive government intervention in an attempt to create jobs. "If we put liberalizing markets and social Europe in contradiction we shall ruin the market and social Europe at the same time," he warned the European Parliament in May 1999.[12]

Europe's arguments over these issues are closely watched by Americans long concerned that the EU, if it fails to overcome its economic and social problems, will resort to fortress Europe policies hostile to U.S. business and economic interests. For now that argument has largely been settled inside Europe, with the case for greater openness carrying the day. Sir Leon Brittan, former European trade commissioner, felt that Europe had unquestionably taken the lead in pushing for greater and faster liberalization of world markets than any of its partners in the last few years.

The war in Kosovo also galvanized EU leaders into attempting new moves to develop common foreign and defense policies. Europeans were shocked by the extent of European military and political dependence on the United States that the war revealed. In April 1999 Ulrich Beck, a professor at Munich University, told the *New York Times* that "Kosovo could be our military euro, creating a political and defense identity for the European Union in the same way as the euro is the expression of economic and financial integration."[13] Prodi has even described a common European army under a European flag and a European commander as "the logical next step," even though he admits it might take "years and years and years."

Some hope that the war will add new urgency to the drive to enlarge the EU into central and eastern Europe, which many, both in the United States and Europe, fear is in danger of losing momentum. Joschka Fischer, the German foreign minister, has gone so far as to describe the Kosovo conflict as a "unification war" that will accelerate European unity and the EU's eastward enlargement.

Opinion polls show a surprising degree of support for intensified European foreign policy and security cooperation, even in Britain.

Most Europeans regard it as more necessary and desirable than the single currency. Once again, as so often before, the aftermath of war may be giving a spur to European unity. Leszek Balcerowicz, deputy prime minister of Poland, says the EU's eastward enlargement "should be seen in a historical perspective as removing the remaining divisions of the second world war."[14]

But it will not resolve all the issues that continue to divide Europeans or provide a final answer to the question of where Europe's eastern border lies. There is no prospect that Europeans will stop arguing over the future shape and direction of their continent—just as they have been doing for more than 2,000 years—any time soon.

4

The Nation-State Redefined

Leif Beck Fallesen

Core functions of the traditional European nation-state are crumbling under the onslaught of economic globalization. But the pace of European integration is still being determined by two nation-states, Germany and France, with the United Kingdom trying to make this pairing a triumvirate. With other nation-states demanding a say, this situation will lead to a confederal, rather than a federal European Union in the twenty-first century. The nation-state is not disappearing, but it will have to redefine itself. And there is a large and potentially dangerous gap between politicians and voters of Europe in their perceptions of both the current and future levels of integration in Europe, with few signs that it is being bridged.

If the nation-state in Europe is dying on the verge of the twenty-first century, someone forgot to tell the Europeans. In politics, the media, and the minds of the people, the nation-state is alive and well. Germany inaugurated its reconstructed Reichstag in Berlin in April 1999, housing its parliament, the Bundestag, and part of the billion-dollar investment in transferring the national capital from Bonn to Berlin.

Indeed, some European nation-states are under severe stress, but the sources are internal. In most EU countries there is widespread disillusion with institutions and political elites, which manifests itself in very large swings of votes and lack of motivation to seek political office. Regions are demanding autonomy, even independence. But there are no signs that loyalties are being transferred to new European institutions.

The latest figures showed that on average 61 percent of Europeans had feelings of citizenship toward their own nation-state and 22 percent

43

felt such attachment to their region, but only 16 percent expressed this sentiment toward the European Union.[1] A United States of Europe is simply not on the popular agenda.

This may seem strange to anyone looking at the European Union from the outside. The signs of progressive integration are obvious: the launch of the euro, the single currency on January 1, 1999; and the forced resignation of the European Commission in March 1999 by the European Parliament are some of the newest landmarks. And in May 1999 Germany's central bank, the Bundesbank, opened a money museum, prompting the satirical wit of the European media to note the official internment of the national currency, the deutsche mark.

There is hardly a more visible symbol of a nation-state than a currency and no stronger example of constitutional change than a directly elected parliament forcing its will on a nonelected executive. A common EU defense and foreign policy has made great strides as a direct consequence of the war in Kosovo. It is difficult to dispute that the elites, politicians, and captains of industry are forging a stronger European Union that will inevitably encroach on the historic functions of the European nation-states.

The gulf between the perceptions of the European voters and the factual state of European integration is not a new phenomenon. The elites have traditionally been in the vanguard of change. Europe is being constructed from the top, not from the bottom. Every major leap forward carries the risk of widening the gulf. It was not bridged in 1992, when the Danes initially rejected the Maastricht Treaty in a referendum, and it was a very close call in France. It could happen again, when the successor to the present Amsterdam Treaty is put to the test at referendums or national elections in perhaps several EU member countries.

Of course, one reason for popular complacency may be that the present surge in economic and political integration looks less impressive from the perspective of the European voter than from the vantage point of the trained eye. The euro will not replace the national currencies of Euroland as a daily means of cash payment until 2002.

The absence at the European level of a machinery of decisionmaking comparable to what exists at the national level may be a second reason. The European flag is widely used but always in conjunction with national flags and very often also in the company of regional flags. Many Europeans might highlight its decorative value, but very few would consider the European flag a political statement of any substance.

There is no European president, no European government, and no truly pan-European, let alone federalist, parties. Nor is there any blueprint of how and when such archetypes of nation building are to be introduced.

It is not possible to take a European oath and assume European citizenship. The passport covers do present the European Union at the top followed by the name of the constituent nation-state. But the only path to such a passport is national citizenship in one of the EU member countries.

The third and probably the most important explanation is that the European voters simply do not believe that the nation-state is in any kind of mortal danger. European integration appears to be firmly under the control of national governments, accountable to national parliaments. The media reflect and probably reinforce this view by reporting events in the European Union with a national bias. Championing the national interest is the standard feature of all decisionmaking at the European level.

There is such disparity of presentation of EU meetings along national lines that many find it difficult to believe that journalists are in fact reporting from the same event. Tellingly, the only magazine explicitly dedicated to unbiased European reporting, *The European,* folded in 1999, just at the time when the pace of European integration was picking up. There was no market for stories written without a nation-state approach.

Cardinal to any examination of what is happening to the nation-state is how such a state is defined. There is no universally accepted definition, but a consensus view of the core functions will include a mixture of legal, ideological, and economic obligations. The right to use state violence to enforce laws within borders, the ability to use violence against intruders, and the right to sign treaties with other nation-states on behalf of all nationals are obvious components of a legal definition.

The sharpest and clearest legal incursion into national sovereignty is the superiority of European Union law to national law. It has been part of EU treaties since the Treaty of Rome in 1957. But until the 1990s, it seldom had any impact outside the economic sphere. That has changed. It is also clear that the dismantling of internal borders—the Schengen agreement—and the powers of the European Commission to represent all the European nation-states in trade matters is an intrusion on these core functions. So is the decision at the Cologne summit in Germany in June 1999 to shape a common defense and foreign policy, a direct consequence of the war in Kosovo.

The ideological ingredients include the duty to preserve and promote the nation as a historical, linguistic, and cultural entity, symbolized by the royal and presidential heads of state. There is a pan-European market for such media material, but the national markets are by far the most important, and they are segregated by language. In Belgium this language barrier between media markets divides the nation-state into Flemish-speaking and French-speaking parts.

English is becoming the common, accepted language of the European Union, despite the strong cultural reservations of the French. Germans no longer expect their neighbors to speak their language, and few do. In the Nordic countries the Finns communicate in English rather than Swedish, formerly the common Nordic platform. Though there are numerous German speakers in eastern Europe, the enlargement of the European Union will further entrench English in the European institutions, with French suffering most, but probably also at the expense of the smaller European languages. But at the nonofficial level this strong tendency toward one working language is much less pronounced, and there are no signs of any of the national languages withering away.

Two factors ensure that a very large proportion of entertainment programming of European television stations is imported. One is U.S. domination of the global entertainment industry, and the other is the business economics of the media, which are able to purchase U.S. material at a fraction of the cost of producing national material. But in all the larger EU countries, virtually no one watches television in any other language than his or her own. Germany, France, Italy, and Spain have whole industries providing national-language sound to imported programming. Even in the Netherlands and the Nordic countries where English is spoken or understood by the vast majority of the people, subtitles in the national language are a must, and English-only television channels have a very limited audience.

There may still be a French-led attempt to limit the amount of U.S. television programming that may be shown in the European Union. Even in France, however, most now concede defeat in the market for television entertainment. But the nation-states retain control of the news markets. Public service stations are the dominant source of television news for most Europeans. Governments attempting to influence the news are so sharply rebuffed that they pose no real threat to editorial freedom. But public service stations are by definition national, not European, public service institutions. On a daily basis there is no perceptible difference between how public service and private television networks select and present news; they share the same national approach. But during election campaigns the public service stations tend to give higher priority to national political news, often the most concrete definition of public service, though promoting national cultural programming with limited audiences usually is part of their official mandate.

It is in the economic sphere that the retreat of the nation-state has been the most marked. Two sets of forces are eroding national economic autonomy: globalization, fostered by liberalization of international trade and technology, and the integration of the European economies, which from the business point of view is a strategy for survival and growth rather than a threat. The nation-state is too small to act in the global economy and too big and unwieldy to deal with local business environments—hence the shift toward regional growth centers, often transcending the borders of two or more EU nations. U.S. management guru Peter F. Drucker believes that the nation-state will survive the globalization of the economy and the information revolution that accompanies it. But he believes that it will be a greatly changed nation-state, especially in domestic fiscal and monetary policies, foreign economic policies, control of international business, and perhaps in the conduct of war. Drucker's perspective is global, not specifically European, but it nonetheless provides a useful approach to what is happening in the European Union.[2]

The single market, established in 1990, transferred substantial power from the state to the market in the European Union. Though remnants still exist, government-erected nontariff barriers between the EU markets have been dismantled and state aids severely reduced. The Maastricht Treaty, ratified in 1993, charted a course toward a single currency that required fiscal policies to converge within certain budgetary limits and stipulated that monetary policy should be turned over entirely to an independent European Central Bank. Disagreements about the goals of monetary policy provided a direct link between economic and monetary union (EMU) and national politics.

The first six months of using the euro exposed the fragility of having a common monetary policy but no common fiscal policy. The euro was much weakened by Italy's inability to abide by the budget rules agreed on by all Euroland ministers for 1999. It is obvious that some kind of common fiscal policy will have to be introduced, but there will be serious problems with member states intent upon preserving their welfare. National fiscal policies reflect the choices of national voters, and most of the money is spent on producing welfare and related public goods. There are major differences among the EU nation-states on both counts.

A Eurobarometer survey in October-November 1998 asked Europeans whether they wanted national or joint decisionmaking in eighteen specified policy areas. In four areas a majority preferred national decisionmaking: health care and social welfare, education, cultural policy, and the basic rules for broadcasting and press freedom and regulation.

The first two are top-priority items on the national budgets, and all four are part of the core functions of the nation-state. They are also very much part of the daily lives of Europeans.

Other policy areas seemed more distant to Europeans. More than two-thirds of them supported EU decisionmaking in seven policy areas: information about the EU, the fight against drugs, foreign policy, science and technology research, humanitarian aid, currency policy, and protection of the environment. This order of priorities is reflected in the EU principle of subsidiarity, which states that nothing should be decided at a higher level than is needed to find a solution.

Subsidiarity could also be called the mutual life insurance system of the nation-states of Europe. Popular support for the principle has actually grown since 1995, from 55 percent in the spring Eurobarometer survey of that year to 64 percent in the fall 1998 survey. This corresponds to a period that showed major progress in European integration and suggests that the subsidiarity principle is what keeps the gulf between popular perception of European integration and actual events of integration from widening beyond the point that will trigger a major counterreaction.

Currency is a classic core function of the nation-state, and the widespread support for an EU currency is, at first glance, a deviation from the principle of subsidiarity. It has been explained as a strong infatuation with the euro. But a better interpretation is probably that most Europeans accept that the nation-state can no longer deliver the economic results that people want and that the euro is seen not as a sacrifice of national sovereignty but as a pragmatic means of improving European competitiveness at the global level, as a response to globalization. European business wants the euro, and European voters are at least willing to give them the benefit of the doubt that it will help create jobs.

Jobs in the European Union are created at the regional level, and regional governments in Spain, Belgium, Germany, and Italy are very active in the economic field. Some even imitate the core functions of the nation-state not only by aggressively promoting their regional flags but also by signing international cooperation agreements and lobbying on their own in Brussels. It is noteworthy that Italy, Belgium, and Spain, three highly regionalized countries, are among the top four countries on the latest Eurobarometer list of those that support joint EU decisionmaking. The fourth is the Netherlands, an ideological stalwart of closer EU integration. But in terms of the social contract in which the state provides the means to maintain a minimum level of health and welfare, the nation-state is not going anywhere, not any time soon.

This observation is supported by the findings of the November 1998 Eurobarometer survey. Asked whether they wanted the EU to play a larger, the same, or a less important role in their daily lives, on average 48 percent of respondents said they wanted it to play a larger role, 27 percent the same, and 14 percent a smaller role. But the average conceals a dramatic difference between Greece, where 77 percent wanted the EU to play a larger role, and the UK, where only 29 percent wanted the European Union to do so.

Interestingly, there is a clear north-south divide in the results. All the Mediterranean countries, including France, are above average in wanting the European Union to play a larger role. All countries north of the Alps are below this average, perhaps surprisingly including the Netherlands. One disrespectful explanation could be that the respondents in the southern countries are hoping for more EU aid to show up. A more respectful interpretation would be that the European Union is seen as a vehicle to allow these economies to catch up with the relatively stronger northern economies. The run-up to economic and monetary union certainly saw a major recovery of the southern economies.

The north-south divide is again present, especially in responses to how the institutions of the European Union should change in the twenty-first century. Only 8 percent of the Danes want a European government, but 71 percent of the Italians support that idea. Only 10 percent of the Danes want a directly elected European president, whereas 70 percent of the Italians say they want one. Even allowing for the fact that neither the powers nor the policies of a European government or president can be defined and that the questions thus are highly hypothetical, there is no denying the pattern of attitudes.

Denmark merits closer scrutiny, not because it is my native country but because it is the only EU country that has formally rejected an EU treaty, the Maastricht Treaty in 1992, and voted not to join Euroland in a referendum in the fall of 2000. It is still, as the cited figures demonstrate, among the most Euroskeptic countries, although no longer in terms of general support for membership in the European Union but as regards relinquishing sovereignty to European institutions. Because Denmark is too small to have regions in a European context, the country is an obvious candidate for nation-state analysis.

Historically, the Danes have been strongly divided in their attitudes toward European integration, in fact, toward any kind of supranational cooperation. From the disastrous defeat in 1864 in the war against the Germans until the beginning of the Cold War, the Danes considered themselves an endangered species. Neutrality was seen as a prerequisite for national independence, in principle absolute neutrality, but with the proximity of Germany inevitably tilting the scales somewhat in that direction in both world wars. Saving the nation-state was imperative for any Danish government, and because there was no credible military option, diplomacy with an accommodative bias toward the realpolitik of the day was seen as the only policy that would do the job.

The emergence of the Cold War in Europe changed all this, and Denmark joined the North Atlantic Treaty Organization (NATO). But this decision was not initially supported by the general public, and the prime minister had to make it a cabinet issue in his own Social Democratic Party to make it happen. Public opinion favored the United Nations, as did a large portion of the usually governing Social Democratic Party and some of the smaller parties needed to provide the majority in the multiparty system of Danish politics.

Almost two-thirds of Danish voters, or 63.4 percent, endorsed Danish membership in the European Economic Community in October 1972, to this day the highest "yes" vote in any European referendum in Denmark. Voter turnout was 90.6 percent, also the highest ever registered. But the issues stressed by the supporters of Danish membership were strictly economic, with the final campaign ads warning that prices of everyday goods would rise by 15 or 20 percent overnight if there was a "no" vote and a subsequent devaluation of the Danish currency. The "no" campaign stressed the threat to the nation-state, likewise with no holds barred, and the jury is still out on who achieved the lowest standards of campaign ethics.

The Single European Act in 1986 posed a dilemma for the Danish political parties that supported EU membership. On the one hand, it was clearly economic, providing the legal basis for a single market that would give European industry a home base similar to or larger than that of the U.S. competition. On the other hand, it strengthened EU decisionmaking by limiting national veto powers, thus diluting national sovereignty. Denmark's largest party, the Social Democratic Party, was in opposition at the time, and perhaps tempted by the near certainty that the government would not survive a referendum defeat, decided to oppose the Single European Act. It was ratified by 56.2 percent of the voters, but voter turnout was a relatively low 75.4 percent.

As with the earlier treaties, the Maastricht Treaty was presented to the Danish voters as an economic treaty with hardly any political superstructure. Economic and monetary union and the single currency seemed eminently marketable, as the Danes had no illusions about the ability of the Danish krone to go its own way. Five out of six Danish parliamentarians asked their voters to say "yes" at the referendum in June 1992. Most of the organized opposition came from grassroots movements demanding that Denmark should leave the EU in the event of a "no" vote, but they were represented in the European, not the Danish, Parliament, and they had virtually no media support. Yet the Danish electorate said "no."

It was a "no" vote with a very slim margin, less than 1 percent. But 50.7 percent of the Danes had rejected the Maastricht Treaty, formally aborting the EU-wide ratification process and erecting a major roadblock for European political integration. A few weeks later Denmark won the European football championship, and the media in Denmark and around the world linked the two events as a unique and successful assertion of sovereignty by a small nation-state. Denmark was the David fighting the Goliath of European Union, and football demonstrated its usefulness as a symbol of national potency.

Politically, however, Denmark was in deep trouble. The conservative-liberal government led by Poul Schlueter, which had deeply committed European and Liberal Party leader Uffe Ellemann-Jensen as foreign minister, no longer had a credible EU policy. If the rejection of the Maastricht Treaty was upheld, as it legally had to be, few had any doubts it would in time be renegotiated with Denmark as a nonparticipant. To prevent this, a new referendum would have to ratify the Maastricht Treaty, despite the obvious problem of seeming to refuse a democratic verdict, and the more practical political problem, that the voters would be so antagonized that they would vote "no" again.

The solution was consistent with the fabric of Danish EU politics but unique in European politics in the way it was initiated. Because the government had been discredited, the opposition negotiated four opt-outs from the Maastricht Treaty with Denmark's European partners, on economic and monetary union, defense, legal and judiciary matters, and Union citizenship. Embodied in the Edinburgh agreement, these reservations became the political and legal basis for asking the Danes to reconsider. They duly did so in May 1993, with a "yes" vote of 56.7 percent and a "no" vote of 43.3 percent.

The latest, but not the last, Danish referendum endorsed the Amsterdam Treaty with a 55.1 percent "yes" vote and a 44.9 percent "no" vote. But it is noteworthy that both Prime Minister Poul Nyrup Rasmussen and the opposition leader Anders Fogh Rasmussen promised the voters that a "yes" to the Amsterdam Treaty would be a "no" to political union. These campaign excesses have mostly been forgotten. But the gap between public opinion and the political elite in Denmark was a problem in the latest referendum on economic and monetary union.[3] It is unlikely but possible that the Danes will refuse to ratify future treaties unless the subsidiarity principle is developed further and anchored firmly in them.

Almost all nation-states of Europe will be led by Social Democratic parties in the first years of the twenty-first century. Because the staunchest defenders of the nation-state in its traditional twentieth-century version were conservatives and parties to the right of mainstream conservative parties, the political shift to the left means that changes in the division of labor and balance of power between nation-states and the European Union will be defined and implemented by parties that generally want the European Union to play a more active role. But there are major differences between the parties, although a commitment to fight unemployment and a willingness to develop a defense dimension of the European Union are unifying factors.

France and Germany have been the principal architects of the current version of the European Union. They are certainly the key managers of economic and monetary union with its single currency. Their views will be taken very seriously by the independent European Central Bank. The United Kingdom has no formal influence on economic policies as long as it remains outside EMU, but an attempt to set the twenty-first-century Social Democratic economic agenda is nevertheless being made by British prime minister Tony Blair and German chancellor Gerhard Schröder after bilateral negotiations fully conforming to nation-state behavior. They are defining a new center or a third way for Europe.

Their agenda calls for further deregulation, easier access to venture capital, and a social security overhaul to promote job creation. Skeptical liberals and conservatives in Europe are still pondering whether their fire is being stolen, and if so, what they can do about it. Equally skeptical left-wingers within the British and German parties and even the French governing Socialist Party wonder what happened to socialist ideology. The simple answer, of course, is that European countries have reached a consensus that private sector growth is crucial. Reform of the welfare state is the most important economic challenge for the European Union in the first decades of the new century. The public budget limits of economic and monetary union serve as a warning to the nation-states that they have to reform, but how they choose to do so has to be decided at the level of the nation-state. By providing a single currency and upholding the fiscal discipline of EMU, the European Union may provide currency stability and the lowest possible interest rate, thus stimulating investment. Breaking down the remaining barriers between the EU markets will further stimulate growth.

It is obvious that the French prime minister Lionel Jospin is not about to endorse the British-German third way lock, stock, and barrel. The nation-state, once the pride of left and right in France, is now a redundant agent of economic change in France, but nation-state interests are still perceptible in the privatization process and highly visible, as when the interests of French farmers are articulated in defense of the Common Agricultural Policy, the great exception to the liberalization of the European economies in the 1990s.

France was also named, directly or indirectly, in the slogans of all three major parties contesting the French elections to the European Parliament in June 1999. "Let us construct our Europe," proclaimed the governing Socialists. "With Europe, let us have a forward-moving France," said the Liberal Union pour la Démocratie Française (UDF), though supporting a federal Europe. "Europe for France," countered the Conservative Rassemblement pour la République (RPR) and Démocracie Libérale (DL). "For France and the independence of Europe," retorted the Euroskeptics led by Charles Pasqua and Philippe de Villiers. All these literal translations do injustice to the grandeur of the French language but demonstrate the political need to approach the European Union from a national perspective. Pasqua also insisted that any treaty changes should be put to a referendum. The last time this happened, in 1992, the electorate narrowly endorsed the Maastricht Treaty, by 51 percent to 49 percent, much to the surprise and consternation of then Socialist president François Mitterand and a large majority in the French parliament.

In the Agenda 2000 negotiations in 1999 on the financial perspectives for 2000–2006, Germany insisted that its net contribution to the European Union be reduced. This is typical nation-state behavior, the last major offensive on this point having been mounted by Margaret Thatcher on behalf of the United Kingdom. It also reflects justified German self-confidence that Germany no longer has to downplay national interests because it lost World War II. The restoration of Berlin as the national capital and the reopening of the old Reichstag parliament building represent this new national attitude. Further, the fall of communism and German reunification have converted German reliance on the United States and NATO from one of subservience to full partnership.

The Kosovo conflict has brought this process full circle. German foreign minister Joschka Fischer was a strong supporter of the NATO bombing of Yugoslavia and a common defense policy for the European Union. Had a land war been necessary, German troops would have been in combat for the first time since the defeat of the Nazis in 1945. The foreign minister's own party, the Greens, had grave reservations on this issue and might have split or forced Fischer to abandon the government if Slobodan Milosevic had not withdrawn from Kosovo.

German politicians of all three major parties are in varying degrees far ahead of popular voter sentiment on defense and euro policies. It is very unlikely that this will surface as a major problem at the next German national election in 2002. Schröder has promised to reduce unemployment in Germany, not the European Union, by 1 million, and Germans will accept no European excuses. And whatever happens at the European level, the means to do so will have to be found at the level of the nation-state.

Will there be nation-states in the European Union in ten, twenty, or thirty years? In ten years, absolutely. A number of new nation-states will join the EU but will be unable to participate fully in integration even if they wanted to, especially in the EMU, which is likely to build at least a minimum common fiscal policy in response to challenges to the euro. Deepening of integration in the European Union is not incompatible with widening; indeed it is probably a political prerequisite. But it means defining the powers and responsibilities of not only institutions of the European Union but also those of various groups of members that are necessarily participating in all spheres of cooperation in the European Union.

Two nation-states, Germany and France, will remain at the helm of the European Union in the first years of the twenty-first century. The United Kingdom will try to make this pairing a triumvirate, but even though Schröder has declared his intention to adopt the economic policies of New Labor, Blair will have to deliver the British pound to the euro before he can claim such status. He will have to win a referendum first, and that is not yet a done thing.

The nation-state will survive, but it will have to redefine itself. The physical barriers are gone, which means that the political borders are crumbling. European law is superior to national law, and like the Supreme Court in the United States the European Court of Justice interprets it in a manner that promotes integration and not a continuation of the status quo. Nation-states can no longer sustain the defense industries necessary for independent security policies, even if they were desirable.

The logic of joint defense procurement, as Romano Prodi, the new president of the European Commission has pointed out, is a common defense policy. The EU summit in Cologne in June 1999 started that process, and may be a milestone in the history of European integration comparable to the Maastricht summit that initiated EMU. Enlargement of the European Union will be preceded by treaty changes that may incorporate defense and certainly will curtail the rights of veto of nation-states, formally speaking reducing the sovereignty of all. In business terms the European Union is already highly integrated and becoming even more so as the number of mergers and alliances picks up to U.S. speed. Cross-border regions operate on free market terms, usurping national aspirations to promote economic growth within the nation-state, and some national regions do not limit themselves to trade, but are developing a political clout to match their economic power. It would seem time that the weaker nation-states of the European Union started thinking about their epitaphs rather than their future.

Any student of the early stages of integration of the United States would be tempted to find parallels in current developments in the European Union. A train seems to have been set in motion that will naturally stop at the federal capital in a United States of Europe. That is certainly a possibility in twenty or thirty years, but it is not inevitable. The Confederate States of Europe is a much more likely name for the station, with what will amount to federal powers in a number of policy areas, most importantly foreign policy and defense. The European Union already has the equivalent of the Federal Reserve.

The real threat to the nation-state lies elsewhere. Currently, the national political systems are the conduits of power to the Council of Ministers in the EU and to the whole set of intergovernmental structures, including the summits of the heads of state at which decisions are made in the European Union today. Decisions are thus born from and legitimized by national parliaments, even if tempered by majority voting. That would change dramatically if the European Parliament was to bypass the national parliaments and replace them as the main source of legitimacy for the decisions of the European Union.

As the resignation of the European Commission in 1999 demonstrated, the European Parliament has reduced the democratic deficit (that is, increased democratic control at the Union level). The extended co-decision rights embedded in the Amsterdam Treaty should further reduce the democratic deficit. But the gap between the ambitions of the European parliamentarians and the European electorate was documented by the low turnout at the elections to the European Parliament and the conspicuous absence of national political figures on the ballots in virtually all the EU countries.

Drucker argues in *Management Challenges for the 21st Century* that the most important social phenomenon in the United States in many years is the emergence of megachurches, which have been very successful.[4] They have analyzed why people do not go church and acted on that information by providing spiritual rather than ritual services.

Finding what spiritual service is demanded by Europeans will be the hard part. It requires a broadly accepted definition of a European identity and a market for that message. Both conditions may in time be fulfilled, but in the foreseeable future the nation-states serve that market as ministers of the national interest.

5

Enlargement of the European Union: How New EU Members Will Change the Shape of Europe

MARTIN WALKER

The maps outside the office of successive EU transportation commissioners may be the best aid in comprehending the real meaning of the European Union's enlargement plans. They feature the grand design of continental transportation that EU experts have been drawing up with the Geneva-based United Nations Economic Commission for Europe. At a conference in Helsinki in October 1998, these experts jointly presented the scheme for two huge new transportation arteries, combining roads and fast rail systems. One runs north to south from Finland to Greece, connecting the Baltic states, Poland, Hungary, Romania, and Bulgaria before branching off to Salonika in Greece and Istanbul in Turkey. The other runs west to east from the Atlantic Ocean at the British Rail network terminus, under the Channel Tunnel, through Brussels and Cologne to Berlin and Warsaw and then to Moscow.

Not the armed frontiers and iron curtains of old but the new arteries of a greater Europe are the defining lines of the new century. They run from the Arctic Ocean and the Baltic region to the Mediterranean and the Black Sea; from the Atlantic to the Volga River and the Caspian Sea. Behind this grandiose scheme lies the knowledge that the countries of central and eastern Europe represent to the plump and satiated economies of western Europe the promise of dynamism and growth. Just as the flood of U.S. Marshall Plan aid inspired Western Europe's furious growth rates in the 1950s and 1960s, so enlargement to the east can and should be the locomotive for future growth in both the old and new parts of Europe.

It will take at least a generation, but by 2020 most of the Warsaw Pact lands should be connected to Europe not just by security pacts and

EU membership but by a shared and common prosperity. An act of historical justice is sweetened by everybody's economic self-interest, in one of the great geopolitical and geo-economic challenges of our time.

At the EU summit in Luxembourg in December 1997, Polish prime minister Jerzy Buzek had tears in his eyes. He was proclaiming the real end of World War II when the European Union formally invited his country and the rest of the old Warsaw Pact nations to join their prosperous haven. It was also, noted his Hungarian counterpart Gyula Horn, the reunification of Europe. For Vaclav Havel of the Czech Republic, it was the fulfillment of that promise made by President George Bush in the summer before the Berlin Wall came down, that the United States was dedicated to the coming of a Germany whole and free in a Europe whole and free.

It has been almost a decade in the coming, but the real aftermath of the Cold War is now plain to see in the double enlargement of both the North Atlantic Treaty Organization (NATO) alliance and the European Union. The division of Europe that followed the defeat of Nazi Germany was finally over, and the collapse of communism meant that the new Europe could insist that the crucial qualification for membership would be not prosperity but democracy, free speech, and free institutions. Thus the countries that brought the music of Frederic Chopin, Franz Liszt, and Bela Bartok, the plays of Vaclav Havel, the science of Copernicus to adorn Europe's culture were coming back where they always belonged. But the European Union will have to twist and wrestle itself into a new shape to absorb them.

The irony of Europe's planned enlargement into eastern Europe is that—despite howls of pain from redundant Polish steelworkers and downsized Czech businesses—by the end of 1999 it was already having more impact on the European Union than on the candidate countries. "We have a serious agenda ahead to reform the European institutions, from the EU budget to the Common Agricultural Policy [CAP]—as the prerequisites to enlargement," German foreign minister Joschka Fischer told the European Parliament as his country assumed the EU's rotating presidency in January.[1] The pressure from the German government was intense to prepare the way for enlargement. The fundamental reality was that the EU was required to reform the CAP and the EU budget system before the Poles, Czechs, Hungarians, and others could hope to join.

This meant that the legacy of Margaret Thatcher has at last begun its grim visitation upon Europe. The British prime minister had made her stirring call at Bruges in 1988, in the year before the Berlin Wall came down. She stated that the United Kingdom would always look on

Warsaw, Prague, and Budapest as great European cities. As always with Lady Thatcher, sentiment blended with the sharpest self-interest. She always hoped that enlarging the EU would preclude its deepening into a federal system. And just as she knew that her own British budget rebate was storing up trouble for Europe's future, she knew that enlargement would require agricultural reform that would eventually wreck the CAP, the central institution of the EU as we have known it.

This Thatcherian agenda began to thrust its way into Europe in 1998–1999, as the European Parliament began its own wrangles into the reform of the CAP and the budget as the essential preludes to enlargement. These issues could no longer be put off because accession talks with the Poles, Czechs, Hungarians, Slovenes, Estonians, and Cypriots had formally begun. But the fissures in European opinion became plain when the European Parliament voted in 1998 for all eleven candidates to be allowed to start the accession talks at the same time. This became known as the "regatta option," after the way rowing races start, with all boats leaving the start line at the same moment but reaching the finish line at their own best speed.

There was more to this decision than met the eye. The European Commission, with strong support from Britain, planned to distinguish between those countries deemed ready for entry and the five who were not. For the Commission, Poland, Hungary, the Czech Republic, Slovenia, Estonia, and Cyprus were all ready for a fast track to membership within ten years or less. (The candidacy of Cyprus was always understood to be complicated by the island's division, along a "peace line" policed by the United Nations between the Greek and Turkish sectors, a partition that had endured since the Turkish invasion of 1974.) Other countries, notably Romania, Bulgaria, Latvia, and Lithuania, were seen as less obviously prepared. Slovakia, which until the elections in the autumn of 1998 was governed by the authoritarian regime of Vladimir Meciar, was deemed not to meet the standards of democratic practice required by the EU. This changed with the elections of 1998, which voted a center-left and democratic coalition into power.

The member states were themselves divided, with Sweden, Denmark, and Greece all supporting the regatta plan, under which all applicants started the process at once. Spain and Portugal, although more concerned about the costs to them of enlargement, also leaned toward this view. Cynics claimed that the regatta plan was a device to delay the entire process of EU enlargement. Spain and Italy supported the principle of enlargement. But in practice the 1998 declaration of Spain's state secretary for Europe, Ramon de Miguel, that Europe could not expand at the cost of dissolving fundamental principles, marked a serious obstacle to the enlargement process. Enlargement would fundamentally change the balance of economic power within the EU. Spain, Greece, and Portugal would at once be replaced as the EU's "deserving poor" by Poland, Hungary, the Czech Republic, and other new members, with inevitable effects on their receipts from the EU. At the same time, this financial worry was deepened by the alarm of the Club Med group of southern countries that enlargement would change the geographical balance of power in the EU. "The expansion toward eastern Europe is an important step, but the region does not have the same critical mass of hundreds of millions of workers and consumers that a Euro-Mediterranean economic zone could have," then Italian prime minister Romano Prodi told Spain's Royal Political Science Academy in Madrid in 1998.[2]

European foreign ministers finally agreed to a compromise under which all eleven central and eastern European countries who wanted to join the Union could start the process together. But in reality only the six chosen nations would then proceed more quickly through the rest of the hoops. This successfully blurred what had begun to look like a new dividing line across Europe between the six deemed fit to start entry negotiations and the five deemed less ready.

The formal process of enlargement began under the British presidency of the European Council, with a formal banquet hosted by Queen Elizabeth II at Buckingham Palace in March 1998, at which she said the process would increase both the European continent's stability and its prosperity. The negotiations then proceeded smoothly, at least in public. In December 1998, the six "fast track" countries began the first accession talks at ministerial level on seven chapters of the *acquis communautaire*, the vast 80,000-page body of EU rules and regulations that all new members are required to adopt. These must be formally introduced into domestic legislation, and the candidate members must also show that they have established the judicial independence and administrative competence, from customs staff to health inspectors, to implement them.

Poland, Hungary, Slovenia, Estonia, Cyprus, and the Czech Republic were told by EU officials that three of these chapters—research, education, and rules for small and medium-sized business enterprises—had been provisionally completed. EU officials then agreed that there did not seem to be serious difficulties with the other four areas: telecommunications, cultural and audiovisual policies, industrial policy, and the move to a Common Foreign and Security Policy.

These agreements simply got the easy bits out of the way first. The real troubles lay in wait, from agricultural policy to border security, from environmental and financial standards to budgets and the introduction of the value-added tax (VAT). And those are only the difficulties that face the applicant countries. Equally tough problems confronted the fifteen existing members of the EU as they addressed the costs and reforms required in admitting the CEECs, the fashionable acronym for the central and eastern European countries.

Hans van den Broek, the Dutch Christian Democrat who ran the enlargement process as external affairs commissioner, became famous in eastern Europe for reminding the CEECs where the real power lay: "The European Union is not trying to join the Czech Republic" was one of his pointed comments.[3] But the fact is that the EU itself would be fundamentally transformed by this process, and in the course of 1999 the costs and implications of that process moved to center stage.

The average European country in 1999 had a per capita gross domestic product (GDP) of around $20,000 per year. By contrast, the 39 million Poles had a per capita GDP of barely one-third that amount, and the 18 million Czechs and Hungarians had less than half. And these are the advanced new candidates, far richer than the Romanians and Bulgarians in the second wave, who are less than half as well off as the Poles. The six new members would increase the population of the EU by 17 percent but would add only 3 percent to its GDP. Even if Poland could maintain the breakneck pace of economic growth it managed in the latter half of the 1990s, it will still be at least fifteen years before its GDP is within striking distance of the EU average. Just as German unification had brought 17 million much poorer neighbors into the new country, with their tragically different tradition of political and social concepts, so the EU's enlargement would add a vast eastern poverty belt of 110 million people.

The admission of the poor easterners would therefore have a dramatic impact on the way Europe financed its budget and paid out its structural funds, which were designed to level out regional inequalities. And it would force a fundamental overhaul of the controversial CAP; the Poles alone had more farmers than Britain, France, and Germany combined. "We have never before faced the challenge of absorbing a new member state, more than 25 percent of whose work force is on the land," EU agriculture commissioner Franz Fischler noted.[4]

Before enlargement became practical, there were three things that the EU had to do. The first was to reform the CAP, which in 1999 still accounted for half the EU's annual $90 billion budget. The Poles, Czechs, and Hungarians all said that they assumed that the prevailing level of farm subsidies would be available to them once they join. That was more pious hope than realistic policy objective. Keeping these levels of subsidies and adding so many new farmers would have doubled the cost of the CAP overnight. And it would have been incompatible with the next round of talks at the World Trade Organization, for which Europe had already committed itself in principle to phasing out export subsidies for food.

Second, the EU had to sort out its own budget payment and transfer system. In 1998, Germany paid out close to 30 percent of the EU budget but got back only 15 percent of the refunds that come through the CAP and structural funds. Net payers to the budget, like Germany, Austria, Sweden, Holland, and the UK, were in effect subsidizing the less wealthy countries like Spain, Greece, and Portugal. Spain, the biggest and toughest of these countries, vowed to block everything rather than forgo its large, annual net income from the EU. Spanish foreign minister Abel Matutes insisted that enlargement was an obligation for all EU members—it should not come at Spain's expense. Germany had sworn it would no longer act as Europe's bankroller, and Britain said it would not give up the annual $3 billion budget rebate Thatcher had won in 1984.

Third, the EU had to work out how it would adapt an institutional system initially designed in the 1960s for six countries to a much bigger administrative operation for more than twenty nations. In 2000 the EU had a total of twenty commissioners, one for each small country and two each for the bigger ones, which most countries agree is already too many. Under the current rules, the next wave of members would mean seven commissioners because Poland reckons it is big enough to deserve two. And then new jobs would have to be found inside the Commission for the Poles, Czechs, and Slovenes who would be recruited, and the various national votes on the Council of Ministers would have to be reweighted. The choice was plain: whether a body of more than twenty countries could continue the system of national veto—the way Greece had long stalled EU policy toward Turkey being a prime example of the problems of the veto system—or whether it was finally time to move toward majority voting. This issue so nearly sank the Amsterdam Treaty negotiations that the heads of government kicked it into the future.

By the year 2000, with the accession talks under way, that future had arrived. These three big challenges were supposed to be resolved by the end of the German presidency of the EU Council in June 1999. They were, rather, only half-settled, with much remaining to be done. Fischler had based his reform plan on the principle that the EU would no longer subsidize food prices but would allow them to adjust to world market levels. Instead, he proposed to subsidize individual farmers in poor areas as a way to maintain the distinctive charms of Europe's rural culture and landscape.

After weeks of argument, including a furious row between France and Germany that severely tested their traditional partnership in Europe, farm ministers agreed to a far more modest version of this plan in March 1999. At their Petersburg summit in February 1999, the EU heads of government had insisted that the farm budget be no more than 40.5 billion euros in its first full year and that costs over the seven-year budget process reach no higher than 307 billion euros. The farm ministers fell short of this target, and at the Berlin summit the following month, French president Jacques Chirac succeeded in defending French farm interests and watering down the CAP reform even further. This development meant that a further reform deal would have to be agreed before Poland and its farmers could hope to become full members of the EU.

The battle over the budget became even more difficult as Spain, Greece, and Portugal simply refused to accept the logic that they would no longer be "poor" countries once enlargement began. And the Germans refused to accept the historical lesson that the EU only functions because they have consistently been prepared to pay for it. The German government, a coalition of Social Democrats and Greens led by Chancellor Gerhard Schröder, insisted on a budget reform to end the annual $12 billion drain from the German federal treasury to Brussels.

The Germans were pivotal to all this because they were both the richest European power and the most troubled. They were rich but weak, in that their military and strategic weight lagged far behind that of France and Britain, Europe's two nuclear powers. They were also at a psychological turning point. Governed for the first time by a generation of leaders who were not wracked by an instinctive sense of historic guilt, they did not automatically reach for their wallets to solve Europe's problems. Nor did they reflexively reach for the easy solution of more European integration to escape Germany's internal rows.

On January 1, 1999, these new Germans, in their uneasy coalition of Greens and Social Democrats (themselves split between Blair-style modernizers and traditional socialists), assumed a place in the sun. They started their six-month turn of chairing and running all meetings of Europe's national ministers, of the G7, and of that fledgling military structure, the Western European Union, by setting themselves a series of tasks. The first was to start the single currency smoothly in the world financial system and in Europe's single market. With luck, they hoped to use Euroland's own stability to anchor a global economy that was still hideously vulnerable to new shocks from those old nightmares of Asia and Russia and the new alarms from Japan, China, and Brazil. In this they suffered an early setback because of the strident campaign by the influential left-wing finance minister (and leader of the Social Democratic Party), Oskar Lafontaine, for lower interest rates in order to create new jobs. But the euro and its interest rates were set by the new European Central Bank, whose charter asserted its independence from political influence. Lafontaine's campaign helped the euro to lose 8 percent of its value against the U.S. dollar in its first ten weeks of life before he resigned in March amid a chorus of denunciation from German banks and industry alike.

Germany's second task was to pass Agenda 2000 during its six months at the European helm. Agenda 2000 was the jargon for the package of budgetary, farm, and systemic reforms required to prepare for EU enlargement. These issues were not insoluble, just very difficult. What made them acute was the new German government's election pledge to stop being Europe's bankroller of last resort, even as the former East German provinces were some of the poorest parts of the EU.

The sums in dispute were, in relative terms, peanuts. The entire European budget was fixed at just below 1.2 percent of GDP. Germany's net payments to Europe, as Helmut Kohl used to point out, were around 0.5 percent of German GDP. This amount was the equivalent of two months spending on the German defense budget and bought a great deal more security and prestige in world affairs. (Britain's net payment was less than 0.2 percent of its own GDP, a strikingly small proportion in relation to the amount of political controversy it generated.) Germany finally accepted a modest reform, which left it still the prime bankroller of the EU budget.

The most serious German task, on which the future of Europe fundamentally hinged, was the ability of the new Schröder government finally to make the country normal and relaxed about its role, identity, and history. Given that normality in the European context embraced a France and Britain that remained obsessed with their international standing, this should not have proved insuperable, despite the uncomfortable echoes that resonated from the shift of the capital from Bonn to Berlin.

Germany has never been a "normal" nation. Otto von Bismarck's unification drive of the 1860s catapulted the place into European primacy virtually overnight. The subsequent self-destructive adventures of the mad Kaiser and the madder corporal Adolf Hitler still dominate Europe's thinking about a country that has been ably and solidly governed by a series of competent and democratic politicians since 1945. The establishment of a German normalcy was thus a central precondition for the EU's healthy enlargement and a key test for the Schröder government.

There were three reasons the climate should have been favorable for this step. First, the euro had so much political and corporate will behind it, in the United States and Europe alike, that Euroland should have enjoyed a stable macroeconomic base for growth in the future. The second was that in French prime minister Lionel Jospin and British prime minister Tony Blair, the new German government was blessed with the supportive partnership of two unusually levelheaded and politically sympathetic leaders in the other two important European capitals. The third reason was that Germany's friends, in the United States as in Europe, were convinced that a stable, prosperous, and self-confident Germany was the key to Europe's future and to the successful absorption of the eleven candidate members.

The overarching context of all this was important, not least for the enlargement process. As the year 2000 began, national governments in Europe decided less and less. The coming of the euro meant that most of the usual levers of economic policymaking were being taken from their hands. The development of a Common Foreign and Security Policy, as mandated by the Amsterdam Treaty, and the new Anglo-French initiative for a common defense identity meant ever more pooling of traditional nation-state sovereignty. The new powers of the European Parliament, again as mandated by the Amsterdam Treaty, to have co-decision powers with the national governments on most aspects of EU legislation, eroded the old role of the nation-states yet further. The new Europe was a new entity; not yet a federal system but far more than a confederation of independent nation-states.

The new member states, who will take the EU's frontiers to the Black Sea, will play a central role in deciding how that new entity develops. For example, the fact that three of the first-wave candidates, Poland, Hungary, and the Czech Republic, were also new members of NATO helped reassert the link between EU members and NATO that had been weakened by the accession of the three neutral states of Finland, Austria, and Sweden in the 1990s.

The new members will also shift Europe's center of gravity, reinforcing that psychological move to the east that the relocation of Germany's capital from Bonn to Berlin had symbolized. In the 1980s, the EU was an essentially Western European institution that naturally looked to the west, across the Atlantic. The Europe of the twenty-first century would be based in Mitteleuropa, with an inherent tendency to look to the east. It would remain an essentially Christian culture, one whose roots lay in Rome and the Reformation rather than in the Orthodox Christianity from ancient Byzantium that prevailed in Russia, Serbia, and most of Ukraine.

After all these efforts to reform the EU, several questions remained: whether the former states of Yugoslavia would eventually join the Union; whether Turkey itself as a secular state with a powerful Islamic tradition would be fully welcomed into an essentially Christian club; and whether Ukraine and even Russia might move from trade associations and partnership agreements with the EU to a more intimate connection. The direction was set in the course of 1999. Under the German presidency, Joschka Fischer laid out a long-term restructuring plan for the former nations of Yugoslavia, which held out to all of them the prospect of eventual membership in the EU and NATO. During the Finnish presidency in the second half of 1999, Turkey was finally accepted as a candidate for membership, in part because of a marked decline in its internal tensions with the Kurds after the decision of the Turkish government not to impose the death sentence on a captured Kurdish separatist leader and also because of a marked thaw in Greek-Turkish relations.

The Commission stated that Turkey should be considered as a candidate country, although it said there was "no question" of opening negotiations at this stage. In October 1999 the European Commission also recommended that the five central and eastern European states of Slovakia, Latvia, Lithuania, Bulgaria, and Romania should start full membership talks, as should the island nation of Malta.

The prospect of full membership for Turkey and for Serbia remained far in the future. However, Serbia's prospects changed dramatically when dictator Slobodan Milosevic lost an election for president in the fall of 2000 to westward-looking Vojislav Kostunica. But as the new millennium began, the new Commission under Romano Prodi was aiming at bringing the first new members into the club during its five-year term of office. Somehow, the farm and budget reforms must be resolved, just as the new intergovernmental conference must agree on new rules on the numbers of commissioners and the weighting of national votes in the Council of Ministers. The EU usually manages to find ways of meeting such deadlines. It may have little choice, since the economic implications of eventual membership are already transforming the countries of eastern Europe. Those maps outside the office of the transportation commissioner point to a commercial and logistical momentum that will give the enlargement process both meaning and potential. The grand new arteries of the new Europe lead to Istanbul and to Moscow, symbolizing new directions for a European Union whose progress has never really stopped because it wisely refused to define the limits to the democratic and prosperous space it had achieved.

Part 2

LOOKING OUTWARD

6

The Future of
Europe's Foreign Policy

MARTIN WALKER

During the forty years of the Cold War, Europe had few foreign policy options. It was a continent divided, and on each side of the Iron Curtain two vast military forces stood constantly to arms. Even the occasional relaxation of a post-Stalin thaw or a Nixon-Brezhnev détente or the West German efforts at carving some independent strategic space through "Ostpolitik" could not fundamentally break the permafrost in which policy was gripped. The end of the Cold War changed everything, although the almost immediate crises in the Gulf in 1990–1991 and the eruption of the Balkan wars throughout the 1990s delayed the full appreciation of the degree to which the strategic environment had been transformed.

President Bill Clinton was one of the first to grasp the most important change, noting while governor of Arkansas in 1991 that "we have moved from the age of geo-politics to the era of geo-economics."[1] The traditional diplomatic minuet of nuclear superpowers discussing missiles at arms control summits was to be replaced by commercial superpowers discussing currency markets and trade agreements at economic summits. Exports, not warheads, were to be the new definitions of power.

In the Cold War world of geopolitics, the shrunken Europe of twelve essentially Western European member states was a subordinate partner to the United States. In the post–Cold War world, the larger European Union of fifteen members, on track to become twenty-one and eventually twenty-six members or more, including the Baltic states, was in some crucial respects the equal of the United States. Its new single currency, the euro, took its place alongside the dollar, an effective du-opoly of money that reflected the fact that the EU and the United States between them accounted for almost half the world's wealth, almost two-thirds of its trade, and almost three-quarters of its investment.

In the final year of the millennium, which saw the birth of Europe's new single currency, three parallel events took place—in addition to the sustained air campaign against Serbia and the subsequent peacekeeping mission in Kosovo—that accelerated and indeed required the develop-ment of a common European foreign policy. These were the ratification of the Amsterdam Treaty; the formal enlargement of the North Atlantic Treaty Organization (NATO) alliance to include Poland, Hungary, and the Czech Republic, which finally ended the Cold War division of Europe; and NATO's formal approval of a "separable but not separate" European security and defense identity. This gave U.S. blessing to the ability of the European powers to use NATO assets in operations that need not require the hitherto-essential presence of U.S. forces.

These various developments unfolded in a context of potential crisis, with European leaders uncomfortably aware that they inhabited a per-ilous neighborhood. The financial implosion of Russia in the summer of 1998 and the consequent enfeeblement of the Russian state system, along with serious fears of winter famines, reminded Europe forcefully of the dangers of a big, destabilized neighbor armed with uncertainly controlled nuclear weapons that might be available to the highest bidder. The fear of Russian nuclear attack had dwindled, but there were more pressing fears of Russia's obsolescent network of nuclear power stations, eight of them built on the ill-fated Chernobyl design.

Russia was just one quadrant of the crescent of crisis that Europe faced. Even closer to home, an hour's drive from the EU's Austrian border, the wars of the Yugoslav succession still simmered. NATO forces maintained an uneasy peace in Bosnia, and after a three-month bombing campaign against Serbia had imposed yet another on the province of Kosovo. Its refugees had long been flooding across the Adriatic Sea to Italy and south across the Macedonian hills to the most southerly EU member, Greece, until the brutality of repression in Kosovo by the Milosevic regime in Belgrade led NATO to intervene. The driving force of NATO and EU policy had been to prevent the Kosovo conflict from getting out of hand, spilling across borders to ig-nite ethnic Albanians in Macedonia, Montenegro, and Bulgaria. Even before NATO's 1999 bombing campaign and occupation of Kosovo, some Albanian and Kosovar militants were demanding the creation of a great pan-Albanian (and Islamic) state. The potential for disruption was manifest.

South of the Balkans, Turkey's own difficulty with its Kurdish minority was but the antechamber to the prolonged Middle Eastern crisis that had begun not with the establishment of the state of Israel in 1948 but with the collapse of the Ottoman Empire in 1918. As the source of most of Europe's oil, many of its refugees, and its intermittent difficulties with terrorism, the Middle East from the Gulf to the length of the North African coastline was a powerful and insistent European security concern. From the stalled Middle East peace process and the on-again-off-again Israeli-Syrian talks to the slaughter by Islamic extremists in Algeria, the region was a deeply uncomfortable neighbor for Europeans.

Moreover, geography imposed another problem for Europe. The northern countries naturally saw the Russian problem and the prospect of EU enlargement into central and eastern Europe as the predominant concern. Europe's Club Med group, whose shores were washed by the Mediterranean, equally focused their own concerns toward North Africa and the Middle East. Even as a common European foreign policy began to form, an inherent conflict of interest persisted between north and south that would require careful management.

There was a further underlying problem for Europe: the worrying distinction between the broadly good relations between the United States and its traditional nation-state partners in NATO and the rather more problematic relations between the United States and the EU in general. Although they shared democratic values, there were important nuances in their approaches to the free market and above all a potential for serious argument in their divergent views on free trade.

As NATO members gathered in Washington, D.C., for their fiftieth anniversary summit in 1999, agreeing on a new strategic doctrine and welcoming the new members from eastern Europe, the display of comity among the NATO allies stood in stark contrast to the heated disputes between the United States and the EU at the World Trade Organization in Geneva. The threats and counterthreats of massive sanctions over the banana dispute (which neither the EU nor United States grew) were themselves but a prelude to looming rows over the use of hormones in beef and the European consumer's deep suspicions of genetically modified organisms, which were becoming commonplace in U.S. food exports.

This contrast between trade rows and security agreements emphasized the deepest problem in forging a common European foreign policy. In the Europe of fifteen, eleven states were members of NATO. Four were officially neutral and thus not alliance members: Austria, Finland, Sweden, and Ireland. France was a halfhearted member of

NATO, still declining to rejoin the military command structure while remaining in political and diplomatic terms a full member of the alliance. Moreover, France seemed least comfortable among the European powers with the dominant role of the United States in the transatlantic security relationship. French foreign minister Hubert Vedrine coined the term *hyperpower* to define the extraordinary powers the United States enjoyed in the 1990s in the fields of global trade and global security, along with global leadership in technology and increasing influence in cultural trends, from Hollywood to fast food.

In short, Europe was poised at the beginning of the new century with a number of dilemmas and had to make some important policy choices, all of which went to the core question of identity: what did Europe's member states want their association to become? It was already a confederal system of associated states with common trade rules, a common legislative and regulatory system, and a common currency. All these implied that Europe had increasingly common interests and would need an increasingly common approach to dealing with them.

This was not a new situation. Europe had repeatedly been confronted with a common challenge in the past and had either failed to meet it or met it only by subordinating its policies to those of the United States. The pattern had been set with the dawn of the Cold War and had become so ingrained that a degree of subservience to and dependence on the Americans had become a habit. This pattern even survived the Cold War's end, when the Luxembourg foreign minister Jacques Poos proclaimed—as the Balkan wars broke out—that the hour of Europe was at hand.

Europe initially mishandled the mission, entangling its troops in Bosnia in a complex and enfeebling dual-key system of command with the United Nations. France and Britain grumbled that Germany had got them into this mess by insisting that the EU recognize the independence of Croatia and Slovenia, thus forcing the breakup of the old Yugoslav federation. In the end, it took a U.S.-brokered peace agreement at a Dayton air base, negotiated by the U.S. envoy Richard Holbrooke and enforced by a U.S.-led NATO force, to control Europe's first war since 1945.

In part because of the lessons of Bosnia and with an eye to the implications of the imminent new common currency, the EU leaders understood that in negotiating the Amsterdam Treaty they would have to devise means to make a common foreign policy both possible and credible. The formal ratification of the Amsterdam Treaty by all fifteen member states in the course of 1999 committed the EU to developing a Common Foreign and Security Policy (CFSP) and established a series of crucial enabling instruments to achieve it.

The first was the appointment of a single figure to run the CFSP. They chose the Spanish secretary-general of NATO, Javier Solana, to be the first high representative, who would finally be able to answer the celebrated 1970 question of Henry Kissinger, then national security adviser at the White House: "When I want to speak to Europe, whose number do I call?" From the French acronym for CFSP, Solana would be known as Monsieur PESC and was appointed by the heads of government at the EU's Cologne summit in June 1999. Monsieur PESC had as his first task the recruitment and organization of his own staff, a policy planning and early warning unit based in Brussels and staffed by and coordinating with the various foreign ministries.

Moreover, the Amsterdam Treaty called for agreement on a series of European foreign policy strategies on major issues. The first to be tackled was EU policy toward Russia, and in its attempt to blend microeconomic aid policies and macroeconomic financial support with security issues and the EU's own enlargement plans, this strategy is supposed to fulfill three functions. First, it should provide a model for the holistic way in which the EU sought to approach the big issues of foreign policy in the future. Second, it seeks to blend the EU's economic and commercial strengths with its potential as a stabilizing regional security system. Third, it is intended to define a broad policy direction that all EU members can individually support while not precluding the development of their own bilateral relations with Russia.

Once such a series of European strategies was agreed on major policy areas like the Middle East, Africa, and the Balkans, taking joint action to implement them would become easier. The Amsterdam negotiators understood that they could not possibly bind member states to join future operations, since the EU was still something short of a military alliance. So they devised a mechanism known as "constructive abstention," which would prevent any one or two countries from blocking EU action while giving them an accepted means of declining to take part. In effect, Amsterdam required that all EU nations adopt a common strategy but left the tactics of implementing it to future EU leaders.

This compromise was probably inevitable, given the differing interests of the various national governments. Consider the following scenarios: a complete breakdown of law and order and of the state's authority in Algeria; a major famine in Russia that unleashed waves of refugees moving to Poland and Ukraine; a militant new government in Albania dedicated to forging a pan-Albanian nation, even at the price of war with its neighbors.

This first crisis in Algeria would deeply concern France, the former colonial ruler, because it would increase the number of refugees seeking to enter France, threaten energy supplies and investments, and create domestic political pressure from many Algerians living in France. It would concern Italy and Spain, again because of refugee pressures but also because of the far greater danger of the destabilization affecting Morocco, Tunisia, and even Libya. Northern Europe, let alone the United States, would have far fewer interests at stake and might be reluctant to join a Franco-Spanish effort to restore stability. They could adopt "constructive abstention."

The second crisis in eastern Europe would be of immediate and serious concern to Germany, Finland, Sweden, and Denmark and could become a mortal threat to state survival for the new EU applicant countries of Poland, Hungary, and Estonia. For Italy, Spain, Portugal, and Greece, the dangers would be far more remote and less compelling. NATO's long habit of concentrating on Russia would probably bring the United States, Britain, and France into the forefront of any international attempts to stabilize the situation. The southern EU members could then adopt "constructive abstention."

These are relatively easy scenarios for understanding how "constructive abstention" might work. But note how weakening they would be to the concept of a European foreign policy; constructive abstention could become a legitimate excuse for the absence of such a common policy, since, in effect, nation-states would be acting for reasons of national rather than European interest. Moreover, the third crisis scenario in the Balkans shows how difficult implementing a common policy could be in practice. Greece would have its fundamental national interests at stake. Britain, France, Germany, and Italy, as members of the International Contact Group on the Former Yugoslavia, would have little choice but to become involved. The United States, fearful of a crisis that might imperil NATO by putting Greece and Turkey at loggerheads and with its own forces already committed to the region, would not stand by and would have great difficulty in deferring to the Europeans. All other EU states would have varying degrees of interest because their troops were deployed in the Stabilization Force (SFOR) mission in Bosnia or the tripwire force in Macedonia or because they felt a general obligation to show solidarity with Greece as an EU member. But that might not be enough to impel distant Portugal or Finland or tiny Luxembourg to join what could be a prolonged, costly, and politically controversial mission.

Still, for all its complications, the Amsterdam Treaty does make a coherent European foreign policy possible and its implementation practicable, without subjecting the Union to the stresses and frustrations imposed by the old rule of unanimous approval. Moreover, two parallel developments, one in Washington and the other in London and Paris, have sharply increased the potential for this practicality. The most important was the Clinton administration's strategic decision in 1995 to take a relaxed and even supportive view of a European security and defense identity. This had not always been so. In 1991, the Bush administration had sent a diplomatic missive, known after its career diplomat author as the "Bartholemew letter," which solemnly warned that U.S. commitment to NATO might have to be reviewed if the EU sought to establish a defense and security policy separate from the Atlantic alliance.

This posture changed because the Bosnian crisis had persuaded the Clinton administration that there were some security issues in which the European stake was more immediate and the U.S. stake was more remote, even though the United States might be dragged in by its priority concern for the survival of NATO. For example, in 1995 the United States realized that its French and British allies might call on NATO solidarity to require U.S. military intervention to help evacuate their troops. Once intervention became inevitable, the United States decided to make it positive and used its massive political and military leverage to force the Dayton peace agreement.

Between 1996 and 1999, the United States made a series of accommodations to promote the emergence of a European foreign policy on the very firm understanding that the Europeans accepted that this would enhance rather than replace or challenge NATO as the core structure of the transatlantic relationship. The United States moved decisively to speed NATO membership for the Poles, Czechs, and Hungarians, knowing that this would dovetail neatly with the EU's own enlargement plans. The United States also agreed that NATO assets could be used for purely European operations that did not require U.S. troops, under the formula that that such European missions and forces would be "separable but not separate" from NATO.

This U.S. accommodation was imposed by the military practicalities. Its $260 billion defense budget, half as large again as the combined defense budgets of the European NATO powers, had given the United States a virtual monopoly on the means of making modern war. It had the network of spy satellites and aircraft carrier task forces, "stealth" warplanes, heavy-lift cargo planes capable of swift force projection, intelligence and logistics systems, tactical air support, and the ability to suppress enemy antiaircraft missile networks.

Of the Europeans, only the British and French had anything remotely approaching this U.S. capability. The French had two medium-sized aircraft carriers: the obsolete one, the *Foch,* was actually faster than the new *Charles de Gaulle.* The British had two small carriers whose usefulness had been demonstrated in the Falklands war but whose limited ability to project force depended on the short and vertical takeoff Harrier jets. The British and French governments were each informed by the general staffs in the summer of 1998 that even combined, their air forces could not suppress the Serbian antiaircraft systems and thus permit a sustained bombing campaign. The limited abilities of the Europeans had been clear since the Gulf War of 1991, when Britain's entire army of the Rhine had to be stripped and its tank brigades cannibalized to field one full-strength armored division in the desert. The French could not even match that, providing only a light division that was boldly handled and capable but was kept on the far west of the battle line for diversionary and rapid-exploitation missions. It was simply not fit for the expected main armored battles around Kuwait.

U.S. support for a distinct (if not separate) European defense identity would have had little meaning, except that the French and British governments also made a policy change as important as that in Washington. The British decided that their long insistence that NATO and only NATO should be the central politico-military structure could be safely modified, and the French decided that NATO itself, in the wake of the Cold War, was changing sufficiently and giving the European powers sufficient strategic space to chart ways to protect their own interests. Thus France could move beyond its traditional suspicion of NATO as a device for locking Europeans into U.S. hegemony.

In December 1998, the French and British governments came together at the St. Mâlo summit to codify the new approach. They concluded that the EU must have the capacity for autonomous action, backed up by credible military forces; the means to decide to use them; and the readiness to do so, which required strengthened armed forces that can react rapidly to the new risks. This declaration was, in effect, the new European defense charter, adopted by its two leading military powers (and the only two with nuclear weapons), and it was formally welcomed by the other EU member states the following week at the EU's Vienna summit. The St. Mâlo summit conclusions were also framed deliberately to reassure rather than alarm the Americans by stressing that the Atlantic alliance was the foundation of the collective defense of the member states of the EU.

NATO's new strategic doctrine, as formally adopted at the Washington summit of 1999, specifically welcomed this new European role and identity. It also committed both sides of the Atlantic alliance to work together to ensure that, in President Clinton's words, "the old Cold War alliance which was designed to confront the Soviet Union develop into a new Euro-Atlantic security system which includes Russia."[2]

In a sense, this kind of U.S.-European security partnership has been in existence since the formal signing of the 1993 Oslo agreements between Israel and Palestine. The United States led the diplomacy, and the EU agreed to lead the fund-raising and development aid strategy that would underpin the peace. In a similar way, the EU took the lead in financial support and trade agreements for Russia, while Washington managed the security strategy with the Kremlin. Although some Europeans sometimes grumbled at a policy of "we pay and they say," this was a rational division of labor that played to both U.S. and European strengths.

Britain and France were not the only European member states to accept that the implications of the end of the Cold War were finally forcing Europe into a new situation with new responsibilities. Dutch foreign minister Jozias van Aartsen summed up the new policy in an important speech early in 1999, which he titled "European Security with the Americans If Possible, on Our Own When Necessary."

"For the last ten years too many people have basked for too long in the apparent comfort of the knowledge that Washington would pull the chestnuts out of the fire if necessary," van Aartsen said. But a number of important developments, not least within European politics, had changed everything: "Since the election of the government headed by Tony Blair, the UK has played a more prominent role on the European stage. France has picked up on this signal, and Paris and London are clearly growing closer together. This is probably related to the emergence of a new Germany that has every right to be more self-assured. The old assumptions that Germany pays and France decides no longer apply."[3]

Naturally, there are no guarantees that Europe's new foreign policy will unfold according to plan because there is no plan as such. There is just a general will and a broadly accepted direction in both Europe and the United States and, for the first time, a series of policy-implementing instruments in Europe that should allow the Europeans to start exercising their long-atrophied ability to take independent strategic decisions. As van Aartsen also noted, "We in Western Europe had grown lazy, so to speak, in the old bipolar world controlled by two nuclear superpowers. We may even have been inclined to take things easy, or perhaps we were at last unwilling to reflect on our common European interests and positions—certainly not in terms of power politics—because for a long time that was done for us. Meanwhile, we tended to focus on our own economic and political construction."[4]

Any number of developments could throw this new European effort off course. A serious escalation of the trade row across the Atlantic could derail it. A failure by the International Contact Group and NATO to stabilize Kosovo would also be a setback. A serious breakdown in U.S.-China relations, followed by a repeat of the European reluctance to support the United States as happened during the Vietnam War, would also create difficulty. Perhaps the most dismaying scenario would be for the Europeans to fail in their first operation without U.S. troops, but one that implicated the United States through the presence of its assets, from spy satellites to airborne warning and control system (AWAC) planes and in-flight tankers. Such a development can be envisaged in the Balkans or in North Africa and would get Europe's new strategy off to a very bad start indeed. Europe's new Monsieur PESC will have to pick his crises with care; Europe has too little strategic prestige to be able to risk it on quixotic ventures.

But by the same token, a successful first operation would make the future development of EU foreign policy all the easier. It is clear that some international situations are understood to be far too dangerous for Europe to tackle alone. A serious crisis between Russia and one of the Baltic States or Russia and one of the eastern European candidates for EU membership would require U.S. participation and probably leadership from the beginning.

Europe does, however, have important strengths to bring to the new Atlantic relationship. It is now experienced in nonmilitary foreign policies, such as the use of development aid and trade diplomacy and its special relationship with the seventy-seven countries of the African, Caribbean, and Pacific group. As the world's leading donors of aid who are accustomed to deploying it in strategic support of a broader Western policy, the Europeans do not come empty-handed to the negotiating table. Moreover, the "ethical" foreign policy that has been pioneered by British foreign secretary Robin Cook, with its stress on human rights and good governance and control of conventional arms sales, has strong support from other member states. The EU is also the leading donor of humanitarian aid around the world through the European Community Humanitarian Office (ECHO) division of the European Commission.

These "soft" areas of foreign policy may not be the backbone of power politics, but they provide an important base of expertise and global involvement that will help Europeans adopt a more robust role in the future. As nuclear powers and permanent members of the UN Security Council, Britain and France ensure Europe some key seats at the main table of world diplomacy, and in addition to their combined vote in the World Bank and International Monetary Fund, the Europeans provide four of the seven leading industrial nations in the G7. In this sense, Europe has had a series of national roles in world policy all along. With the coming of the euro, the new NATO, and the St. Mâlo summit, a series of new and stable foundations have been laid for the fulfillment of the Amsterdam Treaty, in enthusiastic agreement from the still indispensable U.S. ally and partner.

7

The European Union and the World

CHRISTOPHER PATTEN

On May 9, 2000, it was fifty years since the then French foreign minister, Robert Schuman, made his famous declaration proposing the establishment of a European Coal and Steel Community. From that acorn has grown the oak tree of what is now the European Union. The EU is the largest single market in the world and the largest international trader. Together with its member states, it is by far the biggest provider of development and humanitarian aid. The EU represents its member states in external trade negotiations, which makes it a key player in the World Trade Organization. The advent of the single currency, the euro, has added a new dimension to the European Union's international economic role.

Yet since the early failure of the ambitious project of the European Defense Community in 1954, this economic role has never been fully matched by a corresponding role in world politics. Though the European integration process was from the outset conceived to be political, for most of the past fifty years the economic giant has often looked like a political dwarf. International expectations that the EU should make more political use of its economic weight were frustrated by internal arguments about the proper limits of the EU's role. How far could the EU represent its member states on the world stage? How far would they accept limits on their own freedom of action in order to secure the benefits of a strong common policy? The member states were divided, and the consequence was that so-called political cooperation remained a sickly creature. The EU issued ringing declarations from time to time, usually a few weeks after noteworthy international events. But it remained essentially a commentator rather than an actor.

It was the political earthquake of 1989 that made the EU realize that from then on, it had to play a stronger role in foreign policy both within Europe and internationally. The Union found that it was expected to take the lead in shaping Europe's future architecture. It was at once a pole of attraction for the newly emerging democracies and the obvious economic and political focus for an undivided Europe. Yet it was clearly ill-equipped for the task. The bloody disintegration of Yugoslavia demonstrated its weakness. As events unfolded, the EU and its member states recognized with increasing alarm and distress that they were failing to live up to their political responsibilities. The Balkan experience was perhaps the main driving force behind the development of the Common Foreign and Security Policy in the Maastricht and Amsterdam treaties of the 1990s. At the 1999 European Council meetings in Cologne and Helsinki, heads of government took a further step by deciding to develop a military capacity for crisis management in the framework of a European security and defense policy.

The more the EU establishes itself as a single actor on the international scene, the more it must be able to state clearly what it stands for and what it wants to achieve. It must identify its key interests and define its strategic goals. The EU's general objectives, which it must pursue in close cooperation with its allies and partners, are now laid down in the Treaty on European Union. These include

- safeguarding the common values, fundamental interests, independence, and integrity of the Union and strengthening its security in all ways;
- preserving peace and strengthening international security in accordance with principles of the UN Charter as well as the Helsinki Final Act and the Paris Charter of the Organization for Security and Cooperation in Europe (OSCE);
- promoting regional and international cooperation; and
- developing and consolidating democracy, the rule of law, and respect for human rights and fundamental freedoms.

But the proof of the pudding is in the eating. It is easy enough to state objectives. The challenge is to meet them.

STABILITY IN EUROPE

After Europe's experience of two world wars and the long aftermath of Soviet tyranny, the EU's primary strategic objective is clear enough: it seeks lasting political stability and sustainable economic prosperity in a free and undivided Europe. These are interrelated and interdependent goals. They require the solid establishment of democracy and the rule of law, respect for human rights and minorities, and the development of free market economies.

This represents a huge challenge for the countries of central and eastern Europe, which still struggle with the heritage of the communist era. The EU has developed a comprehensive set of policy instruments and mobilized considerable financial resources to help these countries to achieve full integration into the Euro-Atlantic structures that make up "the West."

The strongest incentive the EU can provide to encourage political and economic reform is the prospect of full membership in the EU itself. In 1993 the Union decided in principle to open its doors to central and eastern European countries. Based on a comprehensive strategy (called "Agenda 2000") prepared by the European Commission, the formal enlargement process was begun with the opening of first accession negotiations in early 1998. In December 1999, further accession negotiations were launched. All ten central and southeastern European countries that have applied for membership are now negotiating with the EU, together with Cyprus and Malta.[1] Turkey is another candidate but will not start negotiations until it has fulfilled the political criteria that all applicants have to meet regarding the rule of law, respect for human rights, and the protection of minorities.

Enlargement of the EU—almost doubling the number of members—is an enormous undertaking. This process might be analogous to the United States deciding to incorporate South America. It requires fundamental adaptation not just by the candidates but also by the Union itself, which is having to review key policies, revise its budget plans, and adapt its institutions and procedures. The EU is accelerating its institutional reform so that it will be ready to welcome new members from 2003 onward, but enlargement will continue to figure high on the agenda for many years to come.

Central and eastern Europe do not consist solely of candidates for EU accession. Many other countries that were republics of the former Soviet Union are outside the enlargement process. Yet it is vital for Europe's common future that these countries, especially the two strategically most important countries, Russia and Ukraine, should be firmly anchored in Europe as stable and prosperous democracies. The partnership and cooperation agreements between the EU and Russia and Ukraine should help to strengthen trade and investment, provide advice and expertise, and promote political dialogue. These agreements are

complemented by common strategies, emphasizing the specific importance that the EU attaches to these two countries. The strategies are designed to engage each country in closer cooperation on a wide variety
of issues, including regional security. They should serve as a roadmap
for the future development of relations with the EU.

The situation in the western Balkans presents a specific challenge.
The various successor states of the former Yugoslavia might have participated in the enlargement process from the outset, like Slovenia, had
it not been for the nationalist policies of their rulers—most notoriously
in Serbia—and the resulting wars in Bosnia and over Kosovo. These
former provinces are now shattered economies and shattered societies.
To bring the region back into the mainstream of post–Cold War Europe
requires reconstruction in the broadest sense: physically, economically,
and perhaps most important and most difficult, through the reconstruction of civil society. The EU is convinced that it can best contribute to
stability by drawing the region closer to full integration into its structures. To this end, the Union has offered to conclude stabilization and
association agreements with the countries of the region, provided they
respect human rights, protect minorities, and are willing to engage in
regional cooperation. These agreements will constitute the basis not
only for economic regeneration but gradual alignment with EU legislation, which might pave the way for eventual EU membership. The EU-
sponsored Balkan Stability Pact, which brings together the countries of
the western Balkans and their neighbors in southeastern Europe, is another important vehicle to promote regional cooperation through the identification and implementation of specific projects. (Editor's note: this
chapter was written before the elections in Yugoslavia in the fall of 2000.)

STABILITY BEYOND EUROPE:
THE MEDITERRANEAN AND THE MIDDLE EAST

European stability is linked to stability in its neighborhood. There are
traditionally close links between the EU and the countries of the southern and southeastern Mediterranean. For most of them, the EU is their
largest trading partner. Four major EU member states—Spain, France,
Italy, and Greece—and three accession candidates—Cyprus, Malta, and
Turkey—are themselves Mediterranean countries.

The conference of EU and Mediterranean foreign ministers in Barcelona in 1995 marked the start of a new phase in EU-Mediterranean relations
by turning the network of bilateral relations into a regional partnership
known as the Barcelona process. It aims to create a Euro-Mediterranean

area of peace and stability founded on human rights and democracy, shared prosperity (with the perspective of a Euro-Mediterranean free trade zone to be established by 2010), and social and cultural partnership. These objectives are pursued at a multilateral level as well as at a bilateral one. Regular meetings of foreign ministers steer the multilateral track, and the bilateral track is based on a new generation of Euro-Mediterranean association agreements under negotiation between the EU and each of its Mediterranean partners. Similar to the agreements concluded with the central and eastern European accession candidates, these agreements provide for co-operation in the economic, social, cultural, and financial fields as well as a regular dialogue on foreign and security policy. An EU-Mediterranean summit was held in the autumn of the year 2000 to give further impetus to the EU-Mediterranean partnership.

European policy in the Mediterranean is heavily influenced by the Middle East peace process. The EU has a strong interest in its success. Building on its financial engagement—it has contributed more than half of total external funds—the EU has continuously increased its political involvement as well, underlined by the appointment of an EU special envoy to the region. The EU participates actively in the multilateral track of the peace process, where it chairs the Regional Economic Development Working Group. The Union's unique experience in regional economic cooperation will give it a particular role and an ability to contribute to long-term growth and stability, once a final settlement has been reached and the region sets out to shape a common future.

THE TRANSATLANTIC PARTNERSHIP

The transatlantic relationship, which forms the political bedrock of what is usually referred to as the "West," is perhaps the closest and most deep-rooted alliance that the world has ever seen. It is based on solid values and on solid interests alike. For the United States, its presence in Europe is a key constituent of its status as a global power. For the Europeans, it is a key constituent of European security.

The end of the Cold War marked the beginning of a new era for the transatlantic partnership. Common resistance to the Soviet threat had served as the raison d'être for the partnership for almost half a century. Now transatlantic relations are undergoing a strategic reorientation, as both sides adjust to the new realities. The United States is uncertain of its role as the world's only superpower. The EU, meanwhile, is absorbed in its own continent and in its own development—and there are still those who wrongly define their growing European identity in terms of a rejection of the United States. During such a period, short-term issues of comparatively limited significance, such as trade disputes, tend to take center stage. Yet there are established multilateral mechanisms to deal with such disputes. They must not be allowed to obscure the fact that the common ground on which the EU and the United States stand is as solid as ever. They need to work jointly on a new mid- to long-term strategic perspective for their partnership, in the framework of the transatlantic dialogue and building on the 1990 Transatlantic Declaration and the New Transatlantic Agenda of 1995.

The EU's project on a European Security and Defense Policy (ESDP) should be regarded as an important contribution to such a transatlantic agenda for the twenty-first century. There has been a great deal of confusion about Europe's defense ambitions (and some willful misrepresentation). The EU is emphatically not creating some new mutual defense pact to rival the North Atlantic Treaty Organization (NATO) or to bid farewell to U.S. military engagement in Europe. Rather, Europeans seek finally to make burden sharing a reality by giving substance to the so far rather vague "European security and defense identity" invoked in so many NATO communiqués over the years. Bosnia and Kosovo demonstrated that a post–Cold War Europe could have crises that affect European security but not necessarily vital U.S. interests. In such cases, Europe cannot forever expect the United States and hence NATO to manage on its behalf. Europe has decided to create a—limited—capacity for military crisis management when NATO is not engaged and the United States is understandably reluctant to commit U.S. troops thousands of miles from home. In my view it is not this ambition but the failure to deliver on it that represents a genuine risk to the Atlantic alliance. Thus it is important that EU member states live up to the commitments they made at the Helsinki European summit in December 1999 to create, by 2003, the capacity to deploy up to 60,000 troops to help to manage crises.

CENTRAL AND LATIN AMERICA

The return to democracy, opening of national economies, and pursuit of regional integration across Latin America have renewed the EU's interest in the region and provided a new impetus for political and economic cooperation. In 1999 the Rio summit brought together EU and Latin American heads of state and government for the first time. The EU is Latin America's leading trading partner and the biggest aid donor as well as the chief foreign investor in many Latin American countries.

It has concluded cooperation agreements and leads regular ministerial dialogues with all these countries except Cuba.

Consolidation of democracy and support for sustained economic development in open markets are the overriding objectives of the EU approach to Latin America, though its policy has been adapted to the particular circumstances of each country in the region. Policy toward Central America, too, focuses on consolidating and strengthening democratic institutions and promoting good governance; the fight against drugs is also a key priority in cooperation with the countries of the Andean community. In the mid-1990s the EU embarked on a drive to foster free trade and stimulate international competition in the Southern Cone Common Market (Mercosur), Chile, and Mexico, as well as to promote regional integration. The first fruits of this policy were harvested in March 2000, when the EU signed a free trade agreement with Mexico. Trade liberalization negotiations with Mercosur and Chile are about to start. In recent years, therefore, the EU has laid the basis for extensive cooperation with Latin America. Heads of state and government will have the opportunity to take stock of what has been achieved when they meet for the next Euro–Latin American summit in 2002.

ASIA AND THE PACIFIC

The EU is also heavily engaged in the Asia-Pacific region. After the Asian economic crisis of 1998, the EU was the largest supporter of International Monetary Fund programs after Japan. In view of Asia's growing importance not just as a market but as a driving force in the global economy, the EU adopted an Asia strategy in 1994, which set out a blueprint for a comprehensive EU-Asia partnership. This strategy is based on bilateral agreements as well as multilateral institutions such as the ministerial dialogue between the EU and the Association of Southeast Asian Nations. In March 1996 the Asia-Europe Meeting (ASEM) united heads of government of the EU and ten Asian nations for the first time. This meeting sparked off a multitude of encounters and projects at governmental and nongovernmental levels.

The EU has an important stake in regional peace and stability in Asia, which has fostered a strong political dimension to EU-Asia relations. The EU actively participates in regional security forums, in particular the ASEAN Regional Forum (ARF). It is also involved in nonproliferation efforts on the Korean Peninsula through the Korean Peninsula Energy Development Organization (KEDO).

Events in Indonesia and East Timor in 1999 provided examples of the interdependence among regional stability, respect for human rights, democracy, and the rule of law. The active promotion of these concepts represents another important element in the EU's political engagement in the region, including its relations with China, in which a regular dialogue on human rights provides a forum to discuss critical issues. Political efforts in this field are underpinned by a vast number of EU-funded cooperation projects to support local democracy, good governance, and the protection of human rights.

AFRICA

The 1990s in Africa are sometimes referred to as a "lost decade." The continent's balance of political, economic, and social development is deep in the red—and, sadly, it is often a bloody red. Large parts of Africa are characterized by border conflicts and civil wars, guerrilla warfare and ethnic violence, large-scale corruption, and mismanagement—often all at the same time and in the same country or region. Such developments have extinguished not only human lives but economic and social structures—and they have often obstructed even modest efforts of democratization. The successful transition of South Africa to a multiracial democracy was a remarkable achievement, and there have been other beacons of hope. But the tragedy of the Great Lakes region has been more sadly typical. The end of the genocide in Rwanda and the change of power in Congo-Zaire were immediately followed by new violent conflicts involving all countries of the region. There are continuous instability and violations of human rights in West Africa, where Nigeria's restored democracy is having to deal with religious and tribal unrest. Most recently, we have been witnessing the self-destruction of Zimbabwe.

Africa is not helped by pessimism. But renewed efforts to promote development will only bear fruit if they are supported from within. African governments must be encouraged and enabled to take more responsibility for conflict prevention and crisis management on their continent. Good governance, civil society, democracy, and human rights must be key objectives of the development process, and development must aim at building sustainable economies through poverty eradication and trade.

The traditional links between many European countries and their former colonies in Africa give the EU a specific responsibility in this region. Since the foundation of the European Communities in the

1950s, there has been a special relationship between the EC and the countries of (sub-Saharan) Africa as well as some Caribbean and Pacific states (the African, Caribbean, and Pacific, or ACP group), based on multilateral agreements covering economic, technical, and financial cooperation on a wide range of issues. The last of these ACP-EC conventions was replaced by a new twenty-year partnership between the EU and its seventy-seven ACP partners, signed in May 2000. This will put EU-African relations on a new basis supported by three pillars: the political dimension, development strategies, and economic and trade cooperation. At the heart of the new agreement lies an interactive strategy linking development and trade. The agreement presents a comprehensive and integrated vision of development strategies centered on poverty reduction. It seeks to encourage the involvement of civil society and nonstate actors in the work that lies ahead.

The joint commitment of the EU and Africa to a renewed effort to secure the continent's future was solemnly underlined when the heads of government of the EU and their counterparts from all sub-Saharan and Mediterranean African countries united for the first EU-Africa summit, held in Cairo in April 2000. The Declaration of Cairo sets out guidelines for future joint action with regard to regional economic integration, the integration of Africa in the global economy, the promotion of democracy, the rule of law and good governance, conflict prevention, and management and development in a variety of sectors. A second EU-Africa summit will be held in 2003 to review progress.

GLOBAL RESPONSIBILITY

The EU is not a superpower in the traditional sense, and does not cherish the ambition to become one. Yet its unique experiment in the deep integration of independent countries has made it one of the most influential players on the world stage. Step-by-step it has become a global actor, driven by a growing stock of common interests and by the expectations of its partners worldwide. The international community wants the EU to share its experience and to use its wealth and influence to help prevent conflicts, manage crises, protect human rights, and promote economic and social development.

Faced with these expectations, EU leaders may be forgiven for sometimes feeling overburdened because they know that European foreign policy is still very much a work in progress. The balance between the national policies of member states and of the EU as an institution remains a difficult one. The institutions of the Common Foreign and

Security Policy are still in their infancy. Decisionmaking procedures remain cumbersome. I am aware, for example, that EU management of external assistance is inadequate—and it is one of my top priorities as a commissioner to overhaul these procedures. But of one thing I am certain: hiding at home in Brussels is not an option. Like it or not, the European Union is a major international force. Its member countries and citizens must accept the responsibilities that come with that status.

8

The New Transatlantic Agenda

LIONEL BARBER

Half a century ago, U.S. secretary of state Dean Acheson wrote in his personal diary about his sense of exhilaration at being present at the creation of a new political and economic order in Europe. The Marshall Plan, the North Atlantic Treaty Organization (NATO) alliance, the Organization for Economic Cooperation and Development (OECD), and the Fulbright student exchange program—these were the institutions that built bridges across the Atlantic and paved the way toward reconciliation between former adversaries.

Fifty years on, North Americans and Europeans are engaged in building a new post–Cold War order embracing western and eastern Europe and aimed at filling the vacuum created by the collapse of communism. This process will require a dynamic evolution of existing institutions such as NATO and the European Union; but it also demands a new transatlantic agenda to cement ties between future generations.

Success is by no means assured. Although the official U.S. position continues to be one of support for European economic, even political, integration, a growing proportion of informed opinion has assumed a more critical stance. Some commentators argue that the United States should adopt a "Pacific tilt" in response to the rise of China as the hegemonic power in Asia in the next century.[1] Others are convinced that Europe is trapped in a process of genteel decline in comparison to the dynamic economic potential of Southeast Asian countries. Still others are worried that a more integrated but inward-looking Europe built around the single currency could encourage a fortress Europe, either economically or strategically, which would be less amenable to U.S. interests.

The superiority of U.S. military power, highlighted during the Gulf War, as well as the phenomenal resilience of the U.S. economy during the 1990s have contributed to the impression that there is an imbalance in the transatlantic relationship. The lessons of the immediate postwar era, when farsighted visionaries such as Harry Truman, George Marshall, and Dean Acheson understood that U.S. power depended on alliances rather than unilateral displays of power, risk being forgotten.

From time to time, Americans have displayed a highhandedness toward their European allies that Samuel Huntington, a Harvard political scientist, describes as behavior symptomatic of a "rogue superpower."[2] This behavior cannot be explained solely in terms of U.S. frustration with the relationship—that Europe is a free rider on the back of U.S.-provided security and a feeling in Washington that the European Union itself should take more responsibility for its own "backyard"—one of the big lessons of the Kosovo crisis.

From the U.S. standpoint, the process of EU enlargement to the reform democracies of central and eastern Europe is moving far too slowly compared to the expansion of the NATO alliance (which opened its doors to the Czech Republic, Hungary, and Poland). The United States is also alarmed by the tendency of some European leaders to cold-shoulder Turkey, a strategically vital NATO ally. Americans express frustration at the "business-comes-first" attitudes that Europe displays on occasion toward countries the United States has branded as "rogue states" such as Cuba, Libya, and Iran.

From the vantage point of Europe, U.S. triumphalism could threaten the successful transatlantic cooperation that has endured for half a century and more. U.S. leadership is more unpredictable, more in danger of turning inward now that the Soviet military threat has disappeared. In economic and demographic terms, the rise of the South and the West in the United States at the expense of the East Coast is another unsettling trend.

For much of the twentieth century, the U.S. foreign policy establishment looked east to Europe, not only because of bonds of kinship but also because of commercial ties in the New York banking and law community epitomized by the likes of Acheson and fellow "wise men" such as John McCloy and Averell Harriman. In the twenty-first century, the increasing demographic weight of the Hispanic and Asian-American populations seems bound to encourage countervailing loyalties toward Latin America and the Pacific.[3]

Europeans fret about the unilateralist tendency in U.S. foreign policy. In 1999, it was estimated that two-thirds of the world's population was covered by some form of U.S. sanction imposed by Congress or state and local governments.[4] The most serious trade disputes between Europe and the United States almost invariably stem from U.S. assertions that it has the right to invoke extraterritorial powers to defend its interests, usually employing a broad definition of national security. The same U.S. ambivalence toward multilateralism applies to international law (such as the refusal to recognize the jurisdiction of the International Criminal Court) and international institutions (such as the unilateral refusal to meet its financial obligations toward the United Nations and the reluctance to seek UN backing for military action, say, against Iraq).

What is required is a more adult relationship between Americans and Europeans. The European Union is plainly not ready to act as an equal partner to the United States in political-military matters, but it has considerable economic weight. Its desire to play a greater role in the international financial system is likely to be enhanced by the single currency. Europeans should also work toward a "grand bargain" that offers the prospect of greater burden sharing in security matters while strengthening institutions such as NATO and the World Trade Organization (WTO), both of which engage the United States as sole superpower in the affairs of the continent.

TRADE: CONTAINING TENSIONS WITHIN THE POWER BLOCS

The EU is the United States' largest trading partner, and vice versa, in a combined trade worth more than $230 billion. Some 3 million U.S. workers are employed by European-owned companies. About 51 percent of foreign direct investment in the United States comes from the EU, and the proportion has been rising; more than 42 percent of foreign investment in the EU comes from the United States, which is about nine times the amount accounted for by Japan. As Geoffrey Treverton, a U.S. foreign policy analyst, observes: "Investment across the Atlantic is so long-standing that most of us can barely recall what is 'American' and what is 'European.' In Europe, Ford, IBM, and Xerox are regarded as essentially European. Most Americans probably do not know the European origins of Shell or Phillips."[5]

Those responsible for trade policy in the United States and the EU argue that 95 percent of trade is trouble-free. Indeed, the fears expressed at each stage in the expansion of the European Union's own market—that U.S. exports would face discrimination—have proved wide of the mark. Some trade was undoubtedly diverted from the United States (and others) to the expanded Europe. But in the final resort, the more important lesson for U.S. business is that any diversion was more than compensated for by the benefits of a bigger market. This was true in the immediate years after the founding of the European Economic Community (EEC) in 1957, and it was true when the EEC (now the EU) opened its doors to new members of the club.

Yet there is always a risk of niggling disputes escalating into wider trade wars, especially when one side suspects the other is shirking its responsibilities or failing to play by the book when it comes to submitting to the rules of the international trade system. The risk becomes greater when one side is running a big trade deficit with the rest of the world and the cries for protection among domestic industries become too loud for the politicians to resist.

Toward the end of the twentieth century, the United States consistently ran a large trade deficit, first with Japan and then with China. Surging growth in the United States, compared to sluggish growth in Europe and a sharp recession in Asia triggered by the regional financial crisis in 1997–1998, has encouraged the notion among Americans that they are acting as "consumer of last resort" for Europe and the rest of the world, sucking in cheap imports in order to sustain world growth. In the middle of 1999, for example, the U.S. trade deficit was heading toward $300 billion against a European surplus of more than $100 billion—an uncomfortable and perhaps unsustainable gap, at least in political terms.

The best way forward is to establish certain principles that underscore the pivotal role of both partners in the global trade system and encourage both sides to look outward rather than inward. They would also help to contain the temptation to put sectional and regional interests ahead of a global approach.

The first principle is that the United States can no longer play the anchor role, as it did in the immediate postwar era and the early rounds of the General Agreement on Tariffs and Trade (GATT). It was noticeable that, after a long period of paralysis on the part of the EU, the Europeans and the United States took the lead in driving all sides to an agreement on the Uruguay Round in 1993. In the following years, the Europeans, egged on by Sir Leon Brittan, EU trade commissioner at the time, helped to galvanize other countries (notably Japan) to strike global agreements on the liberalization of financial services, information technology, and telecommunications.

The second principle is that the World Trade Organization must remain the indispensable authority in the world trade system. Whatever its faults, the WTO represents an advance on its GATT predecessor because it contains binding dispute mechanisms. The problem is that both the Americans and the Europeans have found it difficult to come to terms with the WTO's role as the essential safety valve. From the standpoint of the United States, there is no better example than the EU's behavior over bananas.

This cause célèbre stems from the Europeans' defense of a favorable import regime for fruit from their former colonies in the Caribbean at the expense of cheaper bananas from Latin America exported by U.S. companies. Much has been written about the importance of the U.S. banana lobby in Washington, but the fact is that the EU did not comply with two WTO panel rulings and disregarded the impacts on consumers and the wider consequences of ignoring WTO rulings. U.S. officials claimed that the EU's intransigence made it doubly hard for the administration to convince inward-looking, unilateral-minded members of Congress that the WTO is an organization worth fighting for rather than flouting, and theirs remains a powerful argument.

The third principle is that Europeans should become better at spotting issues that risk unilateral action from Congress, such as the Helms-Burton Act banning "trafficking" in Cuban assets and the D'Amato Act penalizing trade with Iran and Libya. The tensions over these extraterritorial laws were barely contained in the mid-1990s. Significantly, they stemmed from the original decision by a weakened president Bill Clinton to respond to the pressure of the Cuban-American lobby in the key state of Florida in an election year. These laws point to another danger: that Congress has emerged as a much more powerful actor in foreign policy, particularly when it can claim domestic issues are driving the foreign policy agenda rather than the need to respond to an external threat such as the former Soviet Union.

The fourth principle is that the transatlantic alliance should forge an agenda benefiting both the United States and Europe and promoting world trade. One idea—pushed hard by Brittan—was to press for a new "transatlantic marketplace."[6] It would fall short of a free trade area, which would involve scrapping tariffs on politically sensitive areas such as agriculture, but it would attempt to address specific concerns both in trade and investment, such as standards, broadcasting, public procurement, and intellectual property rights. Though the initiative has largely been dropped, it seems worthy of revival because it points to the new trade agenda.

THE NEW TRADE AGENDA—REGULATORY COOPERATION

The importance of nontariff barriers has grown in the global trade order. In the past, these issues were viewed as being largely of domestic concern, but today the divergences are widening over matters such as food safety, aircraft noise, and data privacy. Some issues demand special attention.

A foretaste of problems with competition policy appeared in the summer of 1997, when the European Commission announced that it had serious objections on antitrust grounds to the proposed $14 billion merger between Boeing, the world's number one aerospace manufacturer, and McDonnell-Douglas, the civilian airliner and defense business.

The notion that Brussels-based competition authorities could interfere with the merger of two companies often described as "more American than apple pie" took many observers aback, especially those in the White House and the Federal Trade Commission who had cleared the deal. Suspicions were rife in Washington that the Europeans were defending the state-subsidized Airbus Industrie, Boeing's only serious rival.

After a nerve-wracking round of negotiations, Boeing agreed to slightly modify the terms of the merger. The Seattle-based company offered to make available licenses and patents from McDonnell-Douglas's military research programs; it agreed to end twenty-year-long exclusive delivery contracts with three major U.S. airlines and not to sign others for ten more years; and it pledged not to abuse its dominance in the world market.

The Boeing case highlighted European sensitivities about being left behind in the high-technology race, but it also points to the rapid pace of mergers and acquisitions that is increasing the workload of U.S. and EU competition authorities alike. It also underlines the need for regular high-level meetings between the U.S. Justice Department's antitrust authorities and the European Commission's directorate-general for competition, not just to discuss individual cases but to develop a joint policy framework to govern competition questions.

Cooperation on standards and certification of goods is another area that requires more attention. In today's interdependent world of trade and commerce, multinationals are increasingly pressing for more consistency in rules on investment, technical standards, and the removal of obstacles to the free flow of goods, services, and capital.

The Transatlantic Business Dialogue (TABD) is a vital cog in this new form of transatlantic cooperation, as is the Transatlantic Policy Network, a similar grouping made up of parliamentarians on both sides of the Atlantic, businesspeople, and diplomats.[7] In June 1997, the TABD successfully propelled U.S. and European negotiators toward an agreement on mutual recognition of products such as medical devices, telecommunications terminal equipment, and information technology, three sectors that account for some $40 billion of transatlantic trade.

This deal took five years to negotiate and was just a start. Although it does address the problem of certification as a nontariff barrier to trade, it does not deal with governments' practice of insisting on their own inconsistent standards. The real test will be whether the U.S.-EU deal will serve as a model for a multilateral agreement inside the World Trade Organization.

MANAGING THE PEACE

The Cold War was won without NATO firing a shot in anger. Now comes the hard part: managing the peace. The expansion of the NATO alliance eastward, though not without risks, offers the possibility of a new Europe in the twenty-first century in which destiny will no longer be determined by geography. NATO has transformed itself from a defensive alliance whose purpose was to defend Western territory against a Soviet attack into a revamped political-military organization with solid ties across the whole of Europe, one willing to deploy troops to resolve conflicts on the continent, notably in the Balkans.

The admission of the Czech Republic, Hungary, and Poland is the formal acknowledgment that NATO has extended its reach into territory once deemed to be inside the sphere of influence of the Soviet Union. But in many ways, the deployment of a NATO-led multinational force (including Russian troops) in Bosnia was even more significant because it defied the critics who said that NATO acting "out of area" was politically dangerous and legally impossible.

Javier Solana, the former NATO secretary-general, has written that the big new development in the 1990s was that theory followed practice.[8] Instead of waiting to develop a blueprint regulating the deployment of NATO forces to manage the security of Europe, the Americans and Europeans simply created facts on the ground. The same rule applies to the theory that Russia would never accept NATO enlargement. In practice, Russia had little choice. The question was merely to determine the best possible terms of the deal for both sides.

For NATO to further develop its role in the twenty-first century, several features of the alliance will require strengthening and consolidating, especially after the lessons of the intervention in Kosovo. Several European countries felt uneasy about the use of military force against Serbia, a sovereign state whatever its record of brutality and oppression against the Albanian majority in Kosovo.

The most important message underlined during the fiftieth anniversary celebrations in May 1999 is that NATO must continue to be a security relationship binding the United States to Europe and vice versa. NATO must also draw strength from its role as a community of shared interests and values—the most effective means of assisting in the creation of stable, market-oriented democracies in central and eastern Europe, binding Russia into a cooperative role in managing security in Europe, and promoting stability and confidence in the Mediterranean.

The second issue is the development of a more robust and self-confident European defense and security identity (ESDI) under the umbrella of the NATO alliance. The United States dropped its long-standing reservations about ESDI when President Clinton made his inaugural trip to Europe in January 1994; but refining the concept of allowing Europeans to draw on NATO assets and capabilities for European-led peace-keeping and crisis management missions has taken time.

The decisive step forward came in June 1996 at the NATO summit in Berlin. The United States spelled out plans to create a new NATO command on the continent and promised to offer the Europeans a new post of deputy supreme commander of allied forces and to develop the combined task forces. Another important step came in December 1998, when Britain and France announced in St. Mâlo that the development of the ESDI should take priority.

More progress might be made on this issue if European ambassadors to NATO also served as ESDI ambassadors. They would sit in Brussels in a revamped political-military operation under the auspices of the European Council (the forum for EU heads of government). They would handle delicate issues such as how to treat those EU countries who regard themselves as neutral, such as Austria, Finland, Ireland, and Sweden, and how to treat those NATO members who are not EU members (the key countries being Turkey and Poland). For without a satisfactory solution, there is every chance of, say, Turkey blocking a deal because of extraneous issues such as its own frustration at not being treated on an equal footing with the eastern European applicants to the EU.

A third essential step would be for Europe to develop its own defense capacity and thereby reduce its reliance on U.S. technology and capability. Europe has barely begun to develop the strategic lift, satellite intelligence, and communications that would allow it to move an expeditionary force to a secure location and enable the troops on the ground to talk to each other effectively. Out of eight satellites watching over the Balkans multinational peacekeeping operation, only two are European. Similarly, the French were incapable of moving the relief force to the Muslim town of Srbrenica in 1995 without the assistance of U.S. satellite intelligence, according to a senior EU diplomat.[9]

The big question for the twenty-first century is whether the Europeans will decide to try for a "European-only" solution to this high-technology gap or whether the much-needed consolidation of the defense industry in Europe will also include U.S. companies and joint ventures. The initial signs indicate that it will take a long time for European countries to allow their own national champions to be swallowed up in an amorphous European whole, partly because the British, French, and Germans are sensitive about parity in shareholding.

An alternative option is to use the Airbus Industrie consortium as a lever for building a new pan-European defense company, but the first important deal involved the merger of British Aerospace and the UK's General Electric Company, creating a British defense giant that could deal from a position of strength with both the Americans and the Europeans. Though the French—and the Germans through Daimler-Chrysler Aerospace—expressed disappointment at the prospect of more competition, defense experts such as Gordon Adams, a former top White House official, believe that it makes more sense for cooperation and consolidation to take place on a transatlantic basis rather than creating a fortress Europe and fortress America mentality on both sides of the alliance.[10]

EUROPE'S COMMON FOREIGN AND SECURITY POLICY

Much will depend, too, on the EU putting flesh on its own vision of a Common Foreign and Security Policy (CFSP)—a vision first expounded in the Dutch border town of Maastricht in December 1991. Since those heady days, the CFSP has turned out to be less than its name but better than its reputation. Despite setbacks, notably during the civil war in Yugoslavia, the fifteen member states of the European Union are gradually acquiring the habit of working together in an area that goes to the heart of national sovereignty.

The CFSP's greatest asset is money. In 1995, the EU gave Russia $1.5 billion to assist in the transition to democracy, seven times as much as the United States gave for the same purpose. EU humanitarian aid in 1996 was almost $2 billion, one-third more than that given by the United States. The Europeans are also outspending the Americans in central and eastern Europe.

The CFSP's greatest weakness is the unanimity principle in decisionmaking. The rule accentuates individual positions at the expense of a common approach. In addition, its procedures are cumbersome: in major meetings the EU is usually represented by the fifteen foreign ministers, one or two EU Brussels commissioners, and two members of the Council secretariat. Stuart Eizenstat, former U.S. ambassador to the EU in Brussels, sums up the problems this way: "The principal member states are not willing to relinquish their prerogatives. . . . As long as this remains the case, the European Union will not develop a diplomatic and political weight commensurate with its economic and commercial strength."[11]

The Amsterdam Treaty—signed in October 1997—does present the possibility of limited majority voting, but its chief purpose is to repair the structural weaknesses of the Maastricht Treaty. Two important innovations are the new policy planning unit being set up in Brussels and the naming of Javier Solana to the post of CFSP representative to the outside world. (Solana's appointment should help to answer Henry Kissinger's question about which number to dial in Europe in the event of a crisis.) Already, special European envoys have been appointed to deal with Bosnia, Cyprus, the Great Lakes region in Africa, and the Middle East. However, implementing a CFSP will require delicate maneuvering between the European Council, the European Commission, and the still powerful foreign ministries, which treasure national diplomatic prerogatives at the expense of a collective European voice.

A third innovation—separate from the new treaty—may be the most important of all. In the future, the six-month presidency of the EU will always rotate between a big and a small country. This change should improve continuity and reduce eccentricities—especially if the European Commission's functions are streamlined at the same time. Furthermore, when the new European Commission took office in January 2000, a foreign policy leader with the rank of vice president took charge of the sprawling Commission external relations bureaucracy, where as many as five commissioners wear a foreign policy hat, and Javier Solana took on the job of secretary-general to the European Council responsible for foreign policy.

None of the above guarantees that the fledgling EU foreign policy will work better. As Philippe de Schoutheete, the veteran Belgian ambassador to the EU, writes in his new book *Une Europe pour Tous:* "If the instruments [in a treaty] are to be useful, the political will must exist to use them."[12]

A lack of political will often stems from profound differences in perception and interest. Britain's view of China and its human rights record is colored by the colonial past in Hong Kong. Other countries may put more weight on commercial considerations. During the Albania crisis, France and Italy favored intervention, whereas Britain and Germany were reluctant to be drawn in.

In 1914, the competing interests of the great powers of Europe in the Balkans triggered a conflagration leading to a world war. In 1991–1992, the EU was split over Germany's drive to recognize the breakaway states of Croatia and Slovenia. Britain and France were hesitant, apparently tilting toward Serbia. Yet at no point did the conflict in the EU get out of control. The CFSP, for all its weaknesses, remains an important safety valve.

The final element in the New Transatlantic Agenda is burden sharing, particularly in Bosnia. After the successful dovetailing of the NATO-led 50,000-strong Implementation Force (IFOR) with the EU-led civilian reconstruction effort organized by Carl Bildt, the former Swedish prime minister, the follow-up Stabilization Force (SFOR) mission faced steady harassment, especially in the rump Bosnian Serb republic, as did the Kosovo Peacekeeping Force (KFOR) in Kosovo. There are serious doubts as to whether the U.S.-inspired Bosnian-Croat federation can survive and prosper, given the ethnic rivalries in the region. The United States and the EU can point to the practical experience of military cooperation in postwar Bosnia as a measure of success. Once the United States sanctioned a beefy contingent of U.S. troops to stay on in Bosnia, the joint transatlantic effort to stabilize the region continued.

THE CRISIS POINTS

There are at least four potential crisis points in the transatlantic relationship, each of which will require close attention in the first years of the twenty-first century. The immediate threat is that which convulsed Europe twice this century: the Balkans. The Western alliance must find a means of keeping a lid on this powder keg of ethnic rivalry and offering small hostile states the prospect of stability and prosperity. A century ago, the Austro-Hungarian Empire fulfilled this role, offering a "European roof" over a region caught between western democratic states and eastern Orthodox Christianity. Today, the European Union is considering offering partnerships to countries willing to go the extra mile for peace and democracy, and the new president of the European Commission, Romano Prodi, speaks of offering a "European roof" to the Balkans.

Russia presents a second threat to the security of the continent, though not in the same manner in which it menaced Western Europe after 1945. Today, the prospect of the Red Army staging a lightning assault across the northern plains is virtually nonexistent. Russia is no longer a hegemonic power. But it is still a huge, unpredictable, and unstable power, and it must be involved in the creation of the new security architecture in Europe.

A setback to the postcommunist transition to a market economy and democracy would be more than a setback for Western policy. It would either raise the prospect of a revanchist nationalist Russia capable of threatening neighbors such as Poland, Ukraine, and the Baltic states, or it would foreshadow a breakup of Russia into feuding regional clans that would replay the Balkans tragedy tenfold.

The third risk is that the processes of NATO and EU expansion might be mishandled. Both attempt to bolster the central and eastern European states' progress toward democratic market economies that could prosper outside Russia's orbit. Both attempt to fill the security vacuum between Germany and Russia, which was partly responsible for launching two world wars this century. Both need to be handled carefully in order to prevent candidates rejected for NATO membership from clamoring for an EU consolation prize or vice versa.

The fourth and final threat is Turkey, which occupies a geostrategic position on the periphery of Europe, wedged between the volatile Balkans, energy-rich central Asia, Iran and Iraq, Russia, and the tense eastern Mediterranean. As a member of the NATO alliance, a member of the Council of Europe, and a cosignatory to the 1995 customs union with the EU, Turkey is also a key link in the chain of Western security. The EU's offer in late 1999 of membership to Turkey was a useful sign of a shift in attitudes.

Yet Turkey also faces eastward. Because of history and temperament, it has never really joined the West. The secular state coexists uneasily with an Islamist religion. Despite huge strides this century toward a modern democratic society, the country's human rights record is questionable. The "dirty war" with its Kurdish minority continues unabated, and the continuing standoff with Greece over Turkey's occupation of northern Cyprus is another flashpoint.

Ankara's frustrations have grown as the EU and NATO have set in train preparations for the twin enlargements to central and eastern Europe, two historic processes that do not explicitly take Turkey's own interests and sensitivities into account, especially since two former Ottoman provinces—Romania and Bulgaria—are now ahead of Turkey in the application to join the Union.

In 1995, France, supported by its EU partners, engineered a diplomatic maneuver aimed at unblocking the Cyprus impasse while reaching out to the secular forces in Ankara. In essence, the deal involved agreeing to Greek demands for a firm timetable for opening EU accession negotiations with Cyprus in return for lifting the Greek veto over the long-delayed EU-Turkey customs accord and its related financial protocol.

Three questions arise: How can the EU meet the promise it has made to Cyprus on membership? What is to be done about the progressive alienation of the Turkish secular establishment and the slow rise of Islamist fundamentalism? And how can the EU and the United States meet Turkish aspirations to be part of the West without offering Ankara promises that cannot be fulfilled, such as a guarantee of EU membership?

THE UNITED STATES: A EUROPEAN POWER

In the twenty-first century, Europe will still need the active U.S. involvement that has been a necessary component of the continental balance of power for half a century. Conversely, as veteran U.S. diplomat Richard Holbrooke has noted, an unstable Europe would still threaten the vital national security interests of the United States. This is as true today as it was during the Cold War.[13]

European politicians should avoid the temptation to build Europe against the United States, to establish Europe's political and economic identity as a competitor rather than as a partner. The United States is—and should remain—a European power helping to manage the peace after the Cold War.

9

The European Union and Asia

ROBERT J. GUTTMAN

The European Union is rediscovering East Asia. Following in the footsteps of Marco Polo, the EU is developing closer political and economic ties with one of the most dynamic regions in the world. Europe's diplomatic opening recognizes that the global balance of economic power rests on a triangle between East Asia, Europe, and the United States, and that the weakest side of the triangle is the one that joins Asia and Europe.[1]

If satellite cameras could map economic activity on the planet, the resulting image would show three regional "hotspots"—North America, western Europe, and East Asia—forming an enormous triangle. These are the three poles of the global economy, between which the vast majority of the world's capital, goods, and services flow. But if the satellite image could be enhanced to show institutional structures linking these poles, a different picture would emerge. Instead of a triangle, we would see a "V" with a distinct gap between Europe and Asia. Strong institutional bonds connect the United States to its trading partners in Europe and the Pacific Rim. But the Asian-European axis is comparatively weak, amounting to a "missing link." In an effort to correct this institutional imbalance, Asian and European countries launched a bold initiative in 1996. The result is the Asia-Europe Meeting (ASEM).

ASEM was conceived not so much as an institution but as an informal process, "open and evolutionary." It evolved out of a dialogue between the Association of Southeast Asian Nations (ASEAN) and the European Union. In keeping with the informal character of the group, members are commonly referred to as "partners." The partnership's European contingent includes all fifteen EU member states as well as the European Commission. The Asian side consists of seven ASEAN countries—Brunei, Indonesia, Malaysia, the Philippines, Singapore, Thailand, and Vietnam—plus China, Japan, and South Korea. The participation of these latter three countries adds considerable political and economic weight to the Asian grouping.

The acronym ASEM is used to describe the partnership itself, the dialogue process as a whole, and the individual summit meetings. The very first Asia-Europe Meeting (ASEM1) was held in Bangkok in March 1996. That initial gathering was characterized by mutual enthusiasm, with both sides convinced they had much to gain from one another. At that time the Asian tiger and dragon economies were roaring ahead, and the Europeans were eager to extend their interests in a region of spectacular growth. The Asians, for their part, wanted to secure their access to key European export markets, fearing that European economic and monetary union might lead to isolationist trade policies, which fortunately did not occur. With economic issues dominating the agenda, the assembled heads of state and government committed themselves to a "partnership for greater growth."

Improving bilateral trade links was clearly the main objective of ASEM1. But other framework and "softer" issues were also addressed. Expressing their common interest in promoting "peace and global stability," the delegates recognized ASEM's potential as a vehicle for political dialogue. Scientific and cultural exchanges between the regions were to be supported on a far greater scale than ever before. And ASEM members were to do more than simply pay lip service to the need for more cooperation on environmental issues. Concrete measures would be taken to achieve common goals in all these areas.

The ASEM process has spawned several initiatives that have become established elements in the Asian-European dialogue:

- Biannual summits, which involve heads of state and key ministers and alternate between Asia and Europe. Economic and foreign ministers meet separately in the intervening years.
- Asia-Europe Trade Facilitation Action Plan (TFAP), which is aimed at opening up markets between regions and promoting free trade.
- Asia-Europe Investment Promotion Action Plan (IPAP), which was established to promote greater cross-flow investment between Europe and Asia.

- Asia-Europe Business Forum, which hopes to foster greater co-operation between the business and private sectors of the two regions.
- Asia-Europe Environmental Technology Center, which provides research and policy guidance on environmental issues such as pollution control, bioremediation, and disaster management. Technology transfer is a key function. The center opened in Thailand on March 29, 1999.
- Asia-Europe Foundation, based in Singapore, which promotes intellectual and cultural exchanges between Europeans and Asians.

By the time ASEM2 got under way in London in January 1998, the situation in Asia had changed radically. A full-blown financial crisis had struck the region, ravaging the economies of several countries. Thailand and Indonesia were particularly hard hit, but no Asian economy was spared. European companies saw their investments in the region threatened. Loans stopped performing. Construction projects were halted. European exports declined, slowing economic growth throughout the European Union. The crisis, which had global repercussions, tested the strength of the Asia-Europe partnership.

The cause of the Asian financial meltdown became a topic of heated debate within ASEM. Everyone agreed that poor regulation of financial markets and a lack of transparency were contributing factors. It was clear that something had to be done to stop the "Asian contagion" from spreading.

ASEM had gone a long way toward providing a solution. Far from abandoning their partners in need, European leaders at ASEM2 committed themselves to helping Asian countries rebuild their economies. An ASEM Trust Fund was set up at the World Bank, heavily endowed by EU countries. By providing money for technical aid projects, the fund aimed to ease the social impact of the crisis. ASEM2 "also established a network of European financial experts (EFEX) to advise Asian governments in reforming their financial sectors. These projects complement the EU's role as the largest contributor to multilateral agencies (the World Bank, the International Monetary Fund, and the Asian Development Bank) involved in restructuring efforts in Asia."[2]

As ASEM moves into the twenty-first century, it remains committed to its original goals of "peace, stability, and prosperity." Nuclear non-proliferation, good governance, and sustainable development remain on the agenda. Programs already in place are being developed further, and the partnership is developing some clear economic and educational objectives. A report by the Asia-Europe Vision Group, ASEM's plan-ning committee, recommends that ASEM officially adopt the goal of eliminating all trade barriers between member states by the year 2005.

The report also suggests that ASEM commit itself to increasing the flow of exchange students between the regions fivefold by 2025. Cur-rently, the number of Asians who study in Europe far exceeds the num-ber of Europeans studying in Asia, an imbalance the Vision Group feels should be rectified. These and other proposals were considered at the most recent Asia-Europe summit, ASEM3, held in October 2000 in Seoul, South Korea.

Perhaps the largest challenge facing ASEM in the future is the issue of expansion. Other countries seeking to join the group include Australia, New Zealand, India, Pakistan, as well as Laos and Myanmar (both of which became members of ASEAN in 1997). Because the ASEM process is "open and evolutionary," its members expect that the partnership will grow, but some countries are more likely candidates than others.

Myanmar, for example, has little chance under its current military government, which the EU considers an oppressive regime. (EU oppo-sition to Myanmar resulted in that country's exclusion from the ASEAN-EU foreign ministers meeting in Berlin in March 1999.) And human rights issues remain a source of friction within the current ASEM constellation, with China in particular drawing sharp criticism from EU countries such as Germany. Still, the general atmosphere within the group is constructive, as Terry Martin notes:

> ASEM's energies are currently concentrated on helping Asia with its economic recovery. The group's initiatives in the region are encour-aging confidence among its Asian members. European delegates at the ASEM foreign ministers meeting in Berlin in March 1999 noted that ongoing stabilization and reform efforts in Asia had already begun to bear fruit. And despite their many differences—economic and otherwise—the partners have not lost sight of their common goals. European misgivings about China's human rights record, for instance, did not prevent ASEM foreign ministers in Berlin from agreeing to hold their next meeting in Beijing. Determined to explore the synergies of the next millennium, ASEM partners have built a re-sponsive platform for Asian-European relations, a vital link in the geo-political triangle.[3]

According to Ambassador Etienne Reuter, the head of the European Commission delegation to Hong Kong,

> the ASEM process has an important role to play, but at this stage the emphasis must be on bridging the cultural abyss between Asia and

Europe and promoting better understanding of and greater familiar-
ity with each other. The whole process has been affected by the Asian
financial crisis. It is to be hoped that with economic prospects looking again better and political dialogue developing, the ASEM process
will become more dynamic and live up to the expectations and hopes
that were expressed in March 1996 in Bangkok.[4]

Trade and investment are obviously key areas of concern and the
main areas of interaction between the EU member countries and China
and Hong Kong. As Ambassador Reuter mentions, "The accession of
China to the WTO this year [2000] remains a political priority for the European Union. It does not make sense to keep a country with 1.2 billion
inhabitants, which potentially will be the biggest economy in the world
by the year 2020, out of the WTO."[5] And in keeping with this priority, on
May 19, 2000, the European commissioner for trade, Pascal Lamy, announced the successful signing of a Sino-EU agreement. Lamy stated:

> I am delighted to be able to tell you that the European Commission
> and China today have signed an agreement, which concludes our bi-
> lateral negotiations on China's accession to the WTO. And I am par-
> ticularly delighted to tell you that I think it is a first-class agreement.
> The deal is good for EU business. The deal it not just good for China,
> but for Asia, for the region as a whole. And finally, the deal cements
> the close relationship between EU and China in a way which I find
> immensely satisfying.[6]

Since 1978, EU-China trade has increased more than tenfold.
China is now the third most important non-European trading partner
for the EU, and the EU is the fourth-largest trading partner for China.
European firms are actively interested in investing in China if conditions are right. However, China has a long way to go before its markets
will truly be open to foreign investors. In trade matters, market barriers
are one of the key causes of the EU's growing trade deficit with China.
Very high customs duties and quotas are among such barriers, but
problems also arise from the lack of openness in China's legal system.
Improving market access for not only European firms but all interested
global companies would lead to a much more balanced relationship between the EU and China. A 1999 EU publication reports:

> The EU is committed to using all available channels to promote
> human rights in an active, sustained and constructive way. A specific
> dialogue on human rights was set up at China's suggestion in 1995.
> All subjects of concern, even the most sensitive ones such as the death
> penalty and prison conditions have been addressed. The EU attaches
> great importance to respect for the cultural, linguistic and religious

identity of ethnic minorities. It has regularly raised issues on that subject, especially concerning Tibet where the EU sent a fact-finding visit in May 1998.[7]

European Union leaders rebuff suggestions that they are not as strong on human rights as is the United States with regard to China. Not only European commissioners but European heads of state and foreign ministers routinely speak out on any violations of human rights they feel have been perpetuated by the Chinese. The 1989 crackdown by the Chinese government in Tiananmen Square defines how many people in Europe look at contemporary China: "The EU backs China's transition toward an open society based upon the rule of law and respect for human rights and believes this will benefit China's development and lead to greater global stability."[8]

Ambassador Reuter, speaking from the European Commission office in Hong Kong, relates:

> When the former governor of Hong Kong, Mr. Patten [now a European Commissioner], says that the West should behave normally toward China he implies that we should not make allowances for China's poor record on human rights and democracy, but that we should treat it like any other third country. The EU's policy regarding China was redefined in 1995 and we now pursue a twin-track of fostering trade and development cooperation and engaging China in a political dialogue that also covers human rights.[9]

In addition to meeting with Chinese leaders through ASEM, the EU has intensified its bilateral political dialogue with China through other Asian and global forums. The first EU-China summit was held in London in 1998, putting EU relations with China on the same level with those of the United States, Japan, and Russia.

The European Union has established several programs to support China's economic and social reforms, such as the China-Europe International Business School in Shanghai and an EU-China higher education project that supports teaching of and research in European studies in China and provides scholarships and funding for conferences. Chinese-language instruction and business training for young European managers are provided by the EU-China joint managers' project. The EU also has environment, technical assistance, rural education, and agriculture projects with the Chinese, and in 1998 former European Commissioner Sir Leon Brittan began plans while he was in Beijing for a long-term EU-China business dialogue.

When asked if China is a friend or merely a trading partner for the EU, Ambassador Reuter commented: "I would say that for the EU China is a partner, albeit a difficult one. It is a partner for whom we still have a curious fascination like the one experienced by Marco Polo or Matteo Ricci. Trade is, of course, important, but we would also like to see China taking a more active role in the affairs of the planet and sharing concern for political progress, public health, the environment, as well as stability in the region."[10] He adds that Hong Kong has changed very little, at least on the surface, since the resumption of Chinese sovereignty on July 1, 1997. As he reiterates, "The European Union's policy toward Hong Kong continues to be one of visible and tangible support for [the] 'one country, two systems' concept."[11]

Hong Kong is the city in Asia with the greatest number of EU citizens (about 50,000) and also the largest number of European firms (close to 700). Before the turn of the twenty-first century, the EU and Hong Kong signed a customs cooperation agreement, which is politically important because it is the first such agreement concluded by the special administrative region (SAR) and confirms Hong Kong's separateness as a customs territory.

The European Union's relationship with Japan has been dominated for years by the Union's trade deficit with Tokyo. Japan exports to Europe almost 50 percent more than Europe exports to Japan. In 1999, there was nearly a 15 percent fall in Japan's trade surplus with the European Union, although it still stood at 3.6 trillion yen.[12]

There are a large number of factors behind the size of the deficit, including the relative strength of the EU economy and the persistence of mixed economic news in Japan. There are also structural causes, which include regulatory impediments to trade. The European Union continues to engage Japan in a constructive two-way dialogue on regulatory reform and tries to work with the Japanese to remove barriers to the two-way movement of goods and services.

Ambassador Ove Juul Jorgensen, the head of the European Commission delegation to Japan, comments: "While Japanese foreign direct investment in Europe is around seven times greater than EU investment in Japan, the barriers that stood in the way of European investment are gradually being removed. Investment in Japan from abroad is on the increase thanks to a wave of acquisitions by overseas companies prompted by Japan's economic difficulties and the government's steps to simplify and rationalize the procedures for mergers."[13] Recent acquisitions by EU companies include Renault's $5.39 billion stake in Nissan, British Telecom and AT&T's acquisition of a $1.83 billion stake in

Japan Telecom, and the acquisition of International Digital Communications by UK-based Cable and Wireless. Jorgensen adds:

> The deregulation of Japan's nonmanufacturing industries has made sectors such as finance and telecommunications attractive for investors and in the fiscal year 1998 investment in Japan's nonmanufacturing industries increased 140 percent. Overregulation, however, remains a deterrent for investment in Japan and as part of the EU regulatory reform proposals, we have urged the Japanese Government to address the horizontal impediments to foreign direct investment.[14]

The successful launching of Europe's new single currency, the euro, has had a noticeable impact on the Japanese. Former Japanese prime minister Keizo Obuchi visited several European nations in January 1999. In an interview on the eve of his trip, he said that he was "fighting a rear-guard action to help the yen improve its position as an international currency following the launch of the euro."[15]

The former Japanese prime minister, fearing that the yen could become the third-strongest currency behind the dollar and the euro, spoke out in favor of currency cooperation on his 1999 trip to European capitals. He called for a larger role for the yen in the tripolar world based on the yen, dollar, and now the euro, and stated: "If Europe and Japan and also the United States cooperate, it will be possible to build a stable international currency regime."[16]

Despite the normal birth pangs suffered by the euro in its first year, its launch by eleven of the fifteen nations of the European Union was a remarkable and historic achievement. It is quite unlikely that the world will witness the birth of a comparable new Asian currency anytime soon. Neither the desire, nor the determination, nor any type of political structure such as the European Union exists in Asia to unite these diverse nations, much less create a unified Asian currency.

Of the relationship between Japan and Europe, Ambassador Jorgensen says:

> Japan sees parallels with the Europe of today and with the Europe to come. Confronted by the challenges of globalization, Japan often takes a position not dissimilar from the European one. Be it the third way on social questions, be it multi-functionality of agriculture, be it the labeling of genetically-modified organisms, these all reflect a complex view of society. Moreover, the parallel is often drawn between Japan and Europe, both having ancient and sophisticated cultures and both facing similar problems in the future, not least the demographic shift of an older population.[17]

The European Union and Japan interact in a number of international organizations and groupings, including an annual summit meeting between the Japanese prime minister, the president of the European Commission, and the president of the European Council. Japan and the European Union are pursuing cooperation in areas as far apart as Kosovo and East Timor. The establishment of the Korean Peninsula Energy Development Organization (KEDO) provides a good example of multilateral cooperation, comprising as it does the EU, Japan, South Korea, and the United States.

Speaking from the European Commission office in Tokyo, Jorgensen remarks that

> cooperation between Japan and the European Union continues to develop favorably. The EU-Japan Business Dialogue held its first conference in Brussels in October 1999. It is modeled on the Transatlantic Business Dialogue and it aims to promote the flow of trade and investment between the EU and Japan while also giving business and industry a voice in the policymaking process. The two-way regulatory reform dialogue is at the heart of the EU's economic relations with Japan. As the Union's most important trading partner in Asia, it is in our best interest to see Japan's economy return to growth.[18]

In the first year of the twenty-first century, Japan appeared to be slowly recovering from its financial problems. Some Japanese firms were embracing the new high-technology Internet and e-commerce businesses that have propelled the U.S. and European startup ventures to become billion-dollar firms in a short period of time.

If a triangle were drawn from the EU to Japan and then to the United States, the weakest side of the triangle would be that between the EU and Japan. An important objective of EU policy toward Japan, which seems to be showing some positive results, is to strengthen the EU-Japan side of this triangle, which is one of the key relationships in the world economic system.

What does the twenty-first century hold for European-Asian relations, particularly relations between the EU and China and the EU and Japan? The successful signing of the Sino-EU agreement is a major step forward for China's eventual membership in the World Trade Organization. It will provide more contact between European and Chinese businesspeople and government leaders. The Asian financial crisis will become a distant memory, and Japanese firms will most likely roar back as global trendsetters in new fields. There are now some positive signs that the Japanese market is finally opening up, and more European firms are beginning to conduct business there profitably. With the advent of the euro, it is possible that Europe will increase its role in Asia. Certainly, more transactions will be done in Europe's new single currency. The triangle linking the United States, Asia, and the European Union is starting to look more equilateral, with the European-Asian side growing in importance and stature. And just as the European Union is rediscovering East Asia, Asia is rapidly "discovering" and becoming more involved with the new Europe in the twenty-first century.

10

The European Union
and the Middle East

DAVID LENNON

Europe has a very important and influential economic role to play in the Middle East, but not a very influential political one. While the United States as the global superpower seeks accommodation, the Europeans have been helping by providing services, development funds, and humanitarian aid to the needy. The EU describes its role as being complementary to U.S. political leadership: essentially, the United States supports and protects Israel, while the EU provides the Palestinian side with funds and political support.

The European Union has provided more economic assistance to the Israel-Palestinian peace process than any other donor. Its contribution between 1993 and 1997 amounted to more than ECU 1.68 billion (1.68 billion European Currency Units), and the EU will continue to give at that level.[1] These funds are primarily aimed at developing the Palestinian economy, based on the assumption that Palestinian economic development will be Israel's best security guarantee.

Israel has a privileged economic relationship with the EU, according to officials in Brussels: "We trade with Israel like one of us," they say.[2] The 1995 association agreement is gradually establishing a free trade relationship. Europe is Israel's largest trading partner and also provides other benefits: for example, in research and development Israel has a greater access to EU institutions than non-EU European states like Switzerland and Norway.

Despite the strengthening of economic and trading ties, diplomatic relations have long been marred by Israel's perception of most European states as being more pro-Arab, more pro-Palestinian, than the United

States. That is why Israel will not accept European leaders or representatives as official brokers in the political process. However, individual European diplomats and leaders have played facilitating roles, most notably in creating the framework for the peace negotiations that began in Oslo, Norway, in 1993 and led to the Israel-Palestinian accords.

The EU's appointment of a special envoy to the Middle East peace process, Miguel Angel Moratinos, was part of the Union's effort to play a larger role in promoting peace. Moratinos's role was to complement the efforts of the U.S. envoy diplomatically and politically. However, the Commission admitted, "This is an arrangement which has worked imperfectly so far."[3]

More meaningful is the Euro-Mediterranean partnership launched in late 1995, with the declared long-term goal of progressively establishing an area of regional security and free trade. The stated aim is to attain a free trade relationship by the year 2010, with an unstated purpose of trying to stem the flow of economic and social refugees from the Near East and North Africa into southern Europe by helping those nations to develop their domestic economies.

The Euro-Mediterranean partnership strategy consists of concluding association agreements with the twelve Mediterranean states not in the EU: Algeria, Cyprus, Egypt, Israel, Jordan, Lebanon, Malta, Morocco, Syria, Tunisia, Turkey, and the Palestinian Authority. The partnership focuses on three areas: political and security matters; economic and financial assistance; and social, cultural, and community affairs. The main feature of these agreements is the gradual phasing in of free trade in accordance with World Trade Organization rules. Funding for the partnership for the years 1995–1999 was ECU 4.68 billion. The EU has pledged to increase this by 4 percent by 2006.[4]

The Euro-Mediterranean association agreements were meant to pave the way for an influx of private investment. In practice, the stalemate in the Israel-Palestinian arena has meant that this assistance effort has failed to trigger the economic development and the private investment that should have underpinned it. Similarly, an impasse in the peace process has led to a halt in the moves toward regional economic development, cooperation, and integration.

The EU aspiration was to maintain its Mediterranean policy separate from the Israel-Palestinian peace process, but progress in developing Euro-Mediterranean ties gradually slowed because the EU's policy was based on the implicit assumption that the peace process would remain on track. The Commission repeatedly stated that the crisis in the peace process constituted a serious threat to Europe's ambitious long-term policy for the Euro-Mediterranean region.

Just as progress in Euro-Mediterranean economic cooperation slowed, so too the program of economic assistance for the Israel-Palestinian peace process has not yet achieved its original goals. As previously mentioned, the initial five-year commitment of ECU 1.68 billion was provided to develop the Palestinian economy and thus sustain and bolster peace in the region. "The opposite has happened," the Commission says. "All Palestinian economic indicators point at a clear deterioration of living conditions: there are no tangible peace dividends."[5] Nonetheless, Europe has pledged to continue the same level of financial support in the future because it believes that its economic assistance and political support for the Palestinians have succeeded in keeping the peace process alive.

Changes in the political leadership of Israel, the Palestinian Authority, and various Arab countries can be expected in the years to come. What these changes may bring is impossible to forecast. A slight shift to the right in the Israeli elections in 1996 halted the peace process. The 1999 election of a centrist coalition led by Ehud Barak produced a modest swing the other way, bringing renewed momentum to the talks. Slow progress resumed. The death of King Hussein of Jordan in 1999 reminded everyone that the leaders of the Arab world are aging. The ill health of Palestinian leader Yasser Arafat and the death of Syrian president Hafez al-Assad and his son's succession indicate that more changes can be expected.

Oil supplies and markets for its products are the key elements in Europe's relationship with the region today. Both of these depend on stability in the Middle East, which is one of the reasons that the European Union has committed substantial sums in assistance, in particular to support the peace process between Israel and the Palestinians. Having become the world's largest donor of development and humanitarian aid in the 1990s, Europe will step up its economic assistance despite the disappointing achievements of the billions of euros allocated over the past few years.

Europe will continue to be active in the Middle East. The European Union has pledged to provide substantial economic assistance both for the Israel-Palestinian accord and the Euro-Mediterranean framework. It is certain that the motives will continue to be a mixture of economic self-interest, fear of immigration, and genuine humanitarian concern.

11

The European Union and Russia

MARTIN WALKER

In the decade after the fall of the Berlin Wall in 1989, Western governments and financial institutions like the World Bank and International Monetary Fund (IMF) poured a total of just over $122 billion in grants and official credits into the final two years of the Soviet Union and the first eight years of Russia.[1] In constant dollars this amount was rather more than the sums the United States invested in Western Europe through the Marshall Plan in the years after World War II. The Marshall Plan money succeeded almost magically in reestablishing a series of thriving liberal capitalist economies from the ruins of war. So far, the money to Russia has failed.

The essential difference was that in Germany (and also in Japan) in 1945, the victorious U.S. and British troops were in place to require a thorough cleansing of the old discredited regimes and were able to install a new democratic system based on free institutions and the rule of law. Moreover, across Europe and also in Japan could be found experienced businesspeople, bankers, and trade unionists who knew how a modern economy should be run. In Russia in 1991 there was no such economic experience and no such outside authority to install a genuinely democratic political system. The giant state enterprises simply became nominally privatized monopoly firms. Many of the *nomenklatura,* the old Soviet elite, were able to retain political and economic power; a survey by the Russian business journal *Kommersant* found that more than 70 percent of the members of the Moscow stock exchange in its first year had been former members of the KGB secret police.[2]

By contrast, in Poland, Hungary, the Czech Republic, and Slovakia, the crucial combination of political will to transform the system
and sufficient folk memory of capitalist economics developed in the
1990s, allowing these countries to make the transition at which Russia
faltered. So despite all the generosity and good intentions of the West,
the funds proved unable to help the transition from an outdated, cen-
trally planned but still functioning Soviet system to a modern free market economy. Indeed, much of the money seems to have found its way
back to Western banks, after the hemorrhage of private capital that
helped bring about the Russian financial collapse of August 1998.

In at least one depressing way, Russia had returned to the situation
in the Soviet Union before the Gorbachev era, being feebly ruled by its
leader Boris Yeltsin from a Kremlin hospital ward prior to his resignation at the end of 1999. But a terrifying proportion of other things had
changed for the worse. Hunger, homelessness, and unemployment
matched the soaring rise of violent crime in a state that, at least in the
Soviet era, had provided a grim sufficiency of jobs, housing, and food.
And the collapse of state finances in August 1998, with the stunning
default on the debt, had badly dented the one sign of hope, that the privatized economy was finally starting to work.

The state was formally bankrupt, and Deputy Prime Minister Yuri
Maslyukov noted in December 1998 that after ten years of declining
production, Russia would probably soon become an oil importer.[3]
Nothing could be more serious. Russia lived by exporting energy,
mainly to western Europe. The energy sector accounted for more than
half of the value of the Moscow stock exchange, over one-third of what
taxes were paid, and almost one-fifth of the country's entire gross domestic product (GDP). The decline in the oil price, from $24 a barrel in
January 1997 to $12 in July 1998, was the trigger for the debt default.

Above all, Russia was plagued by crime, extortion, and contract
killings. First came extortion of Russia's fledgling businesspeople, and
then contract murders and car bombs became common, first against
rival Mafiya gangs and then against bankers. Finally, the killings
turned political. Veteran democrat Galina Starovoitova, gunned down
in the doorway to her St. Petersburg apartment building in November
1998, was the sixth member of the Duma, the Russian parliament, to
have been assassinated.

The political rhetoric of Russian democracy had always been ugly,
thanks to rabid populists like Vladimir Zhirinovsky, leader of the oddly
named Liberal Democratic Party, who used to boast that Russian troops
would soon be "washing their boots in the Indian Ocean." It 1998 it became rather worse, with naked anti-Semitism being preached in the

Duma. Accusations flew back and forth of fraud and corruption between former president Boris Yeltsin's supporters and the business
leaders and media magnates whose relentless propaganda in the previous presidential elections ensured his return to power.

Galina Starovoitova stood valiantly against all this, just as she lost
her place at Yeltsin's side as his adviser on ethnic policies by oppos-
ing the war against Chechnya. Her last campaign in St. Petersburg was
to try and rally the city's liberals and democrats into a single voting
slate dedicated to cleaning up corruption. Her prime target was Gen-
nady Seleznyov, communist and speaker of the Duma, whom she ac-
cused of extorting funds from St. Petersburg businesses to finance his
presidential campaign.

Were there any hope at all to be found in this political landscape of
desperate gloom, it was the way Russia's battered and dispirited democrats and reformers all gathered at Starovoitova's funeral to say that
her memorial should be a new political coalition to fight the next
year's parliamentary elections on a reform ticket. Three former prime
ministers attended her burial at the Aleksandr Nevsky monastery. With
them came Anatoly Chubais, the reformer who ran the privatization
program and then masterminded Yeltsin's last reelection campaign.

"They are killing our friends. They are killing our comrades," Chubais said over her grave. "They want to frighten us, but they won't succeed."[4] He went on to promise the formation of a new center-right
coalition, dedicated to the free market and democracy. At the same
time, the powerful mayor of Moscow, Yuri Luzhkov, announced the
formation of a moderate center-left coalition party called "Fatherland."
It is to be hoped that Russia is at last moving toward a stable two-party
political system. So far, Russia has known only the politics of the
vozhd—the boss—whether it was czar or commissar, Leonid Brezhnev
or Yeltsin, the autocratic leaders with whom the West has almost always had to deal.

The surprise resignation of Boris Yeltsin at the end of 1999, in effect making way for the little known former KGB agent Vladimir
Putin, continued this dependence on the vozhd that was a central symbol of the essential failure of Russian politics to manage the postcommunist transition. Putin's first act was to intensify the costly and controversial war in Chechnya, conducted with such ferocity that it
imperiled the Western goodwill that was the prerequisite of aid. Putin
then endorsed a new strategic doctrine devised by the Ministry of Defense, which blurred the previous Soviet commitment to no first use of
nuclear weapons. These "nationalist" credentials allowed Putin to win
the presidential elections of March 2000. Although he maintained that

he would follow the course of economic reform, it was clear that his priorities were to reassert the authority of the state and its great-power status in international affairs.

The further problem of the post-Soviet experience was that democracy itself had provided no guarantees of good government. The Russian Duma, or elected parliament, had contributed to Russia's problems, even while its confused mix of old communists and new democrats, of liberals and nationalists, reasonably reflected public opinion. The Duma also refused to enact commercial laws regarding contracts and taxation systems that were essential to attracting serious industrial investment from the West.

All this is the context within which any assessment of the role of the West, whether U.S. or European policies toward Russia in the 1990s, must be judged. U.S. and European leaders, who dominated important institutions like the G7, North Atlantic Treaty Organization (NATO), World Bank, and IMF, had to operate within the constraints of Russian politics and deal with the Russian situation and leadership as they found them. In this sense, their hands were tied. But their thinking and the assessments of their key advisers and diplomats were shaped by two sharply contrasting perceptions. The first was that Russia could not be allowed to fail because it was too big, too strategically important, and too dangerously equipped with nuclear weapons and with unsafe nuclear power stations. The second was that a successful Russian transition to prosperous democracy would be a glittering prize indeed.

A vast market of 150 million people, well-educated and hungry for consumer goods, could become an important locomotive for European growth in the next century. At the same time, Russia's vast reserves of raw materials, including oil, natural gas, iron ore, precious metals, timber, and raw chemicals, could foster a hugely prosperous symbiotic trade relationship. The problem was always how to bring this about despite the failures of the Russian political and economic systems.

Two lessons have been learned since the 1998 financial collapse. That comforting realpolitik, which said that the dominant role of organized crime was just a passing phase and the Mafiya were robber baron capitalists who would soon become wealthy enough to require law and order to protect their own property rights and become a force for stability, has been thoroughly exploded. The Russian Mafiya appeared unaware that the robber barons of capitalism had invested as well as exploited and that the mafia in the United States had learned that there was more money to be made from legal gambling in Las Vegas than from illegal activities. Until Russia's *vori v zakone* (thieves-in-law) understood the merits of honest moneymaking, there was little point in seeing them as any source of hope for the future.

The second lesson was that there was little point in throwing money at Russia. It did not have the skills, legal traditions, commercial contract experience, and investment banking infrastructure that could benefit from a Marshall Plan. Western money disappeared in Russia just the way that the armies of Napoleon Bonaparte and Adolf Hitler once did, swallowed up the forbidding vastness of the place. There was no quick fix to Russia's problems and severe limits on what the West could do except back the reform process in general and invest with great caution in good projects and good people. There was no shortage of either, and they would need all the help they could get to install the structural reforms of the tax and financial systems that are the preconditions of progress.

"The Russian crisis is multi-faceted. So too must be the response of the EU," said Europe's fifteen heads of government after meeting in December 1998 at the Vienna summit. "The EU is ready to help Russia in overcoming the crisis through credible and sustained market-based reforms, while respecting urgent social needs, and a continued commitment to democracy including freedom of the media, the rule of law, and respect for human rights."[5]

The trick was to convert those sensible platitudes into real policies. It is no accident that Russian revolutions have historically come in October and February, when the harvests are in and have been eaten. In late 1998, there was less a food shortage than a series of distribution disasters. But after their worst harvest in a generation, the Russians faced serious food shortages in the spring of 1999. The EU and U.S. donors, however, had great difficulty in ensuring that the food aid stayed out of the hands of the Mafiya and corrupt sectors of government and reached the hospitals and orphanages, schools, and elderly who needed it.

The EU also kept plugging away at those aid programs through which it was making a difference. It funded projects to improve the safety of Russian nuclear power plants and to inculcate the banking, accounting, and financial skills that both public and private sectors sorely needed. Along with these projects (costing about $120 million a year) went a slow, uphill task of education in the basics of capitalism. For example, not only had the Russian farm sector been left largely in the hands of the traditional managers of the old collective farm system, but the basic legal reform of land privatization had not been enacted. Above all, stressed the European Commission, land could not be used as collateral for loans, so there was little that the magic of the market could do for Russia's farmers.

The structures and institutions of the EU-Russian relationship were sound enough. There was by 1999 a partnership and cooperation agreement, under which ministers met regularly at a cooperation council and officials met in joint committees. These solemn occasions published portentous communiqués with little tangible result, except for the ritual statements of EU support for Russian reform and its future membership in the World Trade Organization. But even though EU ministers and their officials could take decisions and send them into a functioning bureaucratic system and know that money and projects would emerge at the other end, the Russians were unable to turn their decisions and promises into anything approaching reality.

Until the 1998 collapse of the ruble and the debt default, the EU-Russian trade relationship was not unhealthy. Europe imported around $25 billion a year in energy and raw materials and exported back a similar value of finished and consumer goods. Since the collapse, the energy purchases continued, but because of falling oil prices Russia's ability to import shrank sharply. The EU accepted the situation and eased some (but far from all) restraints on imports of dumped goods like steel after considerable U.S. pressure on the Europeans to share the burden of managing the Russian and Asian crises by buying their exports. The rise in price of oil in late 1999 offered Russia the prospect of a new economic breathing space.

The EU did have one major new proposal to offer, based on the lesson of the 1990s that the Russian central government in Moscow had proved less than receptive to Western proposals. The EU decided instead to turn to a crucial region of Russia in the hope that local self-interest might secure more cooperation. As a result, in 1999 the EU began preparing the most ambitious central planning project since the fall of the Soviet Union: a $90 billion investment to develop northern Russia and the Baltic states and secure Europe's energy supply for the next 100 years. It was based on a "grand bargain," through which Russia would trade untapped energy resources for an irreversible integration with a European economy that would finance and build the pipelines and develop the giant oil and gas fields of Russia's Barents and Kara seas.

By far the most grandiose act of strategic development that Europe has yet envisaged, the overall scheme is known as "the Northern Dimension" by its authors in the Finnish government, who saw it as the showcase of their first turn at holding the EU presidency in the latter half of 1999. Over the next twenty years they also proposed to clean up the most chronically devastated environment in Europe, in the Baltic Sea and the Kola Peninsula, and build a network of highways and road and energy grids that would bind the plan and the region together. After negotiations with the Swedes, Poles, and Baltic states, the Finnish government drafted the maps and plans and financing systems for the roads and new ports, gas pipelines, and electricity grids that were designed to lock all the countries on the shores of the Baltic Sea into a long-term and supposedly stabilizing interdependence.

"This is all based on the principle that this is an all-Union project in Europe's widest strategic interests, and not just a regional plan," Finnish prime minister Paavo Lipponen said.[6] He spoke just after a Russian ice breaker and specially built Finnish oil tanker had success-fully proved the viability of a year-round Arctic Ocean route to bring gas condensate from Russia's Kara Sea, even when the Arctic ice was at its thickest. Britain, which also supported the scheme in principle, was closely involved through the leading roles assigned to the big oil groups British Petroleum and Shell, who were sponsors of the ice breaker's voyage.

Based on the knowledge that the North Sea's oil and gas fields had already reached their peak and would decline sharply over the next decade and that Europe's alternative gas supply in Algeria contained only eight years of EU energy consumption, those behind the North-ern Dimension plan saw Russia's Arctic gas fields as the only logical solution. The commercial value of the gas and oil meant that more than half of the overall project would be self-financing through the private sector. The road and energy grids were to be financed through multi-national institutions like the World Bank, European Investment Bank, and European Bank for Reconstruction and Development. EU taxpayer funds were crucial to financing pilot schemes and the design stage in the early years and would also help to clean up the nuclear and toxic waste nightmare of the Kola Peninsula.

Although the Northern Dimension explicitly and deliberately ex-cluded all security issues to avoid provoking Russian hawks, a major concern was the pollution problem and the danger caused by old Cold War military structures at the Severomorsk base, where Russia's nu-clear submarine fleet was housed. The U.S. government agreed to join this massive cleanup effort. Finnish sources believed the region still contained some 2,500 tactical nuclear weapons and some 500 nuclear reactors of various sizes, mainly from submarines, ice breakers, and Russian naval vessels. There were serious fears for their stability and equally deep alarm for what is probably the most concentrated, least safe, and dirtiest agglomeration of nuclear waste on earth. The nuclear submarine tragedy involving the crew members of the *Kursk* in the summer of 2000 gave new impetus to reforming Russia's military. Russian officials stated that the *Kursk* submarine posed no nuclear threat as long as it was left on the bottom of the sea.

The Northern Dimension sought to emphasize the positive inter-dependence the project would create among EU, Russia, and the Baltic states, and its planners aimed at "integrating Russia into European and global structures through increased cooperation," according to the Finnish government's own planning paper. "The ultimate objectives of the Northern Dimension are to promote, in a sustainable manner from social and economic points of view, stability in Europe, basic values such as human rights, democracy, the rule of law, market economy, prosperity and high employment, as well as trade and economic cooperation. The objectives also include narrowing the disparities in living standards and preventing and warding off threats originating in the region."[7]

The sharp contrast between the Finnish per capita GDP of more than $22,000 a year and Russian levels of barely a tenth of that meant that the only direct border between Russia and the EU was also the most politically challenging, with the deepest gap in living and social standards. In the long term, Finnish planners insist, this was so dangerously unstable a situation, with such dire implications for refugee movements and communicable diseases like tuberculosis, that development of Russia's northern region, along with the new roads linking Russia with Scandinavia and with central Europe, had to be tackled in Europe's strategic self-interest. The initial part of the Northern Dimension project sought to modernize the sewage system and water supplies of St. Petersburg, which is blamed for 70 percent of the pollution flowing into the Baltic Sea from the Gulf of Finland. It started in 1998, with an immediate EU investment of $120 million and a long-term target budget of $900 million.

Although the Northern Dimension scheme made sense both for the EU and for Russia, it represented yet another triumph of hope over experience and highlighted the stubbornness of the Finns, who keep trying to find ways to help their dangerous and increasingly desperate neighbor. Whether it would have worked or not, it showed that the West's reservoir of goodwill for Russia's future had not run entirely dry.

There was perhaps one missed opportunity. From his new post at the Center for European Policy Studies in Brussels, former EU ambassador to Moscow Michael Emerson devised a bold plan to stabilize the economy. It called for an internationally backed currency board, like the system that had proved effective in Hong Kong and Estonia. It would allow the issuance of no more local currency than was backed by hard currency reserves. Emerson proposed a board capitalized at $35 billion (which would more than finance the current Russian economy) and financed 60 percent by the EU and 20 percent each by the United States and Japan. The idea, while theoretically sound and promising and studied with some interest in the U.S. Treasury, went nowhere because the Russian government refused even to discuss it. It sounded too much, according to one Russian spokesman in Brussels, like "a humiliating imposition upon us."[8]

As British foreign secretary Ernest Bevin said in 1947, when the United States proposed the original Marshall Plan and then Soviet foreign minister Vyacheslav Molotov tried to haggle over the terms and issues of national economic sovereignty, "Beggars can't be choosers." That was the hard and uncomfortable dilemma. In 2000 Russians still did not feel like beggars and insisted on being choosers. In a democracy, even as frail as that of Russia, the reaction was understandable, particularly when the beggar in question still saw itself as a serious nuclear superpower. Russia's neighbors tended to see this nuclear inheritance from the Soviet era as a terrifying and barely controlled nightmare. It made the West take Russia seriously, but in the wrong way. It was not Russian power that Europe feared as the twenty-first century began, but Russia's weakness. And in the end, only the Russians can cure it.

12

The European Union: A Leader in Humanitarian and Development Assistance

DAVID LENNON

Europe is the biggest aid donor in the world, providing 56 percent of all world assistance to developing countries. The EU and the fifteen member states' cooperation policies benefit all developing countries in Asia, Latin America, the Mediterranean, Africa, the Caribbean, and the Pacific.[1]

European Union aid has existed since the European Economic Community (EEC) was established in 1957. The six original member states agreed that there should be measures for pooling resources for external assistance but that they would retain bilateral aid programs. By the 1990s the EU member states had channeled a growing proportion of their total aid programs through the EU, up from under 13 percent in 1990 to more than 17 percent by the end of the decade.

The pooled resources have now developed to the point at which EU assistance is among the world's five leading donor programs. Overall, it manages between $5.5 billion and $6 billion of development aid a year, about the same amount as the official development assistance managed by the UN and similar to the Office of Development Assistance (ODA) component of the World Bank and International Monetary Fund (IMF). The vast majority of EU aid (84 percent) goes to developing countries, and in the 1990s the remaining 16 percent went to the transitional economies of central and eastern Europe and the newly independent states of the former Soviet Union.[2] The experience of giving aid over four decades in a changing world led the EU to review activities in the mid-1990s, with the objective of reforming European policies so that they would be more effective in addressing development needs.

Europe's development cooperation policies and its humanitarian aid have been broad and multifaceted. The EU's aid program increased steeply in real terms, more than tripling as a proportion of Organization for Economic Cooperation and Development (OECD) aid between the mid-1980s and the mid-1990s, while U.S. aid has remained constant in real terms. This disparity has placed enormous strains on the infrastructure of the Commission.

Detractors say that EU aid has become too uncoordinated and poorly managed to have the maximum impact on development. Those more sympathetic to EU aid believe that the rapid growth and diversification of assistance are welcome, even if weaknesses have emerged in its management. A source of much criticism has been that the Commission has four directorates-general dealing with development, mainly on the basis of geographical responsibilities, and a separate directorate for the management of humanitarian aid. The Prodi Commission is creating a new supreme directorate to oversee and coordinate aid.

THE CHALLENGE

One of the challenges of the new century is the elimination of extreme poverty. Adoption of the UN goal of halving the proportion of people living in extreme poverty by the year 2015 is a giant undertaking. Europe is committed to it and, as the largest donor of aid, will play a major role in making it happen.

As the twenty-first century began, almost one-quarter of the world's population of 5.8 billion lived in absolute poverty. This means that some 1.3 billion people, or 23 percent, were surviving on less than a dollar a day. The goal is to halve that percentage to 12 percent by the year 2015, which requires lifting 400 million people above the absolute poverty line. However, because the world population is expected to grow by 1.5 billion in that time, 900 million will still languish in extreme poverty even after that percentage is halved. The population of the world was 2.3 billion in 1945, is almost 6 billion today, will climb to 7.3 billion by 2015, and is expected to reach at least 10 billion before it plateaus.[3]

Although the proportion of the world's population living in extreme poverty has fallen, the number of people enduring absolute poverty has grown. This is one of the great dilemmas of aid: How do donors ensure that improvements brought about by aid outstrip the erosion caused by population growth? In addition to the dramatic reduction in the proportion of people living in extreme poverty, there are associated targets of providing basic health care and ensuring universal access to primary education for all by the year 2015.

Development Policy

The Treaty on European Union, signed in 1992, helped focus policy objectives in granting development assistance. EU development policy now aims at encouraging domestic reform on the basis of four principles: development of democracy, economic and social development, integration into the world economy, and a campaign against poverty.

The EU's development policy consists of a combination of regional agreements under which the recipient countries decide themselves what use they wish to make of the various cooperation instruments. In addition to the various trade agreements and the system of generalized tariff preferences, the EU provides financial, technical, and humanitarian aid in the worldwide war against hunger and deprivation.

Besides participating in collective EU action, each member state conducts its own development policy, which varies according to the traditions, priorities, and financial resources of each donor country. Of course, this process is not entirely altruistic: the national interests of the member states are served by helping developing countries, which both supply them with raw materials and offer markets in which to sell their products.

Many people argue that the EU and its fifteen member states should improve the coordination of their development policies, that is, truly "Europeanize" them. Doing so would be in line with aims of the Maastricht Treaty, which states that the EU and its member states should harmonize their development policies and aid programs. However, national political, economic, cultural, and geostrategic interests stand in the way.

Performance and Reform

The EU performance so far as provider of development and humanitarian aid has come in for very heavy criticism from the European Parliament and many national parliaments, not least the British. Political pressure to appear to be spending at a time when the volume of Community funds being dispensed though Brussels was soaring led to aid commitments that did not take account of the absorptive capacity of the recipient countries and put excessive demands on the EU administration's capacity to implement the tasks. Inefficiencies, slowness in disbursing aid, the multiplicity of agencies in the Commission handling development issues, and a tendency to target the better-off while reducing aid to the poorest are among the many complaints. The European Parliament has also criticized the Commission for drawing conclusions merely in statistical and economic terms and for describing the situation in developing countries solely in the context of macroeconomic functions, disregarding the socioeconomic, ecological, and cultural aspects.[4]

One of the most common weaknesses of past aid efforts was excessive proliferation of aid projects. At the beginning of the twenty-first century, donors are moving beyond the project-by-project approach to the creation of explicit country strategies. There have been fundamental changes in development thinking since the end of the Cold War. For a long time it was believed that the challenge was one of enhancing economic performance plus creating a social safety net for the losers. The effect of aid was measured mainly by the size of the funds mobilized. However, organizations like the United Nations Development Programme (UNDP) have come to realize that it is not that simple to combat poverty. In addition to economic growth, major investments are needed in educational, health, and employment programs. The new criteria have become the results obtained and the viability of the recipient country's policies.

Private Investment

The shift toward privatization and the global market means that development aid is now regarded as something that can facilitate domestic and foreign investment. In the mid-1980s, official development finance was the major part of the resource flow to developing countries. By the mid-1990s, private flows to the developing world were five times greater than the total of development assistance from official sources.

The European Union views the private sector as having a leading role in development and increasingly encourages developing nations to improve the environment for private sector investment. Private investment from the EU to African, Caribbean, and Pacific (ACP) countries more than quadrupled in the 1990s, with particular emphasis in the oil, minerals, and tourism sectors. However, there is scarcely any direct EU investment in export-oriented manufacturing or agriculture. Private flows are highly concentrated in a limited number of countries and sectors and generally do not flow directly to some key sectors of priority needs, such as health and education.

In practice, countries that present promising opportunities attract investors, even against a background of policies and institutions that are far from ideal. Small countries with few exploitable resources find it had to stimulate investment interest, even with sound policies and institutions. Unfortunately, the fifty least developed countries attract little or no private investment, with sub-Saharan Africa getting a mere 5 percent. The current flows are massively concentrated in the twelve most developed of those fifty countries. East Asia and the Pacific attract 40 percent, with Latin America and the Caribbean accounting for more than 30 percent.[5]

Food Aid

The goal of reducing by half the proportion of the world's people who are hungry (currently 23 percent, or 1.3 billion) by the year 2015 was set by the World Food Summit in 1996. It is a tall order—the list of countries in chronic need grew in the 1990s, and the key countries suffering food shortages have the highest birthrates. All this means that their food needs will continue to grow rapidly into the new century.

The EU is the second-largest provider of food aid after the United States, and like the United States its volume of food aid has fallen in recent years. Indeed, global food deliveries in 1997 were half those of a decade earlier. Fortunately, donor countries are getting better at targeting their food aid to the poorest countries.

There are three types of food donations: relief aid to meet emergency food needs arising from natural disasters or armed conflict; program aid, which involves donations that recipient governments can sell on the open market to raise revenue; and project aid to support specific projects such as irrigation or soil improvement. Program aid was the largest category a decade ago but has declined by 75 percent, and project assistance has fallen by half as relief aid grew to account for 41 percent of global food aid.

Sub-Saharan Africa and Southeast Asia are the biggest regional recipients of food aid, but they have much different needs. Half of all food aid to sub-Saharan Africa was relief aid for man-made or natural disasters. In the early to mid-1990s, supplies to central and eastern Europe and the former Soviet states soared because of emergency food needs in the former Yugoslavia and the Caucasus.

By the end of the twentieth century two-thirds of food aid was being delivered through multilateral organizations; a decade earlier most food aid had involved bilateral transfers. The expectation is that this trend will continue in the new century. However, whether the EU will take over more and more of its member states' aid budgets in the new century will very much depend on its ability to reform its operations.[6]

Development Aid—Changing Directions

Development aid decreased sharply in the 1990s, falling by more than 15 percent. One-fifth of the funds goes to a handful of countries, and year after year the same dozen or so countries receive the bulk of the aid. However, even though the recipients have remained the same, the purpose of the aid donations has changed significantly.

In the last quarter of the twentieth century, donations were moved away from industrial and agricultural production and food aid toward the provision of health, education, and welfare services. Economic infrastructure has also benefited with more money going into transportation, communications, and energy. The flow of global aid shifted in the 1990s away from Africa, south-central Asia, and the Middle East toward central and eastern Europe. Some countries received sharp increases in aid, but others suffered dramatic declines. Apart from food aid recipients such as Somalia and Sudan, where aid declined as the crises passed, economic development aid to countries like Turkey, Morocco, and Tunisia more than halved.

The EU initiated two new assistance programs to help the former communist countries: an aid program for economic restructuring in eastern Europe (Pologne et Hungrie: Actions pour la Reconversion Économique, or PHARE), and Technical Assistance to the Commonwealth of Independent States and Georgia (TACIS). When the former Yugoslavia disintegrated after 1992, agencies that had already been giving generously to assist the former communist state adjust to the market economy rushed in with massive injections of aid. Assistance grew from $46.7 million in 1990 to a peak of $2.5 billion three years later.[7]

The European Community Humanitarian Office

More than half of all humanitarian aid in the world comes from the EU and its fifteen member states. The assistance given includes emergency aid, food aid, and aid to refugees and displaced people, and it is used to relieve the effects of all types of crises, from natural disasters to civil and ethnic conflicts. Humanitarian aid is generally directed at victims of conflicts or crises in countries where the local structures cannot meet those needs. "Responding to the needs of victims is the prime objective," explained former European Commissioner Emma Bonino in 1999.[8]

Most of the fifteen member states have been giving aid for decades, and the European Community as a collective entity has been involved since the end of the 1960s. However, it was the significant amount of aid supplied through the Community since the late 1980s that made aid a key element of the EU's international policy. In 1992 the Commission created a new agency, the European Community Humanitarian Office (ECHO), with the aim of centralizing the distribution of aid to nonmember countries.

The volume of funds channeled through the new body grew so rapidly that in 1998 ECHO granted a total of ECU 518 million (518 million European Currency Units) in humanitarian aid. To this must be added the ECU 258 million spent by the EU on assistance to refugees, food aid, and other humanitarian programs. On top of those two amounts comes the direct, bilateral humanitarian aid by the member states, which in 1998 totaled ECU 904 million.

Nearly 30 percent of ECHO aid allocated went to the former Yugoslavia, and ACP countries received more than a quarter of the total. Asia was promised close to 12 percent, with the newly independent states of the former Soviet Union and Latin American countries each sharing just over 8 percent. Eastern Europe received 7 percent, and just over 4 percent went to North Africa and the Middle East.[9]

ECHO normally works through European nongovernmental organizations (NGOs) that are experienced in distributing aid. It has partnership agreements with more than 170 NGOs, as well as with the specialized agencies of the UN and other international bodies like the Red Cross. Approximately 40 percent of aid funding is distributed by NGOs and another 40 percent by UN or other international agencies. The Commission is aware that the delivery of EU humanitarian aid is less than satisfactory because of the lengthy procedure required to release the funds. As a 1997 report put it, "Administrative requirements have sometimes proved to be at variance with crisis needs."[10]

The rapid growth in the funds being disbursed through the EU, particularly for humanitarian aid, appeared to make sense as the Union sought greater cohesion. In practice, however, this growth created a problem because resources at the headquarters in Brussels could not match the needs.

Whatever the criticisms of the efficiency of the ECHO program, there is no argument about the efficacy of its actions. ECHO can respond to a crisis with emergency aid within forty-eight hours and can have a project properly worked out and in place within one to four weeks. When people are dying, this speed is vital. In general, all ECHO projects are limited to three to six months and are then reviewed.

THE EU'S AREAS OF FOCUS FOR DEVELOPMENT AID

Cotonou and the ACP Countries

The Cotonou convention (which will replace the Lomé convention) is a unique treaty covering aid and trade relations between the European Union and the former colonies of its member states. Various versions have been in place for twenty-five years with mixed results, and it is now about to undergo a radical overhaul in line with the globalization of world economies and the growth of free trade.

European Community aid in the 1960s was focused almost exclusively on the former colonies of France, Belgium, Italy, and the Netherlands. When the UK joined the EEC in the 1970s, the twenty Commonwealth countries in Africa, the Caribbean, and the Pacific (the ACP countries) were given the opportunity to negotiate their relations with the EEC. This led to the first convention, which was signed in 1975 in the capital of Togo, Lomé.

By the year 2000 the number of members of the Cotonou convention had grown to seventy-seven countries. There is enormous diversity and complexity among the ACP nations. Some countries in the Caribbean are relatively well developed compared to many countries in Africa. Indeed, three-quarters of ACP aid has gone to sub-Saharan Africa.

Virtually all products originating in the ACP countries have tariff-free access to the Community. Reciprocal arrangements are not compulsory; the ACP countries are merely required to grant the EU states most-favored-nation status. Now the EU wants to bring its trading relationship with the Cotonou countries into line with the policies of the World Trade Organization (WTO). The WTO rules stipulate that the protected and nonreciprocal access accorded to the ACP countries on European markets is discriminatory and must eventually be changed.

The Cotonou trade system was supposed to contribute to an increase in and diversification of ACP exports, with a view to promoting ongoing trade flows. The evolution of ACP-EU commercial transactions over a quarter of a century demonstrated that the objectives have not been achieved and that most ACP countries have not benefited from the Cotonou convention's trade access rules and special protocols.

Globally, the ACP share of total EU imports has declined markedly since the 1970s, falling from about 6.7 percent in 1976 to 3.8 percent in 1996. Their share of world trade has declined even more drastically, from 3 percent in 1975 to 1.5 percent. The competitiveness of ACP countries has progressively declined because their traditional exports are primary products, whose share of global trade has fallen from 50 percent to 20 percent. Although about 40 percent of ACP's exports go to the EU, Caribbean countries tend to trade more with the United States, and Pacific states trade more with Japan.

The year 2000 will definitely be a watershed in ACP-EU relations as the trade preference regime between the two sides gradually undergoes liberalization, moving toward reciprocal treatment of European exports. The implementation of change will be gradual but inexorable. There is considerable concern among ACP countries that adopting WTO rules and ever-increasing trade liberalization will crush their fledgling industries and wreck their economies. They also fear that the establishment of regional cooperation zones will weaken the negotiating strength of the group.

Although some ACP countries reject the idea of regionalization, most accept the inevitability of the changes. Clearly, the adjustment will be harder for those countries that depend on customs duties for much of their revenue. ACP negotiators argued for a long transition period so that there can be progressive integration of the ACP countries into the liberalized world trade system.

An agreement in principle was reached in 2000 when the Lomé convention expired. The EU proposed negotiating free trade areas with regional subgroups over the five-year period 2000–2005, with an implementation period of ten years or more. The Union sees 2015 as the ultimate date for establishing free trade.[11]

The Mediterranean, Asian, and Latin American Countries

Although the Community's activities centered on the ACP countries in the 1970s and 1980s, other developing countries assumed growing importance in the 1990s. In response, the EU created additional cooperation instruments for countries of the Mediterranean region, Asia, and Latin America.

These countries are receiving assistance under separate agreements negotiated or augmented in the early 1990s. The existing bilateral approach was supplemented by a more regional EU policy, such as the New Mediterranean Policy, known as the MED program, and the aid commitments to Asia and Latin America (ALA).

Expansion into Eastern Europe

The collapse of the communist regimes in Eastern Europe and the Soviet Union forced the EU to look eastward to see what it could do to help those countries develop democracy and market economies. For more than a decade the EU has been helping the central and eastern European countries with economic reconstruction under PHARE and TACIS.

PHARE was established in 1989 as a grant program to support the process of economic and social reform in Poland and Hungary. As central and eastern European countries moved out of the Soviet bloc and elected noncommunist governments, the program was gradually extended to additional countries, reaching a total of fourteen by 1990. Within a few years, PHARE was converted into the main instrument for helping the countries prepare for accession to the EU. It focused on restructuring state enterprises, promoting private sector development, reforming institutions, and reinforcing the administration and judicial capacity of recipient countries.

PHARE is the world's largest grant assistance effort for central and eastern Europe and is the financial instrument that will lead these countries to full membership in the EU. The preparation of the first five candidates for membership (Hungary, Poland, the Czech Republic, Estonia, and Slovenia) became a priority in the late 1990s as the EU identified enlargement as one of its major challenges for the twenty-first century. By the end of 1999, PHARE had spent ECU 11 billion in preaccess development aid. It is committed to spending a further ECU 1.5 billion per year until 2006.[12]

In 1991 the Commission launched the TACIS program as a mechanism for helping the transition process in the fifteen republics of the former Soviet Union. Its objective was to support the reform initiatives of the authorities by the transfer of knowledge. By the end of 1999, TACIS had spent nearly ECU 4 billion. Officials admit they have had real problems reaching understandings with the recipient countries, and in the future TACIS efforts will focus on fostering the development of democracy.

NGOs—the Implementing Agencies

The Commission's cofinancing arrangements with European NGOs began in 1976. What was at first a halfhearted and often ambivalent relationship has become a shared commitment. Since then, funds for cofinancing NGO development projects have regularly increased, and in addition NGOs have been contracted to provide specific services. The Commission and Parliament regard the NGOs as an indispensable complement to official cooperation activities. Cofinancing of NGO projects offers a nonofficial approach that is more targeted to specific recipients.

An enormous variety of NGOs have offices in Europe, reflecting the diversity of the world of voluntary associations. They rely on popular support and funds raised from private sources, as well as national and EU cofinancing arrangements and funds from multilateral bodies. More EU development aid is channeled through NGOs than through any other non-EU organizations. To qualify for cofinanced projects, in most cases the NGO must be able to raise 15 percent of the funds from private sources, and the Commission normally gives up to 50 percent of the total cost. In other cases the EU commissions the NGO to undertake a fully funded project. This is known as giving "aid through" the NGOs rather than giving "aid to" them. At times the lines are somewhat blurred.

The projects identified by European development NGOs are often small-scale initiatives formulated by populations in the developing countries. They aim to respond directly to the needs of the most under-privileged groups so as to improve their long-term economic situation.

THE FUTURE

One of the lessons learned since the 1970s is that the old approach of insisting that all aid is neutral no longer applies. Whatever aid the EU provides always has an impact on the situation, be it the result of warfare or natural disaster. Humanitarian supplies such as food and medicine are valuable resources for those in conflict. "No longer can we say that aid is neutral; if you are proactive, you are not neutral," one official in Brussels stressed.[13]

All are aware by now that aid should be targeted to those in real need. It is also generally understood that there is a greater need to link relief to rehabilitation and development. Although the aim of humanitarian action is to improve living conditions that have suddenly deteriorated because of a conflict or natural disaster, development projects are the only way of substantially improving the situation of a given population in the long term.

How can agencies and organizations link humanitarian aid and foreign policy, both of the EU and more especially of the member states? How can the aid bodies influence the political direction of the EU and the national governments? One official explained: "We would like to humanize foreign policy, not politicize humanitarian aid."[14]

Any task that can be implemented more effectively by the EU than by individual member states could profitably be Europeanized. Such tasks might include areas such as food aid, family planning and population policies, structural adjustment, support for regional integration, trade promotion, and conflict prevention.

The bilateral aid packages of the fifteen member states account for 80 percent of the total development aid provided by the European Union: the need for coordination is already understood. Efforts to avoid duplication and ensure that essential sectors are not ignored will continue. There will also be a concerted effort to make European aid more visible. One of the tasks facing those involved in aid is the need to integrate aid, trade, and foreign policy at the multilateral level and bring more coherence to bilateral state policies. At present there are really sixteen European development policies (fifteen national policies plus that of the EU), and no one is certain when or whether they will mesh into a coherent whole and finally into a common policy. Most people cannot foresee such coordination happening soon, but the optimists believe it may come about in the first quarter of the new century, as the single market and single currency move the member states closer together.

The failures of the overstretched Commission to spend the funds allocated and poor supervision of funds spent have led to a serious revision of the tendency of member states to donate a growing share of their bilateral aid through the EU. Many Commission officials and most officials of member states believe that the EU is not yet ready to handle additional funds. Before there is any further growth in the budget, the Commission must develop its own coherent management policy and acquire the necessary skills to manage it.[15]

In the Maastricht Treaty, Europe tried to find a role for EU aid that would be different from national bilateral aid. It sought to be complementary, topping up the bilateral donations of the member states. As one official put it: "The EU has to show what it can do better than the individual states, demonstrate its comparative advantage and then put its resources into that."[16]

Part 3

THE EUROPEAN MARKETPLACE

13

The Euro

LIONEL BARBER

The euro is Europe's great experiment, the most far-reaching development in Europe since the fall of the Berlin Wall. It marks a decisive step in the integration of the economies of Western Europe, the climax of a project more than thirty years in the making. But the euro is also a journey into the unknown. Those in favor of economic and monetary union (EMU) argue that it will act as a catalyst for Europe's slow-growth, high-unemployment economies by offering stable prices, more competition, and greater fiscal discipline. Those against EMU argue that it will foist a straitjacket on divergent economies that have yet to make painful decisions on the deregulation of labor and product markets necessary to make a monetary union work.

The politics of EMU are equally controversial. Will the euro unite Europe in a new U.S.-style federation where power is shared between largely centralized decisionmaking in Brussels and increasingly marginalized national parliaments? Or is Europe on the brink of a painful schism, with EMU imposing intolerable constraints on nation-states and alienating a European public that already harbors doubts about the political legitimacy of opaque and inefficient European institutions? And how will elected politicians manage the relationship with the unelected professionals running Europe's central bank in a manner that will convince citizens about the legitimacy of the enterprise?

The euro zone encompasses almost 300 million consumers and eleven members of the European Union: Austria, Belgium, Finland, France, Germany, Ireland, Italy, Luxembourg, the Netherlands, Portugal, and Spain. (The UK, Denmark, Sweden, and Greece stayed out initially,

141

the first three on political grounds. Greece becomes the twelfth member of Euroland on January 1, 2001, after meeting the necessary economic criteria.) The euro zone will make up the second-largest economy in the world behind the United States, accounting for more than one-fifth of world trade. The euro is widely viewed as a rival to the dollar, at least in the next five to ten years.

Statistics tell only half the story. The euro supplies the vital missing link in Europe's single market (Jacques Delors's project to eliminate barriers to the free movement of capital, goods, services, and people in the European Union that was launched in 1992). The abolition of currency transaction costs should bring greater competition, more efficiency, and better deals for the consumers. EMU has already triggered a wave of mergers, particularly in Europe's financial services sector. It is partly a response to the forces of globalization, which are encouraging the rest of European industry to restructure in a world of instant communications, volatile capital, and ferocious competition.

EMU also marks a cultural revolution, institutionalizing monetary orthodoxy and exporting German-style anti-inflationary rigor throughout Europe through a new supranational institution, the Frankfurt-based European Central Bank (ECB). If EMU advocates are correct, the birth of the euro heralds a second economic renaissance for Europe built on stable prices, iron-willed budgetary discipline, and permanently lower interest rates.

In the run-up to the launch of the single European currency on January 1, 1999, the prospect of entry into an elite grouping inside the EU inspired traditionally weak governments to take courageous steps to meet the entry criteria for monetary union. The most notable example is Italy, where a succession of reformist prime ministers in the 1990s, latterly Romano Prodi, began to restore public finances based on the argument that doing so was the sole means of qualifying for the elite single currency club. The question, however, is whether these incentives will continue to apply or whether "austerity fatigue" will set in as political leaders look to economic growth to tackle still chronic levels of unemployment in Europe.

All these events will be watched closely in Britain, the most important economy still outside the euro zone. The Labor government led by Prime Minister Tony Blair has declared that, in principle, it is in favor of joining EMU. But it remains nervous about the political and economic risks of membership and must win a referendum, most likely to be held in 2001 or 2003, after the next general election. This referendum will be a defining moment in Britain's postwar history, offering a once-in-a-generation opportunity to settle its ambivalent relationship with the continent and European integration.[1]

In this chapter I offer a flavor of the debate in Europe about the pros and cons of the EMU, but I look beyond the political controversy to examine practical questions such as the euro's relationship to the dollar in a new bipolar or tripolar monetary order (including the yen) and its likely impact on other areas of policymaking such as taxation and social policy.

EMU: A BRIEF HISTORY

Whatever the prospects for success or failure of EMU, it is important to remember that the project is the culmination of more than thirty years of planning, debate, and incremental steps toward a commonly agreed goal: a single currency that would finally offer Europeans a measure of control over their economic destiny.

The origins of EMU go back to the late 1960s, when the Europeans were searching for a response to the upheaval in the Bretton Woods international monetary system, in which the U.S. dollar was the dominant currency. In 1970, Pierre Werner, the little-known prime minister of Luxembourg, was asked to prepare a blueprint for the transition to monetary union. Although his plan was derailed by the currency turmoil following the first oil shock in 1973, its spirit and content survived. By 1992—following the launch of the single market and the collapse of the Berlin Wall—the European Union agreed on a timetable for monetary union by 1999 in which the Werner Report was adopted in large measure.

Between 1992 and 1999, the fate of EMU was often in doubt. Even the faith of the most committed supporters occasionally wavered, notably during the currency turmoil that convulsed the European exchange rate mechanism in 1992–1993. But thanks to a combination of political will, a measure of luck, and the occasional piece of improvisation, the project survived. Most important of all, nation-states with divergent political cultures and economic performances such as France, Germany, and Italy were able to bury their differences and agree jointly on the terms, conditions, and membership of the new currency club.

The chain linking these great events was the Maastricht Treaty and its five EMU entry criteria covering interest rates, exchange rate stability, inflation, and the appropriate targets for both budgetary deficits and debt as a proportion of gross domestic product (GDP). In each case, these entry criteria were sufficiently realistic to offer genuine incentives to achieve the necessary targets. But they were also sufficiently flexible to allow a degree of discretion when assessing which countries qualified, thus preventing a north-south divide between the natural deutsche mark zone built around Germany and inflation-prone economies in the south such as Italy and Spain.

The same give-and-take has characterized the formation of rules for the post-EMU world, notably the German-inspired Stability Pact for enforcing fiscal discipline among euro zone countries. Though modified in the summer of 1997 by the new socialist-led government in France to become the Stability and Growth Pact, the agreement nevertheless requires a political commitment to balanced budgets over the cycle. The pact also provides for draconian penalties, starting with public censure and proceeding to heavy fines for countries on a sliding scale of 0.2 to 0.5 percent of GDP.

Most member states believe that these penalties are so politically explosive that they will be impossible to apply; their value is therefore more a deterrent. For the German public, still nervous about surrendering their traditionally stable deutsche mark, the pact was intended to spell out the principle of fiscal discipline more thoroughly than in the Maastricht Treaty (though the new Social Democratic–Green coalition elected in Germany in September 1998 has since displayed a less rigid attitude toward the Stability Pact because of broader concerns about weak economic growth).

Stanley Hoffman, a Harvard University political scientist, has described these complex bargains in terms of the "logic of ambiguity" or the "logic of gambles about the future"—and they can be seen throughout the forty-plus years of European integration.[2] Thus, France saw the founding of the European Coal and Steel Community (ECSC) as a chance to improve the French economy and control Germany's industrial revival; Chancellor Konrad Adenauer saw the ECSC as a step toward German rehabilitation after World War II.[3]

Forty years later, for France, EMU was a means to end the dominant role of a Bundesbank guided exclusively by German interests in the formulation of a de facto Europe-wide monetary policy, whereas Chancellor Helmut Kohl viewed the economic integration of Europe and the sacrifice of the deutsche mark as the strategic imperative for embedding a united Germany in Europe. In the case of the rules for the post-EMU world, the same logic applies: each side has struck a solemn and binding bargain that it hopes will allow its own views to finally prevail.

In a sense, EMU is a recipe for permanent tension and, perhaps, ultimate disappointment. But the primacy of a rules-based system means that the conflict between countries and between interest groups has a reasonable chance of being contained.

AN ECONOMIC GOVERNMENT FOR EUROPE

The success of EMU will depend in large measure on the stability of the macroeconomic framework in which the single currency will operate, which in turn will depend on three factors: the depth of political commitment to EMU-led fiscal discipline and the sustainability of economic convergence within the euro zone; a modus vivendi between the elected politicians leaning toward growth and independent central bankers committed to price stability; and, finally, on more limited steps that will enhance the political legitimacy of the project.

As discussed earlier, a good deal will depend on the willingness of the euro zone members to continue their efforts to achieve greater economic convergence. The area of most concern is budget discipline because five years of pruning the public finances have produced what some call "austerity fatigue." High unemployment (still near 17 million in the EU) and slow growth at first threatened to cast a shadow over the launch of the euro. In fact, the post–Asian financial crisis recovery in Europe was far more impressive than many private sector economists imagined. The only difficulty was that the EU member states risked repeating the errors of the late 1980s, when they ignored the margin of maneuver created by the spurt of growth generated by the single market. The result was that in the good times countries ignored the structural (as opposed to cyclical) causes of the deficit; in the bad times that followed the average deficit in the EU soared to more than 5 percent of GDP.

In the run-up to the launch of the euro, fault lines appeared in the European Union over the issue of fiscal discipline. The Germans took inspiration from their postwar economic success, citing the so-called stability culture. The guarantor of this stability culture was the Bundesbank, whose independence was guaranteed in the constitution.

The French followed a different tradition. Their state may have been compromised in World War II, but it was not destroyed, as the state was in Germany. The tradition of state interference in or state management of the economy is ingrained, going back three centuries to the days of Jean-Baptiste Colbert. Thus, the notion of an independent central bank was new and the idea that all power should rest with unelected central bankers inconceivable. As the French stressed time and again, there must be a political counterweight to the ECB.

In the first months since the launch of EMU, these roles have suffered something of a reversal. Oskar Lafontaine, the mercurial former German socialist finance minister, launched an aggressive campaign to pressure the European Central Bank into lowering interest rates and adopting plans for exchange rate target zones with the yen and the dollar. Lafontaine's abrupt resignation in March 1999 eased tensions, but the argument has enough potency to stage a comeback.

The man in the middle of this confrontation is a tall, chain-smoking Dutchman with craggy features, tousled white hair, and a reputation for monetary orthodoxy. Wim Duisenberg, a sixty-three-year-old former Dutch finance minister who spent fifteen years as head of the Netherlands central bank, is the first president of the European Central Bank. In November 1998, he produced a powerful counterblow to Lafontaine's argument: a coordinated interest rate cut among the eleven future members of the euro zone.

During an interview with the *Financial Times* on the day of the coordinated cut, Duisenberg described the move as "rather sensational."[4] He left no doubt about his pleasure in taking the markets by surprise and answering political critics who have dubbed the ECB as "more Catholic than the Pope" in pursuing price stability and monetary orthodoxy.

In economic terms, the joint reduction in interest rates was driven by fears of a collapse in business confidence in the face of faltering growth in Europe. The slowdown reflected the continuing impact of the Asian financial crisis, which helped to trigger a de facto default in Russia as well as send shock waves through emerging markets in Latin America. All these factors weighed heavily on policymakers in the United States, who have long complained that the U.S. economy has carried a disproportionate burden for keeping world growth going.

Yet the European Central Bank is a new and untested institution that desperately needs to establish credibility. A rush to reduce rates could be interpreted by financial markets as surrendering to political pressure. In this sense, Duisenberg was correct in describing Lafontaine's autumn offensive on behalf of lower rates as "unhelpful" and may even have delayed the eventual cut.

Although the ECB will set the future monetary policy framework for the euro zone, it will leave the execution to the national central banks. The precise balance of power between the Frankfurt center and the national central bank must still be worked out. One outstanding question is who will take the lead role in crisis management when, say, a financial institution in the euro zone gets into trouble: Should it be the ECB or a big national central bank acting in the same way as, say, the New York Federal Reserve?

Third, Duisenberg is still feeling his way as president and public face of the euro zone. His appointment was a close call. French president Jacques Chirac pressed the nomination of Jean-Claude Trichet, governor of the Bank of France. The eventual compromise was at best uneasy.

Duisenberg agreed to step down once the transition to the euro was complete, around mid-2002 after the introduction of euro notes and coins. The exact timing of his departure remains in the Dutchman's hands in order to preserve the notion that his early retirement is a voluntary act, but the uneasy bargain prompted some to dub the first ECB president "Wim Claude Trichenberg."[5]

Partly to establish his credentials, Duisenberg's first public statements included a robust defense of the ECB's independence. He regularly castigated politicians for failing to bring down public deficits and tackle structural economic reform—the real reason for higher-than-necessary interest rates. The straight-talking Dutchman also triggered controversy by refusing to open up the ECB's monetary policy decisionmaking to public scrutiny along the lines of the Federal Reserve or Bank of England. He argued that too much "transparency" could trigger second-guessing in the financial markets and unnecessary currency instability.

The election of a coalition government in Germany led by the Social Democratic Party (SPD) in September 1998 added a new and fissile element to the debate about macroeconomic policy in the post-EMU world. Oskar Lafontaine's high-pressure tactics triggered ill-disguised hostility from within the ECB. A charitable explanation is that Lafontaine was speaking primarily to a domestic audience in the wake of the SPD's first election victory in sixteen years in Germany, but his efforts also looked like an unsubtle attempt to browbeat the ECB into adopting a more accommodating monetary policy than the orthodox hard-liners wanted. Whatever the explanation, the Lafontaine campaign reopened the debate about the appropriate policy mix and the balance of power between finance ministers and central bankers.

Initial impressions were that both sides were pursuing a dialogue with the deaf. The ECB blamed unemployment on structural imbalances created mainly by inflexibility of labor and good markets in the euro zone, resulting in part from excessive regulation, and rigidly defined its mandate as the preservation of price stability. Hence, in its first monthly bulletin published in February 1999, the ECB declared that "effective euro area-wide structural policies would lead to higher trend real growth. Within its monetary policy strategy, the Euro-system would naturally take account of such growth. However, attempting to reduce unemployment by implementing an inflationary monetary policy would ultimately be self-defeating, since such a policy would only undermine price stability over the medium term, which is the basis for lasting and sustainable employment growth."[6]

In the other camp, the Lafontaine lobby argued that the ECB was exaggerating the structural rigidities in the European economy, which it believed to have been exacerbated by an overly restrictive monetary policy. What was needed was expansionary monetary policies along the lines of those pursued successfully by Alan Greenspan, chairman of the Federal Reserve. Dominique Strauss-Kahn, the former French finance minister, offered a variation on this theme, arguing that Europe should follow the U.S. example in the 1990s and implement budget rectitude and a loose monetary policy, rather than implementing the U.S. policy of the 1980s of looser fiscal policy and tight money. "We want Clinton-Greenspan, not Reagan-Volcker," was Strauss-Kahn's favorite slogan.[7]

These arguments are likely to dominate the "launch phase of the euro" and will be fought out in the Euro-11 meetings (the informal gatherings whose membership is restricted to the single currency members), which usually take place before the formal monthly meetings of the Council of Economic and Financial Ministers (ECOFIN). But after Lafontaine's resignation, arguments about interest rates receded in importance in relation to the corporate revolution ushered in as a result of the technology-driven "new economy" in Europe imported from the United States. In some ways, the private sector became a more important force for change than public institutions.

Nevertheless, there seems little doubt that both ECOFIN and Euro-11 will grow in importance, if only to serve as a counterweight to the European Central Bank. They will monitor each member state's economic performance in relation to the Stability and Growth Pact, and they will allow member states to coordinate national budgetary policy more effectively to achieve greater convergence. All this does not make a European economic government per se, but it does take economic governance to a qualitative new level.

THE EURO AS CATALYST FOR ECONOMIC REFORM

One of the key benchmarks for success for the euro will be its impact on labor and product markets. The decisive issue is whether Europe will be able to use the euro as a catalyst for tackling its mass unemployment and reforming its increasingly expensive social security systems. Supporters of the single currency believe that the competitive shock entailed by the introduction of a one-size-fits-all monetary policy will provide governments with a tailor-made excuse to instigate change. The pessimists point to Europe's inflexible labor markets. Without the monetary tools and fiscal leeway to deal with external shocks, the onus will be on the labor market to make the adjustment, most likely through lower wages. Without such an adjustment, the likelihood is that recession will trigger huge job losses and social unrest. This could spell the end of Europe's social model, which combines relatively free markets with a generous welfare state.

Between these extreme points of view, the starting point for debate is that Europe's product and labor markets require overhaul with or without EMU. An increasingly open trading system coupled with the phenomenon of globalization means that capital and production are both footloose and volatile. The first issue, therefore, is whether EMU will accelerate change or, by generating opposition and conflict, exacerbate the changes that are themselves inevitable. The second issue is whether Europe can make the change more acceptable by building a coalition of support through a tripartite alliance of governments, trade unions, and employers.

One of the big surprises about the EMU process is how the majority of trade union and employer organizations support the single currency. On labor's side (particularly in Britain), the trade unions appear to have calculated that they have more chance of prospering in a currency zone where there are minimum EU-wide social policies and safety nets than outside the euro area, where employers (particularly in Britain) pursue a hire-and-fire policy similar to that in the United States. The introduction of devices such as work councils inside companies and other EU-wide legislation covering, say, working time and minimum rights for casual labor and child care workers all combine to offer a reasonable chance of a safety net inside the highly competitive European market.[8]

Having such social safeguards is crucial because many of the competitive stresses created by the introduction of the single currency are likely to affect the labor market. In the absence of monetary and fiscal policy for fine-tuning the economy, much of the pressure for adjustment is likely to fall on wage policy. In this sense, some unions fear a race to the bottom—a downward spiral in which employers use the threat of moving plant and investment elsewhere in the single market. The big question is whether powerful German unions, exploiting a weak Social Democratic–Green coalition government in Germany, can secure high wage settlements, thus setting the pace for others in the euro zone despite difficulties over differential productivity rates and diverse unit labor costs; or whether other sectors and interest groups, especially in the cheaper labor countries in the south, seek to undercut German agreements in the interest of securing comparative advantage.

The European Union—and the European Commission as the EU's executive branch—has sought to create a framework for containing these conflicts that consists of EU-wide norms and standards on training, education, and job creation for youth and the long-term unemployed: the so-called Social Dialogue. None of the above amounts to a revival of the command economy that attempts to regulate every nook and cranny but rather attempts to expand on the model of the Maastricht criteria for entry into the euro club, which encouraged member states to reach common goals through peer pressure and review.

In the case of labor, each state will adopt its own national employment policy and submit it to peer review at the Council of Ministers meeting in Brussels. This approach is much less heavy-handed than the cascade of EU-wide social legislation out of Brussels in the late 1980s and early 1990s, when the pressures for harmonization and standardization were at their peak.

Whether all these disparate pressures will lead to EU-wide wage bargaining coordinated through ever closer ties between national trade unions is more doubtful. Footloose employers are unlikely to accept such constraints. However, the euro zone is more than a single market dominated by a single European Central Bank. It is also a "community of social values" where minimum rules and standards apply rather than the laws of the jungle. In this last respect, the European heritage and the legacy of the European social model appear strong enough to ensure that this will be the course rather than an acceleration toward the U.S. model.

Speculating about the impact of transparency on prices and sectors may be easier than predicting the fate of the labor market. Many experts confidently predict that greater comparative advantage means greater specialization by region and by dominant companies. Without internal barriers to trade, locations that combine high levels of productivity, relatively low costs, available skills, and good transportation links to markets will gain at the expense of others, as *Sunday Times* economics editor David Smith says in his book *Euro-Futures*.[9]

Smith also predicts the "Saville Row" effect—clusters of particular businesses in areas where the proximity of other businesses operating in the same business creates a pool of skilled labor and related expertise. Thus, it is possible to envisage a Europe that will gradually begin to look a little like the United States, with clusters of aerospace and defense companies paralleling the Boeing complex in Seattle; the car industry in Detroit and the Deep South; and the financial services sector built around New York.

THE EURO AND THE DOLLAR: A RECIPE FOR CONFLICT?

John Connally, the hard-bitten U.S. treasury secretary who served in the Nixon administration, used to tell Europeans that the dollar was "our currency, but your problem." Twenty-five years later, the Texan boot is on the other foot. The launch of the euro poses the first serious threat to the dollar, which has dominated the world's financial system since it replaced the British pound during World War I.

Before the euro was actually launched, few members of the U.S. financial and political establishment gave much thought to the implications of EMU or its impact on the global economy. But now that EMU is a reality, the mood has shifted. Many are wondering whether the euro will be to the dollar what Airbus is to Boeing.

Some Europeans, notably the French, have encouraged the idea of the euro as a competitive threat to dollar hegemony. French prime minister Lionel Jospin has likened EMU to an instrument of liberation, a means to achieve a zone of currency stability that will protect Europe against the excessive fluctuations of the greenback.

From a different standpoint, the Japanese authorities have also accepted the proposition that the euro changes the balance of power in the world's financial system. There is a fear in Japan that the yen could be relegated to second-tier status in a bipolar system controlled by the U.S. and Europe. The Japanese want a place at the table.

All this talk of grand monetary strategy begs a number of questions. Has the euro a genuine chance of becoming a global currency? What will determine whether it does? And what impact is its emergence likely to have on the world economy?

Obviously, the dollar's preeminence as a reserve currency is unquestionable. Because of its extensive use by third parties, the dollar's importance far exceeds the U.S. share of world output. The dollar accounts for 56 percent of the world's foreign exchange reserves and about 48 percent of export invoicing and is used in some four-fifths of foreign exchange transactions.

Fred Bergsten, head of the Washington-based International Institute for Economics, argues that the advent of the euro presents the first credible alternative to the dollar.[10]

- The European Central Bank, which has a treaty mandate to fight inflation, will deliver the stability that markets crave.
- The eleven members of the euro zone (twelve members when Greece joins in 2001) have large economies and enough wealth (more than $600 billion combined gross domestic product) to compete with the United States (around $800 billion). The euro zone will be the world's largest exporter and importer, excluding intra-EU trade; if the euro were extended to all fifteen EU member states, its economy would rank alongside that of the United States.

- The euro will also be used in transactions by third countries, particularly those that used the deutsche mark as a preferred currency.
- The United States has built a $1 trillion external debt as a result of running substantial current account deficits since the mid-1980s, and sooner or later this imbalance will count in the minds of investors who will turn to non-dollar-denominated assets.

The contrary view in favor of the dollar's preeminence is that the euro and the ECB remain untested; that the initial performance of the euro against the dollar was dismal; and that the greenback's reserve currency status stems mostly from the fact that the United States has wider, deeper capital markets with far greater liquidity than the undeveloped, fragmented European capital markets.[11]

Moreover, the European domestic security market is only two-thirds the size of its U.S. equivalent. Without a central government bond issuer, euro markets will continue to be fragmented. For this reason, whatever doubts they may have, most EU countries are very anxious for the UK, with its highly liquid capital markets, to join the euro zone as soon as possible.

Certainly, the U.S. ability to finance its current account deficits in assets denominated in dollars is a little like being indebted to foreign countries free of charge. But many economists worry about the impact of a sudden switch into euro-denominated assets, which would risk a substantial appreciation of the euro—not something that export-sensitive countries such as France and Germany would necessarily enjoy.

The underlying reality is that the EU will have to shift from a big surplus to a substantial deficit to accommodate a future shift in favor of euro-denominated assets. Doing so would create some difficulties for ECB monetary policy; and it could force the United States to choose between a sharp drop in the dollar or higher U.S. interest rates.

All these future scenarios will require careful management. They argue in favor of deeper monetary cooperation between the United States and Europe—not least because of the important role that the United States has played in containing the Asian financial crisis. The decisive interest rate cuts delivered by the Federal Reserve helped to keep the U.S. economy going and trade flowing.

Finally, observers question how much political clout the euro zone will command on the international economic stage. In the initial phase after the launch, the impression is less than favorable. First, national sensitivities mean that euro zone countries are unwilling to allow the European Commission to represent their collective interests. France,

Germany, and Italy (as well as Britain) still want their seats at the G7 industrialized countries' table, although they are willing to see the ECB president take his or her place alongside national central bank governors.

A complicated rotation system for other high-level international economic gatherings means that the smaller countries will be represented when they hold the EU presidency. None of this is guaranteed to impress the United States, which speaks with one voice through the U.S. Treasury secretary and the Federal Reserve chairperson. One senior Federal Reserve official noted that European countries were still "overrepresented" at the G7 meetings: "We have never asked the chairman of the Kansas City Fed along to these meetings."[12]

A more fundamental weakness of the euro zone is the division between central bankers and politicians in the EU, which contrasts with the relatively happy equilibrium in the United States between the Treasury and Federal Reserve over the balance of macroeconomic policy. No doubt, the booming U.S. economy has helped to create this equilibrium; but it also reflects the benefits of more than seventy years' experience operating a national central bank in a federal political system.

CONCLUSION

It is too early to pronounce whether the euro is a success. Certainly, the technical preparations have been impressive enough to guarantee a smooth launch. But the early political strains—coupled with unimpressive economic growth performance inside the EU—suggest that the jury will remain out for some time to come.

EMU was a qualitative leap forward for the EU, which seems certain to lead to a further evolution of the Union's political institutions and its standing in the world. But the real issue is whether EMU will act as a catalyst for economic reform, reversing the genteel decline that many European countries succumbed to in the 1990s. In this sense, the greatest challenge for the EU is to harness EMU as a tool for adapting to a new global economic order—in short, to make EMU work for a wider purpose than simple "Euro building."

14

The Single Market

BRUCE BARNARD

SINGLE MARKET, SINGLE MONEY, SINGLE ECONOMY?

Europe is poised to become a single economic superpower, matching and eventually overtaking the United States by the second decade of the twenty-first century. A little over fifty years ago, the war-ravaged continent was sliced in two, its western half propped up by U.S. aid, its eastern side under the yoke of Soviet communism. Today, fifteen EU countries are in a single market, along with Liechtenstein, Norway, and Iceland; eleven share a common currency; and in 2001 it will be twelve. Meantime, six former communist nations, three ex-Soviet republics, and a former Yugoslav republic are negotiating to join the EU.

It may seem overly optimistic to project Europe as the twenty-first century's economic top dog when the transatlantic gap visibly widened as the twentieth century closed. Europe's new single currency, the euro, dropped like a stone against the dollar, and its economy sputtered while the United States basked in its eighth successive year of growth, with unemployment at a thirty-year low of around 4 percent. And while more Americans than ever are working, more than 17 million EU citizens were on the unemployment queue at the beginning of the century, a jobless rate of nearly 10 percent.

But Europe is only at the start of its ambitious project to create a single economy to match that of the United States. The single currency, which is at the core of the project, is still in its infancy—notes and coins will not enter circulation until 2002. The single market, now in its eighth year, has a long way to go to forge a genuine economic unity:

Europe is still fragmented into individual economies with differing rates of growth, investment strategies, taxation structures, and business cultures.

Nevertheless, there are clear signs that a new corporate Europe is being forged that will soon compete as an equal with the United States. A wave of transatlantic mergers and takeovers in the late 1990s created European world champions in such all-American industries as oil, cars, planes, and telecommunications. Equally important, a sudden burst of cross-border merger and acquisition activity in 1999 suggests corporate Europe finally is gelling into a single unit.

The single market and the single currency were not created in a vacuum. They were accompanied by a massive program of privatization of state-owned industries that began in Britain in the 1980s and spread across continental Europe in the mid-1990s. At the same time, Europe and the United States played a leading role in freeing up world trade in goods and services. Meanwhile, globalization continues to spread to an ever-increasing number of industries, forcing European firms to look across their borders to achieve economies of scale.

Despite its shaky start, the euro has established itself as a legitimate global currency with a growing appeal as evidenced by Greece joining in 2001. Britain hopes to hold a referendum on the euro after the next general election, probably in 2001. A large majority of Britons currently oppose membership, but most observers expect the country to sign up to monetary union by the end of the decade. Meanwhile, a clutch of eastern European countries probably will also enter Euroland by 2010–2015.

True, European monetary union is not a guaranteed success. Some commentators play down its potential to transform the European economy; others say it is simply not necessary for the functioning of a single market. A minority warn that a project that applies the same rules to countries as different as Germany and Spain is fatally flawed and will lead to social unrest or even conflict between its dominant economic powers, France and Germany.

But the old continent has an uncanny ability to surprise the pundits, just as the United States has confounded those who condemned it to fall further behind Japan and the Asian tigers. Less than a year before the scheduled launch of the euro in January 1999, when it seemed that few countries would meet the entry criteria, respected economists were urging the project to be delayed, even abandoned. Even the euro's most ardent supporters predicted the euro zone would be an exclusive club of five or six countries clustered around a German core. The idea that Italy, Spain, and Portugal would qualify for the euro was laughable only a year before they did just that.

Europe's leaders kept their nerve, and the euro was launched on schedule, climaxing a decade-long process of economic change spurred by corporate restructuring and government deregulation. But just because Europe has consistently proved the pundits wrong in the past does not mean it will do so in the future. The critics argue that monetary union is an unprecedented exercise: subjecting countries with widely differing economic performances, practices, cultures, and histories to a single monetary policy. Put at its crudest, can freewheeling Italy live with rules-bound Germany?

The launch of the euro transformed the European Union overnight into an economic behemoth that will overtake the United States when all fifteen of its members join monetary union. The current eleven-nation euro zone has a gross domestic product (GDP) of $6.4 trillion, compared with $7.4 trillion for the United States. It has ousted the United States as the world's largest exporter and importer. Nearly one-third of the world's trade is transacted in euro zone currencies, compared with almost half in the dollar.

The EU will pull further ahead of the United States in the second decade of the twenty-first century as more countries, including those from the former communist bloc, join the euro. The wealthy western outsiders—Switzerland, a global financial center, and Norway, a world-ranking oil exporter—also are likely to be members by 2010.

An enlarged euro zone will topple the United States from its perch as the world's biggest economy, but will it do so as a simple aggregate of its member economies or as a single entity? Moreover, will the impact of the single market and the single currency be limited to existing industries? Will the EU draw level with the United States, only to find its rival is building an unassailable lead in the high-technology knowledge-based sectors that hold the key to economic growth in the twenty-first century? To succeed in these sectors, the economies of scale delivered by the single market are less important than risk taking, innovation, and flexible working practices that are in short supply in Europe.

Monetary union is not a panacea, only a respite, and a very temporary one at that, as the United States forges ahead again and Asia recovers from its late 1990s financial crisis to overtake Europe again. Europe's hopes hinge on its ability to fully exploit the potential of the single market, a process that is still in its infancy and has barely scratched the surface of scores of industries, including key sectors such as railroads and electricity that are still largely trapped in national markets. The acid test is whether it will ever be as easy to do business between Dublin and Düsseldorf as it is between Dallas and Detroit. Five years ago, the answer was a definite "no"; at the beginning of the twenty-first century it is "perhaps"; in July 2002 when 300 million Europeans are obliged to buy their groceries in euros because national currencies are no longer legal tender, the answer will graduate to "probably."

The euro dominated debate about Europe's economic prospects as the century closed, but arguably of greater significance was the decision in the mid-1980s to create a single market, an event whose political and economic significance was not fully appreciated even by those responsible for its inception. The European Community, founded by six member countries in 1957, had stagnated by the mid-1970s. It was little more than a single customs area, certainly not a common market. True, the European Commission, its executive body, had power to negotiate trade agreements on behalf of the member states, vet state aids, and enforce competition rules. But further economic integration was not on the agenda.

In the wake of the first oil price shock in 1973–1974, the global recession exposed the limitations of a so-called common market that had lowered customs barriers but left in place numerous other obstacles to cross-border business. The contrast with the open U.S. economy became even starker as European governments sought to protect their vulnerable industries from outside competition by using "nontariff" barriers such as differing national product, safety, health, and environmental standards. A lawn mower made in Detroit could be sold in Dallas, but one made in Düsseldorf was not acceptable in Dublin—different maximum noise levels rigged to protect the local manufacturer made the sale impossible.

A barrier-free market was not a new idea. A senior U.S. official involved in the Marshall Plan called for the creation of a "single large market" in 1949. But it was a long time coming. The 1950 Schuman Plan established a single market for coal and steel. The Treaty of Rome created the European Community, a customs union, that was only completed in 1968.

Meanwhile, the relative economic decline of Europe compared with the United States, Japan, and the emerging Asian tigers convinced its businesspeople of the need to remove the barriers to achieve the economies of scale available to their rivals. While U.S. companies embarked on waves of consolidation that reduced many sectors to four or five major players, European industry was made up of scores of firms surviving in protected local markets but unable to compete globally. Some industries, notably chemicals and automobiles, achieved European and global reach, but these were the exception. In fact, U.S. companies were far more European than the Europeans themselves, treating the continent as a single market in the 1960s and 1970s when they invested tens of billions of dollars in new factories across the Atlantic. As a result, they were better prepared to exploit the benefits of the single market when it was established in 1993.

Many key sectors that represented major costs for business, from air transportation to gas and electricity utilities, were in the grip of inefficient, overstaffed, and lavishly subsidized state-owned monopolies hiding behind protectionist borders. As a result, European businesses were burdened by much bigger bills than their U.S. competitors: airfares, fuel, and telecommunications charges were 30 percent to 100 percent higher in Europe than in the United States.

The single market, agreed by the Single European Act of 1986, basically deepened the original European Community customs union by establishing the free flow of goods, capital, services, and people throughout the member states. The political agreement set in train eight years of tortuous negotiations over 292 "directives" covering everything from the removal of physical trade barriers—such as controls at border crossings—to technical barriers, especially differing national standards.

The aim was to replace national markets with pan-continental ones: a single energy market, a single air transportation market, a single financial services market, often using U.S. deregulation of sectors like railways, trucking, and airlines as blueprints. It was probably the greatest supply-side exercise in world economics, according to Mario Monti, the commissioner responsible for the single market in 1995–1999.

The Single European Act also marked a significant step toward political integration because it involved agreement on the widespread use of qualified majority voting (votes weighted according to a country's population). This practice was intended to stop a country with a vested interest from blocking liberalization under the single market project: And it largely succeeded: countries have watered down proposals, but they have been unable to stop the march toward liberalization. Most measures were in place before the launch of the single market was established in January 1993, and others were phased in to give certain monopoly-dominated sectors time to adjust: telecommunications was not completely open to competition until 1998, and the electricity market was only partially liberalized in 1999. Progress has been uneven among differing sectors, but the key point is that the process toward a genuine single market is irreversible. If governments cannot finish the job, market forces will.

Some of the most far-reaching results of the single market are so deeply ingrained that they are taken for granted today. The massive lines of trucks at border crossings disappeared on January 1, 1993, when internal customs checks were abolished. So too have technical barriers such as the requirement to relabel and repackage goods for different national markets, the registration of cars and pharmaceuticals with national authorities, and the constant retesting of products to comply with local health and safety rules.

The establishment of the single market unleashed competitive forces and closed hiding places for protectionist governments. Some countries, notably Britain, had a head start on their neighbors because they embarked on deregulation and privatization well before 1993. Others followed suit in the mid-1990s, partly influenced by the new emphasis on free markets that accompanied the removal of borders and partly motivated by the need to raise cash from the sale of state assets to cut budget deficits to qualify for the euro. These were the unintended spin-offs from the single market and the single currency.

Equally important, claims by U.S. and Asian companies that Europe was using the single market to create a "fortress Europe" by rigging rules and standards to favor its own firms were unfounded. True, the EU did set limits on Japanese car imports until the end of 1999 to give its own manufacturers time to adjust to the single market and imposed quotas on U.S. movies. But the Japanese are making cars in Europe rather than shipping them from Japan, and Hollywood has tightened its grip on the European market.

Indeed, it can be argued that U.S. companies are the biggest beneficiaries of the single market to date. The United States and the EU form the world's largest trading relationship, with two-way trade and investment flows adding up to more than $2 trillion a year and supporting 14 million jobs. This has buried the perception that the United States was turning its back on Europe to focus across the Pacific and suggests the relationship will grow even stronger in the twenty-first century, as the enlargement of the EU single market to the east enhances opportunities for U.S. companies. U.S. firms in the Standard and Poor's 500 stock index are estimated to generate between 15 percent and 20 percent of their sales in Europe.

The EU has some way to go before it can claim to be a completely open economy. Some analysts feel it is as protected as it was ten years ago, with import restrictions doubling the price of many goods, especially food. The Institute for International Economics, a think tank in Washington, D.C., estimates the cost of protection at around $600 billion, or 7 percent of the EU's GDP. The United States and Japan also are guilty of protectionism, but the costs for their citizens are not as high as those borne by the European consumer. The single market formula is beginning to work, although it is difficult to draw up a list of winners and losers or calculate the impact on economic growth, the number of jobs created, or the number of jobs that would have been lost in the absence of liberalization. With European economic growth lagging behind that of the United States and unemployment stuck at just under 10 percent, the gains seem to be minimal. But the single market is still in its infancy, and Europe is two or three decades from its goal of creating an economy as open as the U.S. economy. Many sectors are still fragmented: Europe had fifty tractor manufacturers in 1999, compared with four in the United States; sixteen locomotive makers versus just two in the United States; and forty battery firms, compared with five across the Atlantic.

Europe's banking sector has been engulfed by a wave of mergers, yet it remains extremely fragmented compared with its U.S. counterpart. Thus ABN-Amro controlled nearly half of its domestic Dutch market but accounts for less than 2 percent of euro zone deposits, and Germany's mighty Deutsche Bank, which owns Bankers Trust in the United States, controls a mere 3 percent. By contrast, the domestic market share of the five leading U.S. banks surged from 12 percent to 22 percent in 1998 following a massive consolidation of the industry. But fiscal, regulatory, and cultural differences will inhibit the growth of a fully integrated European banking sector well into the twenty-first century.

In some areas, the single market is nonexistent. Thus it is impossible to run a nonstop freight train from the port of Rotterdam to, say, Milan in northern Italy. The rail gauges are the same, but signaling, safety systems, and electric voltages vary, and trains can be idled for hours—occasionally days—at border crossings awaiting a change of locomotive and crew.

The most glaring evidence that a single market does not exist is seen in the massive differences in car prices across the EU. A survey by the European Commission in 1998 showed that a Ford Mondeo was 58.5 percent more expensive in Britain than in Spain, and an Alfa Romeo 156 cost 47 percent more in Britain than in Ireland. The gap was almost as large in 1999. The Commission is cracking down—it fined Volkswagen, Europe's largest manufacturer, more than $100 million in 1998 for telling its Austrian dealers not to sell cars to bargain-hunting Germans. It also took action against DaimlerChrysler for stopping dealers in four EU countries from supplying cars to nonresidents.

Price variations are not restricted to cars. Farmers in Britain pay 40 percent more for tractors than their Spanish counterparts, and Belgian farmers pay 165 percent more for a pesticide than German farmers across the border. A pair of Levi's 501 jeans that costs 56 euros in Italy could cost up to 75 euros in Germany. A Japanese Canon camera retailing for 200 euros in Germany goes for 300 euros in France. A Belgian credit card costs three times as much to acquire as a Dutch one.

The single market will not function properly until the EU roots out the massive subsidies that distort competition—$55 billion per year on the manufacturing industry alone. Agreement is very difficult because the EU's three biggest economies, Germany, France, and Italy, account for two-thirds of all handouts. Competition is also distorted by state guarantees, most common in Austria and Germany, that allow regional banks to borrow at reduced and effectively subsidized rates of interest. But perhaps the most telling indictment of Europe's failure to bury nationalism in favor of a single economic entity is the failure to agree on a single electric plug for the continent!

Moreover, there is very little mobility of labor across borders in the EU, a key ingredient for a successful single market that mirrors the United States. The number of EU nationals resident in another member state is only 5.5 million, or 1.5 percent of the bloc's 370 million people. The United States, by contrast, is a very mobile society. The U.S. Census Bureau estimates that about 7 percent of all Americans move in a typical year, and 3 percent of the population, some 7.7 million people, change their state of residence.

The single market, Mario Monti has remarked, is not so much a legal framework as an attitude of mind. And it will take much longer than eight years to change the habits of generations of Europeans.

But the market is already having an impact on the lives of ordinary people. Germany, for a long time burdened by sky-high telephone charges, now has some of the cheapest rates in the world following a 70 percent plunge in charges in 1998, the first year of totally free competition. And the winners have outnumbered the losers: for example, Deutsche Telekom, the former state monopoly, shed 12,000 jobs in the first year of competition, but newcomers created 40,000. Airfares have also tumbled as scores of low-cost, no-frills carriers take advantage of deregulation. Again, the performance is patchy: on more than 90 percent of the routes in the EU, only two competing airlines provide service.

SINGLE MONEY

The successful launch of the euro marked the end of a twenty-five-year drive for monetary union and the beginning of the final phase of Europe's bid to create a seamless single market from the Arctic to the Mediterranean. The euro has transformed Europe into the world's second-largest economic unit after the United States: the euro zone's $6.4 trillion GDP trails the U.S. $7.4 trillion GDP, but the EU accounts for nearly 19 percent of world exports, compared with the U.S. share of 14 percent.

The new currency has already established itself as a junior partner to the dollar in the global financial system and may eventually challenge the greenback's role as the world's reserve money and the main invoicing unit for global commerce. There's little doubt the euro has the potential to topple the dollar from its perch. The only question is how long this process will take—the consensus is two decades. For the moment, however, businesspeople are more concerned about whether the euro can fulfill its potential as the missing link in the single market.

Monetary union carries a big upside: price stability, low interest rates, fiscal discipline, greater transparency, and easier cross-border mergers. But it also comes with a potentially risky downside: the implosion of the euro zone as the one-size-fits-all monetary policy becomes untenable. Critics never tire of recalling the collapse of Europe's exchange rate mechanism, the springboard to monetary union, in August 1993.

Monetary union is already paying off by getting rid of exchange costs—the values of the euro zone currency were irrevocably fixed on December 31, 1998. The savings could be as much as $12 billion a year, equivalent to 0.4 percent of the EU's GDP. But these savings pale in comparison with the euro's potential long-term spin-offs. Freed from currency risks, small and medium-sized firms are exporting to the euro zone for the first time. But most small firms will require some time to adjust to the new currency: companies are free to, but not obliged to use the euro either exclusively or along with national currencies until 2002.

Monetary union is also increasing price transparency, sharpening competition between companies, and cutting prices. The impact will be muted until January 2002, when euro notes and coins enter circulation, and will gather momentum six months later when national currencies in the euro zone are no longer legal tender. All goods and services, from northern Finland to southern Spain, will be quoted only in euros, enabling 320 million consumers to compare prices at a glance. Cross-border price variations will not disappear overnight, but they will broadly converge by the end of the first decade of the twenty-first century. The euro's impact will not be restricted to consumer goods: wages, taxes, insurance premiums, and welfare payments will become instantly comparable. This unprecedented price transparency combined with the growth of Internet shopping will be a powerful spur to creating a genuine single market. The laggard companies and protectionist governments that have tried to restrict the impact of the single market will be swept aside.

Ironically, although the euro may eventually topple the dollar from its perch, the most immediate impact of the new currency has been the "Americanizing" of continental European business. European firms are adopting U.S.-style employee stock options and stock buybacks. Multinationals are adopting U.S. accounting and governance standards and listing their stocks in New York. Hostile takeovers, a rarity in continental Europe, became all the rage within weeks of the euro's launch. Monetary union is not the spur to these changes, but it is certainly the accelerator.

Monetary union is creating a massive liquid single capital market, forcing companies to compete for funds on a Europe-wide basis and allowing financial institutions to be more choosy in providing loans. But Europe will not match the United States anytime soon: Europe's capital markets are even more fragmented than its industries. Less than one-fifth of financial assets in Britain, the most open European country, are invested abroad, whereas the figure in France, Italy, and Germany combined is barely 5 percent.

The arrival of the euro also has enabled investors to select stocks in the euro zone countries without currency risks, freeing them to focus on corporate management, strategy, margins, and profitability. This advantage, in turn, is forcing firms to improve their returns by selling noncore businesses and merging with and taking over rivals.

Although the single market prompted companies to rationalize their production, marketing, distribution and transportation, the single currency is forcing them to change the way they raise money and run their operations. Continental European firms raise about three-quarters of their finance from banks and only one-quarter from the capital markets. In the United States, by contrast, banks provide only one-quarter of firms' financing requirements.

A growing number of European firms have switched from banks to bond markets to exploit the historically low interest rates that accompanied the launch of the euro. The volume of euro-denominated bonds issued by firms in the first quarter of 1999 surged sevenfold compared with the 1998 period. More important, the average credit rating fell sharply after the launch of the euro, suggesting European investors have a greater appetite for risk.

But Euroland has a long way to go to catch up to the United States. The corporate bond market in the euro zone at the beginning of 1999 was valued at around $160 billion, one-sixth the size of the U.S. market. Its stock markets' capitalization was less than one-third that of the U.S. markets.

But thanks to lower transaction costs, the end of currency risks, price transparency, and lower interest rates, Europe is heading toward a U.S.-style equity culture. Regarding individual investing, Europe still trails the United States, where 45 percent of the stock market is directly owned by individuals, and it lacks U.S.-style pension plans that allow individuals to invest directly in their chosen shares. But the differences will melt away in 2000–2010.

The tough membership rules of the euro zone also promise action on the biggest impediment to U.S.-style growth: labor market reform. Unable to devalue or run budget deficits to counter economic slow-down, governments have no option but to undertake tough structural reform. Florida and California may grow at different rates, but unlike in Europe, there is a federal government to raise and redistribute taxes. Moreover, if a recession hits one state, Americans can—and do—move to where the jobs are. However, differences in language and home financing, pension, and welfare systems make this an unlikely option for Europeans who lose their jobs.

There is a danger that the European Central Bank could face pressure from individual countries that are suffering economic difficulties. Even in the United States there is some evidence that local conditions influence the votes of Federal Reserve districts. The ECB could be more vulnerable in this regard. But in its first year, the ECB stood firm in the face of pressure by politicians to cut interest rates to stimulate economic growth in their countries, enhancing its credibility in the financial markets.

Some EU governments have already undertaken labor market reform. The Netherlands, for example, slashed its unemployment rate from more than 11 percent to under 5 percent by easing hire and fire rules, which allowed a huge increase in part-time jobs, and by cutting taxes—without undermining the country's social welfare system, among the world's most generous. Germany, which feared it might have to follow the laissez-faire U.S. system, is pinning its hopes of reducing its 10 percent–plus jobless rate on replicating the Dutch model, which has nailed the claim that economic growth and job creation can only be achieved at the expense of welfare protection.

Europe will remain divided into distinct national and regional economies for decades despite the advent of the single market and single currency. Some European countries are set to outperform their neighbors and the United States. Britain will be the second-best place in the world to do business in 2000–2003 after Hong Kong, and the Netherlands will be third. Both will edge out the United States in fifth place, according to a survey of sixty nations by the Economist Intelligence Unit, using indicators such as tax and labor market policies, infrastructure, market potential, and political background.[1]

15

Business and the
Technologies of the Future

BRUCE BARNARD

There are two conflicting views of Europe at the dawn of the new millennium. It is either an economic also-ran, condemned to permanently trail a triumphant United States that has built up a commanding, seemingly unassailable, lead in the high-tech industries of the future; or it is a contender for world economic leadership as it builds on its single market and single currency to remove the physical, cultural, and psychological barriers that have hobbled its economic performance since the 1970s.

The answer will become clearer before the end of the first decade of the twenty-first century. There's no doubt that, measured by crude output statistics, Europe will overtake the United States. But will it match the United States in the statistics that really matter, job creation and per capita income? The gap between the United States and the larger European economies, such as Germany, France, and Britain, was steadily narrowing until the mid-1990s. It started to widen again as U.S. companies consolidated their lead in high-growth sectors such as computers, telecommunications, and multimedia.

The United States is the clear favorite to win the global economic race because the new industries of the information age put a premium on innovation and flexibility, quintessential U.S. virtues that are lacking in Europe. But the betting odds are based on an increasingly outdated perception of Europe, which is further distorted by the fact that its most public symbol, the euro, has initially performed miserably against the dollar. Europe's slow growth and high unemployment, in marked contrast to the booming U.S. economy, also suggest the heavily touted single market is failing to deliver an economy to match that of the United States.

Europeans can take heart from the fact that in the late 1980s the United States too was being written off as a spent technological force, condemned to lag ever further behind seemingly unstoppable Japan and the Asian tigers in the twenty-first century. Then came the Internet, catapulting the United States back to the top of the league just as Asia was snared in financial turmoil. Other U.S. industries that were losing ground to leaner, fitter, and more flexible Asian rivals, notably the auto industry, had also staged a revival that was underpinned by the commanding U.S. lead in computers.

Europe is evolving, however, with the pace of change accelerating in the late 1990s under the combined influence of deregulation, globalization, and privatization. The value of European mergers and acquisitions doubled to $1,213 billion in 1999, compared with a record-breaking $1,730 billion in the United States. In 2000 Europe is expected to overtake the United States for the first time, as barriers to cross-border deals crumble. Vodafone AirTouch's record-breaking $183 billion acquisition of Mannesman, a rival mobile phone operator, in January 2000 was the first successful hostile bid in Germany and opened up Europe's largest economy to international investors. A highly leveraged $65 billion bid by Olivetti, an Italian telecommunications group, for Telecom Italia, a firm five times its size, gave Italy its first taste of Anglo-Saxon business culture. Only France resisted the invasion of these "alien" corporate practices, but it too will have to fall in line to keep pace with its two big neighbors.

Europe is also drawing abreast of the United States in key industries after Daimler-Benz acquired Chrysler; Britain's Vodafone beat off Bell Atlantic to buy San Francisco's AirTouch Communications for $62 billion; British Petroleum swooped on two U.S. oil companies, Amoco and Arco, to rub shoulders with Exxon; Bertelsmann, the German media group, took control of Random House, the most prestigious U.S. publisher; and Airbus began the assault on Boeing's monopoly on jumbo jets by starting work on a double-decker airliner that will carry up to 650 passengers.

But these European gains are all in mature industries and are matched by equally large U.S. acquisitions of European firms. Achieving parity with the United States in these industries doesn't give Europe automatic entry into the information age. Moreover, the deals suggest that in spite of the attractions of the single market and the euro, European firms prefer to invest across the Atlantic rather than just beyond their borders. That is hardly a good advertisement for Europe.

To catch up with the United States, Europe must create its own Silicon Valleys. Until fairly recently, the superior U.S. performance in job creation—30 million new (net) jobs since 1980, mostly in private companies, compared with 3.5 million in Europe, most in the bloated public sector—was largely attributed to the country's flexible labor market. This realization posed a dilemma for European governments who were desperate to shrink the continent's dole lines and sought a halfway house between the easy hire-and-fire culture across the Atlantic and the tightly regulated labor market at home.

Now governments realize that the massive leap in technology, rather than temporary factors such as a strong dollar, is largely responsible for the phenomenal U.S. performance to which they aspire. Technological innovations centered on computers and information processing machines have enabled companies to work more efficiently, controlling costs and raising profits without increasing prices. Almost all the advances have been pioneered by U.S. companies, which are now exporting them abroad.

Can Europe catch up to the United States in the high-technology race, or has it left this task until too late? The United States has built up a daunting lead thanks to the Internet-based information revolution: it supplies almost all the software, a large slice of the hardware, and the main "portals" through which consumers enter the Net. The United States is also far ahead in the next phase of the revolution—electronic commerce.

A clutch of remarkable success stories suggests that there is no reason Europe should throw in the towel. The fact that a company in one of Europe's most isolated countries, whose largest trading partner was the Soviet Union until the early 1990s, transformed itself from a manufacturer of toilet tissue and electric cable into a world leader in a futuristic cutting-edge technology shows nothing is impossible. That is what Nokia, Finland's mobile telephone manufacturer, achieved in a decade, overtaking Motorola on the way. Other would-be Nokias can do the same if their governments get out of the way.

Europe can create new Nokias if it gives budding entrepreneurs room to breathe. European startups have to contend with a risk-averse culture, a severe shortage of venture capital, stifling bureaucracy, a thicket of obsolete regulations, protection of former monopolies, rigid hire-and-fire laws, an unforgiving attitude toward bankruptcies, and high personal taxes. The Organization for Economic Cooperation and Development (OECD) calculates that between 1984 and 1991 the United States created new businesses at four times the rate of France and eight times that of Denmark.

It is little wonder that many young Europeans with an idea have fled abroad—usually to the United States—in search of finance and the chance to meet like-minded entrepreneurial innovators. Equally telling, U.S. firms took five of the top six positions in a survey of the most popular employers among European business graduates.

But Europe was a beehive of invention and entrepreneurship until World War II and only ceded leadership to the United States in the second half of the century, when business culture was stifled by the growth of big-government regulations and restrictions that accompanied the establishment of the welfare state. There were occasional breakthroughs such as the invention of the audio- and videocassette by Philips, the Dutch consumer electronics group.

But the United States set the technological pace during the 1970s and 1980s and stretched its lead over Europe in the 1990s with the rise of computer and Internet-based industries. Europe has no one who compares with Bill Gates and Steve Jobs. But Europe can compete with the United States in the right conditions. The success of Nokia and Ericsson of Sweden in mobile phones was no accident. The companies got a head start because the Nordic countries were the first to deregulate their telecommunications markets and set a common standard throughout the region, which in time led to the establishment of a Europe-wide system. The United States, by contrast, adopted a laissez-faire stance, letting multiple systems battle it out for supremacy. Economic theory suggested the U.S. system was superior, "but it hasn't worked out that way," according to Nokia chief executive officer Jorma Ollila. Europe has consolidated its global leadership in wireless telephony and will probably set the world standard for the forthcoming generation of video cell phones. Europe is also positioned to lead the United States in the next big jump in telecommunications—the delivery of data over mobile phones that are set to replace the personal computer as the main link to the Internet.

European firms have outsmarted U.S. rivals in sectors as diverse as computer software and health foods. One of the most remarkable U.S.-style success stories of the 1990s, the business software group SAP, was founded in one of the least promising markets, Germany. Since its start in 1992, SAP has enjoyed explosive growth and is now the world leader in its market. The company pioneered the technology that gels companies together, making information on everything from accounts and inventories from different corners of the globe available on a computer screen. In effect, SAP is helping to restructure global corporations and now wants to connect its systems with those of its suppliers and customers.

Europe also leads the world in the production of smart cards (credit cards with computer chips) and is matching the United States in design systems for everything from data search to online banking. Some small firms have built blue chip client lists within years of setting up: Munich-based Tecoplan, which develops software that allows companies to build and test digital prototypes of their products, is helping Lockheed-Martin to design the next-generation space shuttle.

Europe scored a rare victory over the United States in the food market, with Raisio, a Finnish chemicals company, launching Benecol, a low-cholesterol dietary spread, on the U.S. market in 1999. A rival product, Take Control, was produced by Unilever, the Anglo-Dutch consumer products group. Europe is also achieving critical mass in typically twenty-first-century businesses: the world's biggest life sciences company, Aventis, was forged in 1999 by the merger of Germany's Hoechst and France's Rhone-Poulenc. And with projected sales of $18.5 billion in 2000, Germany's Bertlesmann is the world's third-largest media company behind AOL-TimeWarner and Walt Disney.

Europeans, from giant corporations to individuals, are still good at inventing new products. Philips launched the Alto, the world's first environmentally friendly light bulb, in the United States in 1995, under the nose of General Electric. James Dyson, a British businessman, invented a bagless vacuum cleaner in 1978, put it into production in 1993 after more than 5,000 prototypes, and now claims global leadership with sales topping $1.5 billion. Dyson's other inventions include Sea Truck, a high-speed air-lubricated hull for navy ships and oil industry tankers; a wheelbarrow that does not make lines across a lawn; a crumb-free toaster; and a superfast washing machine.

Prospects for would-be entrepreneurs improved considerably during the late 1990s as European corporations adapted to globalization by adopting U.S. business methods, and governments desperate to generate jobs made life easier for startups. But the most important breakthrough was the increased flow of finance from venture capitalists and the establishment of secondary stock exchanges, like Easdaq, the electronic Brussels market based on Nasdaq in the United States, and Germany's Neuer Markt, a spin-off from the Frankfurt bourse.

The venture capital market is small compared with its flourishing U.S. counterpart—the bank overdraft remains the most popular way of financing startups in Europe. But a steady stream of spectacular successes is encouraging financiers to open up their wallets to U.S.-style garage startups.

Entrepreneurship has become fashionable in Europe, but there are still huge cultural barriers to be overcome before it matches the "can do" attitude that is a vital ingredient in American business. U.S. entrepreneurs accept bankruptcies as a way of life, but a big social stigma still attaches to business failure in Europe. Many university graduates still prefer to work for big corporations instead of themselves. Bumper rewards for successful managers are still frowned on, but this is changing rapidly. Klaus Esser, the head of Mannesman, was "paid off" with $33 million after Vodafone took over his company.

Europe boasts universities with second-to-none reputations in science, like Germany's Max Planck Institute and France's Institut Louis Pasteur, but unlike their U.S. counterparts, they have been slow to forge links with business. This too is changing, with leading institutions like Cambridge University establishing world-class science parks and forming private companies with outside entrepreneurs to exploit the commercial value of their research. And in another significant move, the U.S. computer giant IBM teamed up with ESC Grenoble, a French business school, to jointly develop master's degrees in e-commerce.

As the public buys computers and hooks up to the Internet, Europe is starting to close the information technology gap with the United States. Sales of personal computers rose by more than 21 percent in 1998, a growth rate that continued into 1999 and grew even faster in 2000, making Europeans the population with the highest rates of computer purchases in the world. International Data Corp, a technology research company, says that in 1998 online business in western Europe was $6 billion, trailing the United States sales of $31 billion, but the gap will narrow in 2002 to $291 billion in the United States and $223 billion in Europe. Some countries are approaching U.S. levels of computer literacy: in Britain, computer science is now the second-most-popular degree subject at universities.

Europe is also eroding the U.S. lead in several high-technology sectors, thanks to easier access to seed capital and a more enlightened government attitude toward startups. The European biotechnology industry, for example, is still only a quarter the size of its U.S. counterpart, but it is growing twice as fast and has made some significant breakthroughs, according to a 1999 survey by consulting firm Ernst and Young.

European firms are concentrating on genomics—finding out how genes combine with environmental factors to cause diseases and using the information to develop new treatments. They are able to compete with the bigger U.S. firms by focusing on specific genes and diseases rather than covering the complete human genome. They are also concentrating on population-based studies, capitalizing on the fact that Europe's centralized public health systems have more comprehensive records on patients than the fragmented private system in the United States.

Germany, for a long time a no-go area for individualistic entrepreneurs, is changing rapidly. By April 1999 it had 225 biotechnology companies, compared with none five years earlier; it had the fastest growth rate in the world and was poised to oust Britain as Europe's top biotechnology nation. The catalyst was the so-called Bioregio initiative, which allocated federal funding and encouraged states to provide matching funds and soft loans to startup companies. Venture capitalists often are able to triple or even quadruple their initial investments by applying for government funds. The industry also had to overcome public apprehension over genetic engineering. When Morphsys of Munich was founded in the mid-1990s, it chose a name without the word "gene" to avoid controversy.

The change in public attitudes was highlighted by the decision by the Icelandic government to approve a controversial plan by a local firm, deCode Genetics, to build a commercial database from the genetic, health, and genealogical records of all 270,000 Icelanders to locate disease-related genes.

Proof that European nations can compete in U.S.-dominated industries if they join forces is provided by the spectacular success of Airbus, a consortium of companies from Britain, France, Germany, and Spain, which is on target to split the world order book with arch-rival Boeing. The United States has always attributed Airbus's success to massive government subsidies, but its own firms have benefited from equally huge indirect handouts from the Pentagon. Airbus is planning to spend more than $10 billion to launch a new 550–650-seat super jumbo jet in 2005 to break the monopoly of the Boeing 747. It is also challenging Boeing at the smaller end of the market, with a 100-seat regional jetliner that will compete head on with the new Boeing 717.

In other high-growth sectors, however, the gap between the EU and the United States is widening as U.S. firms exploit the advantages of consolidation and European companies pay the price for fragmentation. The United States is expected to dominate the global pharmaceuticals market, with one report predicting that European drugs firms will supply only three of the world's twenty-five top-selling drugs by 2002.

These gloomy forecasts, however, could soon be overtaken by events as European firms embark on cross-border mergers and alliances that are creating new world leaders in scores of sectors, from steel and cars to banks and telecommunications operators. European firms are compensating for their slow start in the high-technology race by buying U.S. companies. Britain's General Electric Company, Nokia, Siemens, Ericsson, and Alcatel of France have spent billions of dollars acquiring U.S. Internet-based firms in a bid to stop industry leaders like Lucent Technologies, Cisco, and Nortel from building an unassailable lead.

Globalization, meanwhile, is eroding the importance of nationality as European and U.S. firms that are fierce rivals in some businesses join forces to develop new technologies and standards. The world's three top mobile phone manufacturers, Nokia, Ericsson, and Motorola, teamed up with Psion, a small British high-technology firm, to develop a standard operating system for the next generation of handheld wireless devices to challenge domination of the market by Microsoft's Windows CE operating system. Microsoft, in turn, has courted Nokia and other European high-technology leaders.

Such transnational alliances, which are likely to include Japanese firms, will become increasingly popular in the coming decade. And Europe must ensure it does not miss out.

16

Creating Jobs for the Twenty-first Century

SUSAN LADIKA

A decade ago, Ireland struggled with sky-high unemployment. The standard of living stood well below the European average, and vacant, crumbling warehouses dotted Dublin's Docklands' areas. Young people by the thousands packed their bags and headed to the United States or the United Kingdom in search of brighter economic prospects.

Today, Ireland is a land of immigration. Those who left during tougher times are returning home, and multinational firms by the hundreds have established operations there. Nicknamed the "Celtic Tiger," Ireland has seen stunning average growth of 8 percent per year through much of the 1990s, and annual growth rates of 6 percent are projected to continue well past the year 2000. Dublin has become a city of construction cranes, with commercial and residential properties rising along the waterfront and in the suburbs. Gross domestic product (GDP) per capita has more than doubled, from 6,500 Irish pounds in 1988 to nearly 16,000 pounds a decade later. Unemployment has tumbled by nearly one-half, falling to less than 7 percent in 1999, propelled by the 300,000 jobs created in the second half of the decade.[1]

It certainly wasn't the luck of the leprechauns that brought this change to the Irish economy. Instead, the remarkable record of economic growth and job creation accompanied a shift from tradition to innovation. Developments such as a revamped educational system, low corporate tax rates, and aggressive courting of foreign firms helped make Ireland an island of economic and employment growth within the European Union.

Similar pockets of growth can be seen in countries such as the Netherlands, where a boom in part-time work and temporary employment

175

has halved the country's unemployment rate in less than a decade. Agreement between the country's social partners has kept a lid on salary increases in exchange for a slightly shortened work week. Denmark, meanwhile, has one of the highest employment rates in the world. A generous social benefits system, coupled with few regulations on hiring and firing, has helped Denmark reduce its unemployment rate by 4 percent in the 1990s. The bulk of the workforce is employed in small and medium-sized enterprises, and a popular paid leave program allows the jobless to gain valuable work experience while full-time employees are on sabbaticals.

In this fast-paced era of globalization, tradition must merge with innovation if Europe wants to maintain its place as one of the world's economic powerhouses. The development of service industries and entrepreneurship must be encouraged, and labor market regulations must be loosened. "Our problem is that the European Union has substantial growth potential within the working-age population. Our employment rate is still below 60 percent. In the United States and Japan it's more than 70 percent. With this employment rate, we are out of sync with the rest of the competitive world," said Padraig Flynn, the EU's former commissioner for employment and social affairs.[2]

Throughout the 1990s, Europe and the United States have followed markedly different paths. The U.S. economy bottomed out in the early 1990s, pushing unemployment rates up to 7.5 percent in 1992, according to the U.S. Bureau of Labor Statistics. Tens of thousands were laid off, including many middle and leading managers, sending shock waves through the business community. But as the service and high-tech sectors boomed, so did the U.S. economy. By 1998, the unemployment rate had tumbled to 4.5 percent, the lowest level in years.

In contrast, the European Union still registered more than 16 million unemployed, or a cumulative rate of 9.6 percent, in early 1999, according to Eurostat, the EU's statistical office. Unemployment remained stubbornly high in Spain, where 17.4 percent of the population was out of work, compared to Luxembourg, where the jobless rate stood at 2.8 percent.

Only five of the fifteen EU members had unemployment rates anywhere near that of the United States, and a wealth of factors have been blamed for Europe's employment deficit. A key stumbling block is Europe's failure to develop lower-level service sector jobs at a pace comparable to that of the United States. These are sorely needed to replace manufacturing jobs that have been lost as industries pull up stakes and move to cheaper markets in Asia and eastern Europe. A European Commission report shows only 39 percent of the EU population employed in the service sector in 1997, compared to 54 percent in the United States.

Part of the problem is that lower-level service jobs are not readily accepted in some European countries. For example, "people have tried to offer shoeshine service in Düsseldorf, but have given up in a week or so. No one dared to sit down in public and have their shoes shined. Germans are hesitant to consume this service," said Axel Schimmel-pfennig, an economist with the Kiel Institute of World Economics in Germany.[3] In addition, many workers in high-paid industrial jobs, such as steel manufacturing, do not have the skills necessary to become a bank teller but are unwilling to settle for the loss of pay and prestige that can accompany the shift to a job in the fast-food industry. Some older workers will instead opt for unemployment, Schimmelpfennig said. "Given the European social security system, it's almost an attractive option. You don't work, and you get a decent amount of money."

In some countries, these generous social security benefits have hindered employment efforts. According to Eurostat, the EU nations spent nearly 29 percent of GDP on social protection. In the Netherlands, disability programs were essentially used as an early retirement scheme, and by 1991 only 22 percent of men between the ages of sixty and sixty-four were employed, a fall of nearly 50 percent within less than twenty years. In Germany, social security contributions, paid jointly by employees and employers, total 42 percent of gross wages. Another cause of concern is labor market rigidities, particularly strict job protection laws that make it difficult and costly for employers to fire workers. In addition, legislative barriers or union intransigence can limit the hours or shifts that employees will work, often making weekend or night work taboo. High-wage and nonwage costs also take a toll. A production worker cost $28.28 per hour in wage and nonwage costs in Germany in 1997, compared to $18.24 in the United States. In Ireland, the cost was only $13.57, according to the Bureau of Labor Statistics.

In response, European nations have spent much of the 1990s grappling with the issues of unemployment and job creation. White papers have been drafted and national action plans drawn up under the auspices of the EU. But some countries have simply gotten down to work, adopting innovative strategies to get their residents out of the unemployment lines.

Among the most aggressive has been Ireland, which has seen its unemployment rate nosedive in less than a decade. In 1990, unemployment stood at 14.4 percent—among the highest in Europe. By March 1999, that rate had slid to 6.9 percent, putting it in the lower ranks of the EU. Much of this turnaround can be credited to Ireland's decision to become a mecca for international investment. Generous financial incentives, low corporate tax rates, and an updated educational system helped lure hundreds of foreign firms to the country.

The Industrial Development Agency of Ireland (IDA), which has the express charge of attracting foreign investment, already works with nearly 1,200 international corporations. In 1998, these firms provided 116,000 of the country's 1.6 million jobs. More than one-third of the multinationals are U.S.-owned, employing more than 74,000 workers. In 1998 alone, foreign-owned corporations created 16,000 new jobs, with more than half in the electronics and engineering sectors. In addition, these firms accounted for 55 percent of Ireland's industrial output, 76 percent of its exports, and 18 percent of the country's GDP. "They are the engines driving the economy," said Finn Gallen, media relations manager for the IDA.[4]

Ireland's boom did not happen overnight but was a conscious decision made by representatives from government, employers, unions, and farmers, who realized that "we didn't need castor oil, we needed strong medicine," according to Gallen. A series of agreements beginning in the late 1980s worked to slash government spending, put a brake on wages and inflation, and trim personal taxes. The country has received a generous helping of structural funds from the European Union, which have reached as high as 7 percent of gross national product. One-third of the money has been channeled to education and training programs.

Ireland's youthful population—40 percent of the population will be under age twenty-five in the year 2000—has developed sophisticated technical skills. Almost 40 percent of high school students attend college, and 60 percent of college students major in engineering, science, or business. Foreign-language skills also have been emphasized, which has helped Ireland become the base for dozens of international call centers.

Another magnet drawing multinationals is Ireland's low corporate tax rate, which stood at 10 percent. A new tax rate of 12.5 percent is being phased in, which may remain in place till 2025. A wide range of grants also are available, which can pay for up to 45 percent of the fixed costs of an investment. But each grant is tailor-made, based on the number and the quality of the jobs created. For some services, such as call centers and data processing centers, half of the grant is paid when a job is created, with the remainder paid out after a year, if the job still exists. Grants to fund training programs are available. The IDA also may build factories to lure industries to remote areas, or it offers rent-free or rent-reduced facilities. But if a firm shuts its doors within ten years, it may be required to pay back all or part of the grants it received.

Multinational corporations also have spurred spin-off growth in the local economy. For example, 600 small high-technology companies have been launched in recent years, many of them linked to the multinationals operating in Ireland. These international corporations pumped 8 billion Irish pounds into the local economy in 1998. The multinationals also bring the most modern technology, manufacturing skills, and industrial practices, which then are diffused throughout Irish industry. With these experiences, Irish companies are better prepared when they set up their own operations abroad.

Intel is the largest private investor, pouring $2.5 billion into Irish operations since 1989. The Santa Clara, California–based corporation entered the Irish market because it feared the arrival of the single market in 1992 might make it difficult to do business without an EU presence. Although those fears proved unfounded, Intel found Ireland a good place for operations. From its first factory, employing 100 people producing motherboards for personal computers, Intel has expanded to three factories with 4,000 employees. Although other countries offered similar grant packages, Ireland's low corporate tax rate was a major draw. "For a company like ourselves, the tax rate is more interesting to us, rather than [extra grants of] $5 to $10 per employee," said Liam Cahill, media relations manager for Intel Ireland.[5] He added: "Ireland is distinctive because of the huge investment it made in the last twenty years in higher education." Two new universities and about a dozen technical institutes have opened nationwide, ensuring that enough young people with computer skills are available to fill industry demands. "Other countries had a more mature semi-conductor industry. But the problem was they couldn't guarantee the supply and work force as needed," Cahill said.

Not willing to rest on their laurels, Irish officials keep a close eye on industry trends. Part of their focus is on e-commerce, which is expected to generate business worth $300 billion worldwide by 2003. Because multinationals will invest in countries with the best skills and telecommunications systems, plans are in the works to develop Ireland's broadband communications capacity and extend it throughout the country. In addition, Ireland is planning to boost the number of higher-education places for those who want to study information technology. "We try to predict what skills will be required over the next three to five years, and try to put them in the place within the educational system," Gallen said. "We're a small country, so we can react fairly quickly and influence the system."

Another small country that has received high marks for revising its system is the Netherlands, which has seen its unemployment rate halved, from 7.7 percent in 1990 to 3.6 percent in early 1999, according to Eurostat. Often referred to as the "Dutch miracle," employment growth has averaged 1.6 percent per year since the mid-1980s, with much of it fueled by a boom in part-time jobs and temporary work. Part-time work accounted for 80 percent of the jobs created between 1989 and 1994, and by 1997, 38 percent of employees were working less than thirty-five hours per week. Many women prefer part-time work because it allows them to spend more time with their families, and the perception of part-time employment has shifted. Rather than being sneered at, it has become something valued. Companies have realized that it is often better to allow someone to work part-time than to lose them completely. Today, 70 percent of women and 19 percent of men are employed on a part-time basis. "If the same level of social security is attached to the jobs, they become more accepted by the people who work those jobs, and more accepted by the average citizen," said Anton Hemerijck, professor of policy and politics at Erasmus University in Rotterdam.[6] For those who desire full-time work, part-time jobs are often "entry tickets to the regular labor market."

The Netherlands also has overhauled it social protection system, putting more people back on company payrolls. In the mid-1980s, the unemployment rate was close to 14 percent. Rather than boosting the rate even higher as manufacturers moved to lower-cost markets, leaders chose to use the country's sickness and disability schemes as a means to facilitate early retirement and industrial restructuring. If a worker was unlikely to find a job similar to the one he had lost, he was classified as "disabled" and was able to collect sickness benefits for one year before being put on disability. The disability program, designed for 200,000 participants, soared to 900,000 by 1990. Those considered "disabled" in the fifty-five- to sixty-four-year-old age group outnumbered those with jobs. In the 1990s, the system was revamped, and many saw their benefits trimmed or were forced to find work. At the same time, priorities started to shift. Rather than focusing on keeping unemployment rates down, the government began to emphasize "jobs, jobs and even more jobs," according to Hemerijck. Now firms that hire long-time unemployed can receive a break in their social security contributions, and unemployment benefits are linked to a person's willingness to take a job or enroll in a training program.

Employment also has been influenced by the 1982 Wassenaar agreement, in which trade unions and employers organizations pledged to support wage moderation in exchange for reduced working hours in a bid to bolster profits and create jobs. Since that time, wage increases have generally kept pace with inflation, while the average work week fell from forty to thirty-seven-and-a-half hours. According to a report written by Joop Hartog for the International Labour Organization (ILO), unit wage costs in 1996 were the same as they were in 1981, compared to a 40 percent increase in Germany and a 15 percent increase in the EU during that time.[7]

Denmark also has made steady progress in decreasing joblessness, which slid from 8.5 percent in 1990 to 4.7 percent in early 1999, according to Eurostat. From 1993 to 1998 alone, 164,000 new people were employed, an increase of 6.5 percent. With 75 percent of the population employed, Denmark has one of the highest employment rates in the world, behind only Switzerland and Norway. Much of that success can be attributed to Denmark's extensive state-financed child care facilities, allowing thousands of women to return to the workforce.

Unlike other countries whose extensive regulations make it difficult to start new firms or to hire and fire workers, Denmark has a strong tradition of self-employment, with nearly 10 percent of the workforce self-employed or working for a spouse in a family business. Historically, craftspeople, farmers, and shop owners have worked for themselves, but today the trend is spreading to service providers such as computer software firms and advertising agencies. This spirit of independence also is illustrated in the prominence of small and medium-sized enterprises in the Danish economy, with 70 percent of the workforce employed by firms with less than 250 employees. Very small firms with less than ten employees are surprisingly common, employing 30 percent of all workers.

Perhaps these practices have allowed Denmark to maintain few hiring and firing regulations. Despite its strong social safety net, many workers can be dismissed with only a few days or weeks notice, and workers are able to leave their jobs at will. With this high level of mobility, nearly 40 percent of all jobs open up each year. According to the Organization for Economic Cooperation and Development (OECD), the average employee tenure is eight years in Denmark, second-lowest in the industrialized world, behind the United States.[8] In contrast, the average tenure in Italy and Belgium is close to twelve years. Slightly more than 40 percent of Danes say their job is secure, compared to nearly 80 percent in France and more than 70 percent in Germany, Sweden, and Belgium, according to the OECD.

With this highly mobile labor force, the Danish government has devised an unusual way to reduce the ranks of the unemployed through the introduction of paid leave. Under this scheme, both the employed and the unemployed are encouraged to take up to a year's leave, giving both groups an opportunity to upgrade their skills. The time off can be granted for child care or educational reasons or simply to take a sabbatical. "One strong argument supporting the introduction of paid leave was the idea of job rotation, where employed persons going on leave would be substituted by unemployed, who would thus get a chance to return to ordinary employment," Per Kongshoj Madsen wrote in a report for the ILO that reviewed Denmark's employment policies.[9]

That policy seems to be working. More than one-third of those hired as a substitute wound up with a full-time job with the same employer. In 1996, more than 120,000 people took paid leave. Unemployed persons who take leave do not have to be involved in job-seeking programs during that time, while still receiving unemployment benefits of 100 percent for those on educational leave and 60 percent for child care leave or sabbatical. The paid leave scheme also has an impact on unemployment rates, according to Madsen: "The number of registered unemployed decreases by one person, every time an unemployed person takes leave. If an employed person takes leave, the decrease in registered unemployment is related to the share of vacancies being filled with substitutes."

Denmark isn't alone in its efforts to get the unemployed back to work. The United Kingdom, for example, has launched the New Deal, with one program focusing on those between the ages of eighteen and twenty-four and one for those twenty-five and older who have been out of work at least two years. Introduced in 1998, the programs are designed to assess the skills and experiences of each unemployed person and help each one draw up a plan to ease entry into the job market. This may result in quick leads to a new job, courses in resumé writing and interview techniques, full-time education or training to learn new skills, or subsidized employment for six months. Employers must pay the going rate for those hired from New Deal programs, but they are eligible for subsidies of 75 pounds a week for a full-time job or 50 pounds a week for part-time work.

Germany's 100,000 Jobs for Youth program does everything from providing vocational training courses to paying young people to complete their high school education to helping with the job search. The government will even cover up to 60 percent of wage costs for an employer who hires a young person who has been unemployed for more than three months. France's controversial move to adopt a thirty-five-hour work week has drawn a mixed response, with some criticizing it for not getting the unemployed back to work and others praising it for improving labor market flexibility. Italy also has seen an increase in flexibility. In 1998, the country created 110,000 new jobs—virtually all coming from part-time and temporary work.

The European Union also has put its muscle behind back-to-work efforts. When employment started to climb in the early 1990s, officials thought the slowdown was cyclical and that a growth spurt would be a "panacea to solve all our problems," former EU Commissioner Flynn said.[10] But things did not work out that way. By 1993, leaders began to realize that structural reforms were sorely needed and gradually started to chart that course. In a 1993 white paper, EU officials called for a review of labor laws and tax and social security systems and urged more training and part-time employment. Those calls still are being heard today.

Four years later, at the Luxembourg summit, officials agreed that efforts were needed to fill the skills gap. Already, the information technology sector has 500,000 job vacancies, and that number will soar to 1.4 million by 2004 if training and lifelong learning programs are not put into place. Officials also agreed to encourage adaptation to meet the needs of a changing, global society; promote entrepreneurship; and foster equal opportunities for all EU residents. These goals were to be converted into reality through national action plans drawn up for each country. The plans must be submitted each year to EU officials for evaluation, and targets would be added, subtracted, and adjusted. The best practices were also held up as examples for others in the Union.

During 1998, EU countries created 1.7 million jobs. But that still was not enough. "We're way behind" when it comes to the creation of service sector jobs, said Flynn, who sees plenty of room for growth in areas such as education, health care, finance tourism, leisure, and culture. The former EU commissioner acknowledges that growth is deterred by high wage and nonwage costs. "We mustn't price our workers out of work," he said. "We have to lower taxes on labor, no question about it. We also have to cut out red tape." Bureaucracy must be eased to make it simpler for someone to found and operate a business and to receive training.

Special emphasis is being put on serving the crises of youth unemployment and long-term unemployed. In countries such as Spain and Italy, about one-third of young people are out of work, and the overall youth unemployment rate in the EU totaled 19.5 percent in 1998, according to Eurostat.

Flynn said the EU wants to see job training offered to every young person before he or she has been out of work for six months. "We want to stop the flow into long-term unemployment and give the work ethic to young people," he said. In addition, costs should be cut for firms hiring low-skilled workers. Lifelong learning also must be emphasized, as Europe grapples with an aging population and fewer young people enter the job market. "We're going to need to keep people in the labor market longer," Flynn said.

Many of Flynn's views are echoed by those in industry, who call for greater flexibility and urgent labor market reforms. According to Dirk Hudig, secretary-general of the Union of Industrial and Employers' Confederations of Europe (UNICE), EU member states need policies "putting the emphasis on the integration of outsiders [those without jobs] rather than on strengthening the rights of insiders [those with a job]."[11]

UNICE, which represents 16 million enterprises, most of which are small and medium-sized, has called for structural reforms that will bolster the creation of new firms and deep cuts in indirect labor costs, which can cost 70 percent more than an employee's actual salary. "The effect of this has been to price people out of the labor market, especially in the service sector," Hudig writes.

Some businesses have taken their own measures to boost employment and liberalize the working environment. Palmers Textil AG, an upscale Austrian lingerie retailer and manufacturer with a prominent presence in Germany, central Europe, Turkey, the Middle East, and South Korea, has developed flexible scheduling for its sales staff. For example, an employee may be paid to work thirty hours each week. But if business is slow, she may be sent home early and put in only twenty-five hours. If the next week is busy, she may work thirty-five hours instead. "In the beginning, this was very unusual for them. Now they're starting to like it," said Martin Zieger, a member of the Palmers board of directors.[12] "Our attitude is to make our people happy. Then they have a better attitude on the job."

Along with developing new methods to cope with restrictive labor markets, companies are finding alternatives to deal with restrictive capital markets. Small firms "tend to be injured by the typical kind of banking relationship. Without an established relationship with a bank, it's very difficult to find funds," said Francesco Giordano, an economist with the London office of Credit Suisse First Boston.[13] Although capital markets have gradually been deregulated, huge differences remain between Europe and the United States. European stock markets were capitalized at 31 percent of GDP in 1995, compared to 95 percent in the United States, and the European debt market was capitalized at 103 percent of GDP, versus 152 percent in the United States. One glimmer of hope is the development of stock markets for growth companies such as Germany's Neuer Markt, launched in 1997, which has seen the index returning 175 percent in 1998, compared to Nasdaq's 39 percent in 1998. Yet Neuer Markt is capitalized at just $44 billion, compared to $2.8 trillion for Nasdaq. Although Neuer Mark has only about eighty listings, primarily small and medium-sized enterprises, those firms created a total of 14,000 jobs in 1997 and 1998.

One agency advocating the development of alternative financing sources is the European Venture Capital Association (EVCA). Although Europe trails far behind the United States in the use of venture capital at a ratio of 4:1, "the gap has been decreasing quite significantly," said EVCA secretary-general Serge Raicher. "One of the issues is to find worthwhile projects to invest in and to find entrepreneurs in a position to take risks."[14] Since the late 1970s, the European venture capital industry has raised more than 60 billion euros in long-term capital and has invested in approximately 20,000 privately owned companies. To foster even more investment, EVCA advocates low capital gains tax rates, tax deductions for losses, and no tax on the issue or exercise of stock options. It also calls for the spread of funded pension systems, which are allowed to invest in capital markets and not be prevented from cross-border investments. A survey of 500 companies backed by venture capital shows average sales revenue increases of 35 percent between 1991 and 1995, double that of the top 500 European companies. At the same time, staff increased an average 15 percent per year, compared to 2 percent for the largest firms, and exports rose by 30 percent per annum. Eighty percent of the respondents said the company would not exist or would have developed far more slowly without private equity.

Although the ideas for getting Europeans back to work are nearly as numerous as the population itself, one thing is clear: maintaining the status quo will not earn EU residents places on company payrolls. Yet at the same time, what works for one country may not work for another because each is shaped by its own history and traditions. But that doesn't mean each country should turn a blind eye to what the others are doing. Many policies can be picked up from other countries, and adapted to fit local situations. The EU is trying to foster this exchange of information by focusing on benchmarking and best practices.

In a report for the ILO on the policies of four countries with low unemployment rates—Ireland, the Netherlands, Denmark, and Austria—economist Peter Auer found that dialogue was the key to reducing spiraling joblessness or preserving already low unemployment rates: "It is most important to have a climate where everybody agrees there is a problem, and something should be done together."[15] Even though all the EU countries with low unemployment rates besides the United Kingdom have relatively small populations, having a small population is not enough to guarantee a low unemployment rate. But a smaller, more homogeneous power elite can make it easier to win support for policy shifts. These smaller nations also rely heavily on international trade rather than a large domestic market and must retain their flexibility to compete on a global scale. They can also boast of a growing service sector. Ireland alone has a growing manufacturing base, but it is fueled by the investment of high-technology corporations. According to Flynn, the EU's long-term growth will be a result of introducing the right mix of macroeconomic policy, economic reforms, and implementation of guidelines outlined in the national action plans: "It all has taken since 1993 to put it together. It's not working flat out 100 percent yet, but it's seen now as the solution to the European problem."

Part 4

PERSONAL VISIONS

17

Young Europeans: Speaking Out on the Twenty-first Century

We asked a young person from different walks of life in each of the fifteen EU countries to write about the following: "Do you feel European? If so, why? Describe an experience that made you feel European. If not, tell us why not." Here are their experiences.

AUSTRIA

Isabelle Walters, English teacher, 29 years old. One way to find out more about ourselves and to help us determine our own identities is to learn about other people's reactions toward us. Similarly, we need other nationalities to determine our own national identity. Thus the best way to find out about our feelings about our own nationality is to go abroad and get to know people of other nationalities.

I, personally, have never felt Austrian myself. (Only whenever I was addressed as a German did I have strong feelings about my being Austrian.) But did I ever feel European? And how does it feel to be European?

When I was about twenty I started to learn Hungarian because I wanted to learn another language. One reason why I decided to choose Hungarian was that even if the language is difficult to learn, I would at least easily understand the Hungarian mentality, which might then help me with my language-learning progress. I thought that since Austrians and Hungarians once shared a monarchy, they must also have shared a certain mentality, a fair amount of which should still be found in both peoples. However, when I finally left to live and work in Budapest for some months, I soon realized that the developments that divided Austria's fate from that of Hungary after World War II also had its result on the mentality of the people and that if there were to be found similarities between Hungarians and Austrians at all, they were only to be found in traces.

It is certainly easier to make out common traits among the peoples that had to live through a period of communism. Whenever I listen to people of my age from eastern European countries talk about their past lives and experiences, I can recognize bits and pieces that are common to most of these stories. No matter whether these are told by young Hungarians or Bulgarians, very often I will be able to relate to their stories because I will have heard very similar ones before. Listening to these stories makes me feel "Western European" (as opposed to "Eastern European") because the stories of my own past are distinctly different. However, my being able to relate to most of these stories at the same time makes me somehow feel more "Eastern European" than my fellow "Western European" listeners.

When I lived and studied in Edinburgh I made observations of a very different kind. The people I spent most of my time with were a group of international postgraduate and mature students.

The "Europeanness" I experienced there was of a "continental European" kind. One evening I recall particularly well when I, together with two American friends, was invited to have supper with a Swedish friend of ours and her English boyfriend. Sophie, our host, and I were the only people from the continent that evening, and I strongly felt that we shared a certain kind of experience, way of upbringing, or habits that were not familiar to the other people around. Not only did I recognize Sophie's way of cooking (healthy, vegetarian food) as very familiar, but her way of setting the table made me instantly feel at home. Her way of cooking and setting the table for me symbolized values that may characterize people from continental Europe and distinguish them from those of Great Britain and non-European countries. Now, however, if I look at it from a distance, I have started to question the feeling I had on this evening. First, Sophie had been living in England for more than ten years, before we met in Scotland, hence one could argue that she should rather be regarded as an Englishwoman than a Swede. And second, it was my American friend Rebecca with whom I ended up philosophizing on politics, nationality, family, friends, our studies, and our futures night after night, and to whom I have always felt emotionally more close than to my Swedish fellow students or roommates.

It seems that at the end of the day what counts is not where we come from, but whether we have lived through similar experiences, have had to cope with similar problems, and have some interests in common (and maybe have read the same books and seen the same films). I have always wondered how smoothly the living together of so many people of so different nationalities and cultures worked when I looked at the various student flats during my time in Edinburgh and heard other students' experiences. They all said that the one motivation and goal to go and study in another country equipped them with a common ideal that led to a common bond making them respect, most often understand, and very often even love each other. Thus, not our national or cultural backgrounds seem to count but the goal we have in common.

May a common goal "Europe" be the motivation, incentive, and value to live side by side in respect, tolerance, and peace one time, despite the very many differences which characterize us as individuals and which make life within Europe and the whole world interesting, exciting, and generally worth living for.

BELGIUM

Eve van Soens, nanny and photographer, 24 years old. My name is Eve van Soens and I'm twenty-four years old. I am Belgian. I was born and raised in Brussels. Although I lived in a Flemish country, I always spoke French.

When I graduated from high school, I went to California, where I stayed for eight months. This is important because this is how I learned English, which is quite useful in Europe. I currently live in Washington, D.C. Living in the United States has changed my views about Europe.

I now think it is still too early to declare yourself as a European. Of course, you are European when you go to the United States or Australia, meaning you come from the European continent. The problem is you do not have too many concrete "European facts" to rely on. The euro currency will for sure clear things up for everybody. Money has and will always interest people.

When you are far away from your country, you realize you are European, especially when you come from a little country like Belgium. People don't seem to know where it is and it makes everyone's life easier when you say you come from Europe's capital.

I have been given the opportunity to travel a lot across Europe, and it's true that sometimes I had the feeling I had not left my country as there are no borders. As long as you spoke English, you could always find your way. The only problem was the money; now that problem will disappear.

You cannot deny your origins. You do not realize that immediately, but it is something you can't go against. For instance, even if you're not a big sports fan, when you see a countryman win a medal, you're proud that he or she comes from your good old country.

But that's not all. There are bad sides to it, too. If terrible political scandals occur, you feel bad, even ashamed. Then you suddenly feel a bit more European.

I do not know European political matters too well (not to say not at all). Therefore, if someone attacks Europe, the only way I can defend it is by defending my own country.

I'm a photographer. I guess you could say I'm more of an artistic type. I sure have great hopes for Europe. As a new "nation" Europeans must realize how art is important in a society. Why wouldn't Europe promote something that has been left on the side for years in many countries? This might be a little naïve but as a citizen, that is one of the things I'm really looking for.

I think someone has killed the patriotic instinct of my generation in Belgium. For instance, a lot of countrymen my age do not know the national anthem and they simply do not care about it. I don't sing the national anthem every morning, but I think, in a way, it weakens the feelings for one's country.

Anyway, the European Union is a great thing.

DENMARK

Lone Ryg Olsen, journalist, 28 years old. It is early morning. The ship MS *Poseidon* approaches the Greek island of Corfu, and as the sun rises hundreds of youngsters on board the vessel come to life.

They are completely covering the upper deck with color: yellow sleeping bags, purple rucksacks, red bandannas, white t-shirts, and tanned bodies. The journey across the Ionian Sea has been entertaining: 2-liter red wine bottles—now empty—roll around between ghetto blasters and travel books. Not everybody welcomes the morning sun. But slowly voices are rising: "Come look, we are almost there." "Regardez." "Der ist die hafen." Little by little, we all gather along the railing.

As the ship reaches the harbor, we are met by cheers from an equally young crowd waiting to embark. They have had their share of sun and sand and are ready to move on. Greetings, advice, and warnings jet back and forth until it is time to go: "adieu," "goodbye," "farewell." The arriving crowd is absorbed by Corfu's camping site and youth hostels, while the departing group follow the trail to Athens, Rome, or the Côte d'Azur, and a week or two later you might meet a group of those fellow travelers again beneath the Eiffel Tower or in a Munich Beerhalle.

Those summers were totally European. To buy a Eurail pass ($200 for a month of unlimited transport from the north of Norway to the south of Spain) and hit off had been the thing to do in Denmark for about ten years and would keep that status for a few years more until cheap plane tickets made traveling in Asia more popular.

This way of getting around changed the way I, and probably many other young Europeans, looked at Europe. Before leaving I had regarded the debate about the European Union as at its best "boring" and at its worst "meaningless." It had nothing to do with my life. But traveling out there, sitting in a train compartment sharing Italian wine and French cheese with German students and Spanish guitar players, did make the thought of a common Europe seem pleasant. And then there were the Acropolis, the Roman Forum, La Sagrada Familia, and the Sacre Coeur . . . all representing cultures I would be happy to acknowledge my relation to. Europe, I discovered, was cool. Europe was fun.

The Eurail affair turned into lasting love. I would travel around Europe summer after summer with family, friends, or on my own, by train, plane, boat, car, or thumb! I figure that altogether I have spent more than a year exploring the continent, covering about 100 major cities, islands, and regions. Some of the trips lasted for several months, once I literally worked my way through Italy and Greece, hitchhiking and bartending and living—for periods—on bread and tomatoes to get as far as I possibly could on a next-to-nothing summer budget.

When I finished my studies, the time span became shorter and the expenses higher: shopping in London, skiing in Austria, wine tasting in Italy, dining in France. I also tried to venture further: Africa, the United States, and Asia. Yes, it was nice. No, it did not compare to Europe.

I always missed the evening stroll through the narrow streets of the city center, looking at the old houses, and the children playing soccer, wondering whether to have an ice cream, a café latte, or a drink to close the day. The easy pace, the pleasure of doing nothing but filling the senses. In Asia there was too much traffic or too much livestock, Africa's streets were teeming with hustlers, and the North American cities had no cozy centers to stroll in.

For sure, these parts of the globe had many other things to offer, and I want to see more of the world south of Sicily, west of Lisbon, east of Hungary, and north of the Polar Circle. But the craving for European cities, European art, and European food and wine will always be there.

I've even become fond of the European people. In Denmark as in many other countries, it is common to regard the domestic as the best without thinking twice, especially when it comes to the country's citizens. As a Dane you might admit that food is better in France, but the French are rude. You will agree that the sun shines more in Spain, but the Spaniards are aggressive. The Italian architecture sure is impressive, but the people living in the beautiful houses cannot be trusted. And so forth.

Now I am reaching a point at which I am willing to trade some of the Danish in me for something European (even though it, of course, is best to be Danish).

In other words, I have become addicted to Europe, I am proud of Europe, and I would be proud to call myself a European citizen.

FINLAND

Mirja Sitila, international business student and former player on the Finnish national basketball team, 26 years old. "I am European." This expression, which only a short while ago was not natural to me, has become a very normal part of who I am today. My awareness of being European has not, however, lessened the sense of my own nationality: I am a Finn, and I feel very strongly about it. But my new European identity has changed the way I view the world and the way I see myself as part of it. I feel European, just like Britons, Germans, or Italians. I consider this a big change for a Finn who grew up planning to take trips to Europe.

My years with the Finnish national basketball team showed me how strongly one can feel about one's roots and one's own country. Wearing the blue-and-white Finnish uniform and hearing the national anthem brought new intensity to the game. It was no longer just a question of pride as in an ordinary game but a question of our national pride. At the arena, there were us Finns, and there were the others. The sense of our nationality was very strong.

The cultural differences existed even on the basketball court. We faced the Greeks, the Spanish, the Italians, the Danes, and the Swedes, who all brought their own national features to the game.

With my team, I experienced the thrill of victory and the devastation of loss. The win after two games that ran into overtime over the Swedes and the two-point loss to the Dutch, which resulted in our disqualification from the European championship tournament, remain still clearly in my memory. The games against our "old rivals," the Swedes, were always extremely intense. You could not find the otherwise "cooperative Scandinavians" present at the arena, nor did you find any neighborly love. The Swedes were time after time our toughest opponents, and therefore a win over them was as appreciated as the tournament championship. The intensity of the game was almost untouchable.

These differences and the rivalry, however, almost disappeared when we participated in tournaments in other parts of the world. Even the global game of basketball was played differently in Asia and in North America than what we had been used to in Europe. The experience of the new cultures and different approaches to the game gave us a true comparison.

We Finns and our rival Europeans were all of a sudden amazingly similar. Instead of being a distinguishing element, our backgrounds became a cohesive force. There were us, the Europeans, and there were the others. We Europeans, we understood each other, and our differences seemed to become less significant. The new angle of looking at things brought us closer together.

I am a Finn, but I have realized that at the same time I can also be a European. That is a new perspective in my life. I have learned to look at things on another scale, as a European. It is important to be proud of our distinguishing traits and our roots, but it is also a richness to acknowledge our similarities. We can pull all these traits together and turn it into something positive.

For many Finns the decision to join the EU and the monetary union raised the question of losing our own national identity. But to me it is not a question of losing identity or giving up what we have. It is a question of bringing the best out of us. To me, Europe is a team of different players who complement each other and work together toward a better future; together, as Europeans. That is our future.

FRANCE

Ondine Millot, student, 23 years old. They say a lot about my generation. They say we stay in our parents' houses forever. They say we lack motivation, we're not interested in politics anymore.

Thirty years ago, our parents were in the streets demonstrating. We are in the living room watching television. They fought the fight. We benefit from it. But is it really our fault? What remains to get involved for, anyway? They tell us that we lack patriotic sense. France, this great historical nation, how come young people don't commemorate its past anymore?

I think they are wrong. Most of the young French people I know love their country. And I am like them. I believe in France, and I want it to be great. I feel French.

I have never really felt European. But that's the difference. I want to be European. I want to become a European citizen as a result of a conscious and willing process. To my mind, Europe is *the* great political cause that is worth fighting for.

One cannot be born European. And despite all that my American friends are telling me, I don't think there is a European type or profile. People are just different—want some examples?

As with many people of my age, I have experienced traveling with a bunch of international students. It's one of my best memories ever. We had a great time because we just didn't care about differences. The Danish girl would go swimming at eight in the morning, and the Spanish guy would still be in bed at noon. But when it came time to party, everybody was there. The Germans would drink beer, whereas I would desperately look for a glass of wine. The Italian boy would fall in love every five minutes, and the Irish girls would organize crazy dancing contests. And in the middle of this big mess, something would bring us together.

It's incredible indeed how you realize, when you are 6,000 kilometers [3,726 miles] away from home, how close you feel to your German or Spanish traveling mates. You suddenly discover that they are your neighbors. You have studied similar stuff in school, worshipped the same rock bands, hung out in the same kind of places, played the same kind of silly games.

Of course we did not always understand each other at first try. Luckily, we all spoke English. But did you know that there are many more kinds of English than one thinks? There is German-English, which is grammatically the best. There is also a French-English, well known for its strong and particular accent (luckily I was asked to write and not to make a speech). In Spanish-English, you say many more things in one sentence than in any other kind of English. It is very expressive but not very picky about tenses and structure. And Italian-English, it is very visual.

I could go on with languages and cultural barriers. Speaking is not the difficulty. But what is really important is that we somehow managed to overcome those barriers. Nobody really changed. There were still Britons, Austrians, Belgians, and Danes. But all of us also gained a new identity. We became parts of the group.

I see Europe as a similar enterprise (even though a more difficult one, since its purpose might not be fun only). Europe is about bringing people together to create a new thing. The media talk about economic agreements. They write about the euro. But you cannot separate the economy from the people. I see Europe as a process that involves all its inhabitants in a continuous attempt to improve European citizens' conditions. Europe is about trying. Everything may not work instantly, but you still have this will to go further, to do better.

Europe is a great adventure, and I want to be a part of it. We young people have been lucky enough to be born at a time of peace between European nations. This peace, we owe it to Europe. It's up to us to continue this direction, and to bring that great project further.

GERMANY

Claudia Hellman, journalist, 26 years old. For many years, the idea of Europe was for me no more than a vague political concept that had little to do with my own life. It wasn't until I moved away from the continent that I began to understand, for the first time, what Europe meant and how I was part of this place. In the beginning, it was often irritating to me to be called a European instead of a German, but after a while, I noticed that my own perspective on Europe was gradually changing through my stays abroad.

Meeting and discovering commonalities with French, Italians, and other young Europeans overseas created a new sense of unity. We did, in fact, have much more in common than I had previously perceived.

Standing on the inside, I had not been able to see Europe. Only from the outside looking in did I discover that a European identity existed and that I was a part of it. To discover that Europe could actually convey a sense of belonging was one of the valuable experiences of having lived away from home. Today, I still consider myself a German first, but I am also proud to be part of that prospering, larger community.

Over the last ten years, the unification of European countries has come a long way. It is exciting to see a vision take shape. There are a handful of events that in my opinion have shaped this process. The recent introduction of the euro currency was one of the most defining steps toward a truly integrated Europe, and of all the countries it was probably most difficult for Germans to accept that their beloved deutsche mark would have to be sacrificed on the altar of economic unity. But as with every relationship, this one too can only work through compromise.

Prior to the official starting of the monetary union, distrust and opposition to the euro were widespread in Germany. Initially, I used to share the general feeling that the new currency might lack the strength and stability of the deutsche mark. After a short but heated debate the country assumed a wait-and-see attitude. The introduction of the euro was then met with surprising calmness, which has meanwhile even turned into guarded optimism. The euro will certainly still have to stand the test of time, and the consequences on the economy cannot yet be fully assessed, but I see it as a unique chance to both establish a second major international currency and to initiate the long-necessary structural reforms within the German economy.

Although skepticism has not completely vanished, I am convinced that optimism is increasingly taking hold. For example, I recently encountered an elderly lady in a bank who was genuinely disappointed to learn that she could not yet withdraw any euros from her account.

The introduction of the euro is a bold and unprecedented economic experiment. But it is not a revolutionary coup overrunning the people of Europe. I see it as one crucial step in the evolutionary process of the formation of a unified Europe. It is a challenge we must accept if we want this union to progress. I also see the internationalization of business that will doubtlessly follow the creation of a single, large market as a unique career opportunity. Changing from a job in Cologne to one in Glasgow, Milan, or Stockholm will become even easier than it already is. Just as introducing a common currency has been a definitive step, other important issues lie ahead, such as opening the EU to new member states. There will be difficulties, and there is no magic formula to make this union work, but respecting each country's individuality while embracing common ground should bring us a long way.

GREECE

Angeliki Papantoniou, consultant, 31 years old. Writing this essay a week after the 1999 elections for the European Parliament, my first thought is to say that the issue for my generation is no longer if we feel European, but whether we feel ourselves to be citizens of a united Europe.

Being European is a characterization that we take for granted. Being Greek still has precedence in our hearts, but we also feel European, and it is this feeling that distinguishes us from our parents' generation. The keys to this notable change have been peace, education, communication, the growing globalization of culture, and Greece's membership in the European Union.

We are, after all, a generation that grew up in a peaceful Europe—in fact, we take peace in western Europe for granted. Even when war broke out in the Balkans (Bosnia, Kosovo), or when Turkey talked about the "gray zones of the Aegean," somehow everything seems distant from our everyday life. Our education was better than that of previous generations, lots of us had the opportunity to study abroad—today more than 30,000 Greek students study in European or U.S. universities—and almost everyone speaks English (and often a third European language).

Traveling throughout Europe is simple—London, Rome, or Paris is no longer an expensive distant dream. Either by Eurail passes, cheap airfares, or simply as students studying abroad, we traveled to foreign places. Similarly, the hordes of young tourists that "invaded" our land every summer got to know Greece and we their ways. When friendships grew on a Greek island or in a youth hostel somewhere in Europe, discussions about music, films, and TV shows came out naturally. We were not so different after all; in fact, we were quite similar. Back at school or work, we kept in touch through the Internet that we all love to surf so much to this day.

Without a doubt, stereotypes endure: to Greeks northerners are reserved and lack temperament, the British drink too much beer, the French are too chauvinistic, and so on. In a company of Italians, Spaniards, French, and Greeks somewhere on a U.S. university campus, we could argue all night long about which country has the best wine, cheese, and food. In comparison to our American friends, however, we, the Europeans, knew so much more about gourmet food! At the end of the day, there was a feeling of "us" meaning "Europeans"; we felt the proximity of culture, and now I feel how fortunate we were to have known each other.

The notion of "Europeanness" was also reinforced by Greece's membership in the European Union. My generation essentially grew up during the eighteen years of membership—fourteen years ago when I was starting my university education, I was so impressed by all the talk about the Single European Act that I chose (like many of my friends) to study European affairs. Today, the European Union is part of our life whether we flash our red passports at Heathrow or Frankfurt, have the right to work in any of the fifteen member countries, notice the infrastructure works (partly funded by the European Union) that are changing Greece, or argue about the benefits of the euro.

At the same time, although our parents' debates about whether or not to join the Union seem irrelevant, we are becoming increasingly critical of or indifferent toward the operations of the European Union. The reason is that the European Union has become a bureaucratic economic organization that, despite the treaties of Maastricht and Amsterdam, has failed to involve the citizens in its operations or to proceed with solid steps toward the promised political union.

The European Parliament is the only institution of the Union that is elected directly by the people of Europe, yet it remains the least powerful

European organization. As a result, most Europeans know very little about its daily operations, and the European elections are fought on national issues. A few days ago, in the last elections of this century, national issues prevailed for one more time, and the elections were reduced to a midterm test for the ruling party. As expected, voter turnout, especially among the young, was the lowest ever, while protest votes to fringe parties and the anti–European Union Communist Party increased. Similarly, the case of Kosovo and previously Bosnia has proved that, despite all the talk about a Common Foreign and Security Policy, European leaders are not prepared to follow an independent European foreign policy. Last but not least, when the euro will be a reality and the European Central Bank will influence the fiscal and monetary policy of Greece, we want to know more about the issues and to have an opinion.

My generation is "more European" than all previous ones and thus readier for a "closer union," a democratic union with checks and balances that will involve us—meaning all European citizens—in the decisions for our future.

IRELAND

Emer O'Beirne, university lecturer, 33 years old. As a teacher of French in Ireland's largest university, feeling European is almost part of the job! There's a distinctly polyglot character to our part of the university, as the French conversations in the corridors mingle with those of colleagues and students in German, Spanish, and Italian, not to mention Irish. I work side by side with people from all corners of France, some permanently settled in Ireland, others on one-year exchanges from French universities. For all of us, making the French language and Francophone culture accessible to the 800 or so students who have chosen to study with us means staying in close and regular contact with life in France.

In recent years, communication developments have made maintaining links with other European countries ever easier, overcoming Ireland's geographical peripherality and perhaps diluting the cultural introspectiveness that went with it. Indeed, our students today need no reminding that they are Europeans—since the advent of cable and satellite television, French, German, Spanish, and Italian TV programs have taken their place alongside English- and Irish-language channels, and the Internet makes European newspapers and radio stations more easily available than ever before. For young Irish people, Europe is an extracurricular reality too: DJs play a European circuit and bring a correspondingly European selection of music to Irish clubs (followed closely by the artists themselves in concert), and a combination of low-cost airfares and a new economic prosperity have made other European capitals increasingly accessible.

One tangible effect of this drawing closer of cultures is that Irish students are no longer intimidated by the idea of studying for a year in another European country but embrace the possibility with confidence. In fact, those who go to Paris and who stay in the Collège des Irlandais are continuing a centuries-old tradition. But you no longer need to be a seminarian to study in Europe. The EU Socrates and Erasmus schemes, which established a single, Europe-wide system of credits, have enabled students to incorporate a year in another European university into their degree program (and have also subsidized their travel expenses). This year alone, 250 students at University College Dublin are studying abroad on Socrates-Erasmus exchanges, and we have welcomed 350 students from other European countries; the feedback from both "camps" is, as always, overwhelmingly positive. However, there's no danger of the different educational traditions merging in an amorphous mass: not even the EU can get European academics to agree to apply the system in the same way! I spend a lot of time trying to ascertain the numbers of credits assigned to courses taken by our students abroad and trying to explain the workings of our own system to disoriented visiting Erasmus students. Overall, though, the Socrates-Erasmus scheme works well, and even the problems and disparities are in a way reassuring, for they remind us that despite economic convergence, cultural divergence is "thankfully" alive and well!

ITALY

Antonio Corsano Leopizzi, marketing manager, 35 years old. Five years have passed since the company I work for, Birra Peroni Industriale (Dannon Group) began to develop the Crazy Bull Café project. What began as a marketing innovation has evolved into one of the most original franchise restaurants in our country.

With the Crazy Bull Café, we committed to a restaurant concept that diverged completely from the traditional Italian locale. In the process we created a restaurant designed for those who love American-style cuisine and specifically targeted to young adults, who come to Crazy Bull for its engaging environment, good music, and good food.

The importance of a young audience to the success of this project has made me an attentive observer of this unique world. I have found Italy's young generation to be filled with enthusiasm and constantly searching for new ideas, styles, and trends but also filled with uncertainty and facing a complicated world with ever-changing problems.

I see the enormous success of Crazy Bull and other restaurants based on the food and cultures of other countries as evidence of a strong desire on the part of Italy's young adults to explore new worlds and approach new cultures. These young people are constantly comparing and contrasting their own experiences with the world around them. What better place to find this new type of social contact than in an environment that is more international, not typically Italian, and that gives them the idea that they could be anywhere in the world, in Rome but also in Paris, London, or Brussels.

The environment in which I work represents a significant test case for understanding the inclinations and preferences of Italy's youth: the choice of a certain kind of restaurant is a clear sign of a trend that underlines, if not illustrates, young Italians' evolution toward a new way of thinking.

It is an evolution that also clearly illustrates aspects of our culture that may even be more significant. Just think of the rising numbers of young people who decide to complete part or all of their education and training abroad, taking advantage of university programs like the Erasmus project or signing up for language programs. This does not even include the increasing competition among airlines, which for some time have been offering significantly reduced fairs for international destinations. I see this as a tangible sign of the rising numbers of people who leave Italy each day for other European destinations as tourists or businessmen and -women, often just to attend sports events and concerts that involve only short stays. Europe is becoming smaller and more accessible.

These observations lead me to believe that Italy's young people are reaching out to new cultures and lifestyles, are developing an outlook that is becoming more and more European, and are less and less constrained by the old ways of thinking that made it so hard to accept the idea of "abandoning" one's home country and family. Today the possibility of a move abroad is no longer viewed as a last resort by those lacking any other opportunities, but rather as a valid opportunity to be jumped at for the benefit of one's own cultural and professional growth.

Italy's younger generations are heeding the call of Europe and are preparing themselves to be part of a more international society.

LUXEMBOURG

Antoine Kremer, intern, 26 years old. If you take a look at the map of the European Union, Luxembourg is right at the center, half the distance between the southern tip of Greece and the most northern part of Finland, and from east to west right in the middle between Germany and France.

Historically, there has been in Luxembourg a long and continuous presence of foreign powers, like Spain, France, Prussia, the Netherlands, and Belgium, interested in the fortress of the city. The people of the grand duchy have learned to get along with all these foreign people coming and going.

Modern Luxembourg, independent since 1839, has often invited people coming from abroad to work first in its industrial sector and nowadays in the service sector of the country. This explains why, according to recent statistics, 35.6 percent of the population are non-Luxembourgers coming mostly from other EU countries but also from outside the EU.

By the way, you shouldn't forget that Luxembourg city is home to several institutions of the European Union and its 16,000 officials and their families from all over Europe.

Being born into such an international environment; growing up with German, Belgian, and French television; trilingual because of the school system; and having studied in Belgium for four years and lived in Italy for nearly a year, I couldn't think of myself as being just a Luxembourger and nothing else. In all these years, I have learned to accept and respect the differences of other people and nations, discover their originalities and strong points, and work together with them. This diversity, which occasionally can reveal itself as a difficulty, is also a fantastic source of creativity and one of the motors of European integration.

As a young European, having grown up as a Luxembourger in an international environment, this diversity seems to me an essential part of our European identity. Every single one of us is entirely Spanish, Irish, Greek, or Finnish. But more and more there is a consciousness growing in the whole of Europe that we also belong to something else crossing the borders of the different national states: the consciousness of being European alongside and beyond our respective national identity.

Over the past thirty years, we have spent our holidays more and more in some other European country: Germans going to Spain, the Dutch to Luxembourg, Danes to Greece, and Belgians to the United Kingdom. At the same time we hear about the politics of the European Union every day on the news, and newspapers have daily pages dedicated to European affairs. Since the end of 1998 and the introduction of the euro at the beginning of the following year, people are conscious of having another thing in common. From 2002 onward, Europeans all over the euro zone will be doing their daily shopping by paying in euro notes and coins. The European integration, which sometimes appeared a little bit abstract, will become more tangible.

That's why I feel Luxembourgish and European too. I think this growing consciousness of being also European is a chance for Europeans themselves to open their minds more and more to other peoples and nations, not only in Europe, but in the world at large. We shouldn't miss this opportunity.

THE NETHERLANDS

Ingelies Strick, university student, 26 years old. Living in Europe does not make you feel European. Instead it confronts you with the differences between all the European countries. Living in the Netherlands makes me feel Dutch. Together with my friends we joke about our close neighbors—the Belgians and the Germans. For the summer we go on holiday to Spain, France, or maybe even Greece to experience something different. We play tourists for two or three weeks and sigh on return, "Oh, it's good to be home."

Funnily enough, in order to feel European one has to leave Europe. A real sense of being European hit me the first time I entered the United States. Standing in the long line at Newark airport in the line of non-Americans, I looked around and sensed that I was different. This whole country was going to be different from what I had experienced at home, in Europe.

At university in a small town in Missouri called Mount Pleasant, I met some really nice people. With them I could talk about my experiences in the United States. They would understand if something would irritate, confuse, or amaze me. They were feeling the same thing. But they were not Dutch; they were German. At that moment, I started to realize that there was such a thing as feeling European.

Feeling European pops up when you least expect it. For example, when you see someone trying to eat a hamburger with a knife and fork. The person doing this could be German, French, Belgian, Spanish, or Danish; in other words, European. At this time, I'm living in an international student house. So I can observe every day how we Europeans differ from them, the rest of the world.

Before I came to the United States, I had never been aware of all the information we get in the Netherlands about Europe. Through television, radio, newspapers, and magazines, we gather a lot of information about all the European countries. In my experience, most Europeans are well informed about the whole of Europe. Sharing knowledge about Europe is part of the European feeling.

It is hard to explain what feeling European is all about. The definition of a nation is a group of people with the same history, language, and religion. European countries do share a common history. In the past this shared history has mostly been about wars. From the Middle Ages until 1945, wars filled our history books. But luckily things have changed. At this time European countries share a new common interest, the European Union.

The European Union has caused a lot of people to speak out, either in favor of or against the EU. Some are afraid the individual countries will lose their cultural identity and blend into one big uniform monster. Others think that the EU is not taking things far enough, that in order to compete with the United States and Asia, our economic plans should be even more extreme. In my opinion, a country has to have self-confidence in order to become part of a union. Extreme nationalistic views are an obstacle on the road to a union.

Nationalism always flares up in countries that have had a history of oppression. When Tito ruled Yugoslavia, he used the communist regime to keep all the different ethnic and religious groups quiet. Unfortunately, this resulted in an outburst of violence after the fall of communism. Its results are still visible today; all one has to do is turn on CNN and watch the Serb army burning down Kosovo. Kosovo presents both a danger and an opportunity to the EU. It could be the beginning of a series of nationalist uprisings, the first in a long line of civil wars. Or it could be the end of the old Europe, the one from the history books, and the start of a new peaceful Europe.

The future of the EU will depend on the citizens of the European countries. My friends and I will belong to a group of people who will be able to travel without a passport and pay with the same currency in each country we visit. My guess is that people who have not experienced the European feeling will discover it while working or traveling throughout Europe. The EU, the Union with unlimited opportunities, the Union of the free. That does sound kind of familiar, does it not?

PORTUGAL

Diana Rochford, international law student, 25 years old. I have always thought of myself as European. I was brought up bilingually in an English school in the heart of Portugal and have been taught to look at the world, family, life, and career through two perspectives. My father taught me to dive into every opportunity in that go-getter Anglo-Saxon fashion, and my mother taught me the importance of creating a network of family and friends, the skills needed to survive in a Mediterranean country.

Having parents from different countries has made me feel worldly, but I'm not really European. I'm a cake that has been sliced in two, not in fifteen, nor, if we look at it financially, in twelve. If I were placed in Thessaloníki in Greece or in the midst of reindeers in Finland, I would be lost. I would have to spend many lost hours staring at people's expressions and habits to understand what makes them tick. I am certain I'd miss sipping my black coffee at some small tiled cake shop. It's hard to escape the frame of mind with which one is injected with during one's formative years.

Yet, when one is outside of Europe one seems to realize just how similar the different European counties actually are. Being plonked in the midst of Greece or Finland would bear no resemblance to being left alone on a busy street in New Delhi. My sense of survival would be different.

Despite our differences within Europe, our languages and customs are bound by a common thread. People in general in Europe look determined; they have an opinion or just something to say. They are quickly overcoming any specter of a repressive and dictatorial past that has plagued many European countries this century.

And contagion is rife among European countries. Europeans work and present their arguments on the basis of comparison. While the north is invading the south with its strong environmental concerns and egalitarian political rights and duties, the south has tweaked at the north's human side with its coffee, pasta, sun, and general love of life.

A Portuguese person now knows that in the north of Europe, citizens do not have to wait for hours in a queue in order to buy a simple white-faced document, only to get to the front of the queue and be faced by that gray expressionless creature and be told the document is out of print:

"Can you please tell me when will you receive more
    documents?"
"I don't know."
"Do you know another place where I can buy the document?"
"I don't know."
"Can you find out for me?"
"I don't know."
"Can I kiss you?"
"I don't know."

A typical conversion, but one that now provokes a different reaction than a few years back, when the man would have turned his back, sighed, and walked away. Today, he scrunches up his face and shouts out: "It stinks, do they think I have nothing better to do . . . !*?# uncivilized country."

With European elections at bay, I share the Portuguese people's disappointment with the current political campaigns. Like the people around me, I am more interested in hearing what the various candidates are willing to fight for in Europe, as opposed to the usual exchange of verbal abuse.

Having always leaned toward Portugal's wide-eyed incredulous admiration of the European Union for all the obvious benefits it has brought, I am concerned with how Portugal will be represented in Europe's official bodies.

On a basis of comparison, I do not wish Portuguese Europeans to be considered less than Dutch, Swedish, British, or Spanish Europeans.

SPAIN

Belen Vidal Villasur, university student, 24 years old. I come from Spain, which is the same as saying from the borderland of Europe. My experience of Europe is thus peripheral, southern, and Mediterranean. For years, a well-know cliché has read Spain as different; but what nation does not feel in some way different and eccentric when confronted with the intimidating European project? I've never found such difference threatening to my sense of identity.

My education has made me think of Europe as a state of being at home abroad; as a Spanish student with a degree in English, who has lived in London and been lucky enough to travel across several European countries, I've had the opportunity of choosing to which cultures I want to belong. I have made myself at home in Europe by doing my work in English, watching French films, trying to learn some German, and being friends with a Croatian. I consider the European cities I love as much a part of my identity as my birthplace and upbringing. Europe demands of us to overcome historical and geographic divides through the desire to take part in a larger community. In my case, such desire has manifested itself as a voluntary state of exile, but one that reverses the condition of being perpetually away from home into the joy of finding a little bit of home everywhere.

Nothing is going to prevent me from being, first and foremost, Spanish: my accent betrays me and my long paragraphs tell about the romantic shaping of my linguistic cast of mind. But my Spanish legacy does not set the limits of my personality; it is, rather, the starting point of a journey that has always led me back to my cultural skin feeling enlarged and enriched.

Why worry about embracing difference? Sameness crops up spontaneously. Being a graduate student in the United States, I soon discovered that the European colony shared a language that prompted a special sense of bonding. My best friends are Europeans in mental exile as I am, passing and cheating on cultural borders: a Romanian with a transparent accent and an English girl doing her Ph.D. in Spanish. It is not only mutual understanding that brought us together but the fact of having made ourselves comfortable in cultural places other than our own.

Against the barren immobility of nationalism, the best way of building Europe is through exchange and circulation. The economic union is a crucial aspect, but equally important is getting to know your neighbors. The real dimensions of Europe are still unknown to its citizens, and too often history has been abused in order to draw arbitrary borders inspired by fear and hatred, as the tragic conflicts in eastern Europe have come to prove.

In this respect, multicultural education plays a role as fundamental in the construction of Europe as the access to work and capital. The power of circulating cultural products to bring cohesion has yet to be fully realized. It is in a Europe without mental locks that the key for union truly lies.

SWEDEN

Helen Holst, student of business administration and economics, 22 years old. There is a war in Europe. I am almost becoming numb to the falling of bombs and the burning flames on the television set. Empathy from a distance is difficult. Still, the people in Serbia and Kosovo are not very different from my friends and me in Stockholm. I wish there were a simple solution to the war, but there is not. Instead, my life goes on while theirs ceases to exist in a normal way.

The young and well-educated people of Kosovo flee the lives they have made for themselves to meet an uncertain future in crowded refugee camps. I worry about my future. What do I want to become when I grow up? In Kosovo the worries are different. Will there be enough food tomorrow? Will there be a tomorrow to grow up in and a future to live? When the television set is on I feel concern for the future of the refugees, but when it is off, the falling of bombs and the burning flames of a European country are also absent from my consciousness.

In a few weeks I will vote to elect the Swedish members of the European Parliament. The debate is tepid. Facts on what is accomplished in the European Parliament and by what parties are difficult to get a hold on. As usual, the political debate held in public is superficial. I will vote for the same party as I did in the election for the Swedish Parliament because I expect that party to represent the same values in the European Parliament as in the Swedish. There are issues that I care about, but what difference can I make? Together with the Swedish majority, I am passive in the debate. Whatever parliament, my future will remain bright because I am young and well educated.

Amid falling bombs in a burning inferno, being young and well educated does not help. There, political actions and protests are a better way of securing one's future. In safe Sweden, I can cast a vote for whatever party, and my life will go on as usual. At the moment I prioritize my studies to graduate by Christmas. I want the EU to help me with my worries and offer me opportunities to work outside Sweden and to travel. I also want the EU to take care of the young of Serbia and Kosovo, to give them peace and all the opportunities that I have. I want everyone to be able to share the safety I feel in being European.

In the future I hope that the EU will encompass every European nation and that we together can keep peace and high living standards in Europe. There is also a necessity not only for Europe but for the entire world to cooperate on environmental issues. I regard the EU as a step toward a global world. Therefore the EU needs to look more for breadth than depth and deal with large issues in many countries rather than small issues in a few countries. The EU should represent freedom, not restrictions. As to my own near future, I wish to find a job in Sweden or elsewhere in the world if countries outside of the EU would open their labor markets to me and offer some freedom for a world citizen.

UNITED KINGDOM

Peter Droussiotis, lawyer and Labor Party councilor, 39 years old. I was born and spent my formative years on a small island called Cyprus on what some may see as the periphery of Europe. My father worked at the British sovereign bases in Cyprus for many years and had British citizenship.

When I was a teenager, my parents, my two sisters, and I moved to the UK—another, much larger island that some may also see as being on the periphery of Europe.

I came of age in England. I went to school in North London and then to the University of Birmingham. I was called to the English bar.

As a lawyer, I have worked in a number of large multinational organizations in the City of London. My work meant that I had to travel extensively throughout the continent. I have interacted with people of many different nationalities in Europe, including French, Italian, German, Czech, Swiss, Swedish, and Finnish people. Some of them became friends of mine.

In my early thirties I met and married my wife. Her name is Carolyn, and she comes from Yorkshire—a beautiful region of England with its own distinctive identity and people. My father-in-law is proud to be first a Yorkshireman, second an Englishman, and then British. He says he feels less European than I do, which is consistent with the findings of British opinion surveys that show that we, the younger generation, are happier with a European identity than our parents and grandparents. My wife and I have two daughters: Isabella, who is four years old, and baby Alexandra, who is one.

I sometimes wonder which identity they will feel most comfortable with when they grow up. We live in North London, a very multicultural area with people from every conceivable ethnic background. I love the rich diversity of the place where I live.

Most of my life, I have been surrounded by diversity. People are different. Each one of us is unique, with his or her own ambitions, hopes, and fears. Most of us are happy with a multilayered identity. We are comfortable with having plural allegiances. And yet, what strikes me time and again is that the vast majority of all of these different people have something very important in common: shared values. A sense of justice, tolerance of others, a love of freedom, and a feeling of comfort in a pluralist society—intangible values that some of us may take for granted but that underpin our laws; our institutions; our ethos; the way we live, work, and play.

Whether we are lawyers or businesspeople, housewives or teachers, nurses or politicians, black or white, all of us have a common point of reference called Europe. But Europe is more than a place on the map. It is a collection of ideas and ideals, a concept and a reality; Europe is the now but is also the vision for tomorrow. We live in an increasingly interdependent, synthetic world. Problems and solutions cut across national boundaries. Creating new jobs, alleviating poverty, protecting our environment, and fighting racism and xenophobia are all pan-European challenges requiring European solutions. When I think of Europe in this context, I think of the European Union and of what it can or should achieve. I think of its institutions and its vast resources. I think of the potential to create a Europe that derives strength from its diversity, a Europe focused on the common good of all its citizens.

This is part of the vision that in so many different ways drives my passion for politics, my membership in the British Labor Party, and my work as a local councilor in the London Borough of Haringey. Improving the quality of people's lives in Haringey is no longer solely a local or even a national objective. It is a European goal.

I am emotionally attached to London—ever changing and yet always the same; I am proud of my Greek origins and equally proud of my sense of Britishness. I also know that Europe itself inspires me: its history, its music, its architecture, its politics, its art, its literature; its people; its sports; its myths, its diversity, and its constancy. When I think of these things, I have no doubt that in the journey of my life so far, no matter where I may have been physically, I have always been at the heart of Europe. That feeling gives me a certain reassurance about who I am as well as confidence in the future.

18

Europe's Leaders of Today
Discuss the Europe of Tomorrow

We asked leaders in various fields across Europe questions about Europe in the new century. In addition to other questions, we asked each respondent: "What does it mean to be European in the twenty-first century?" "How do you think Europe will look economically and politically in the year 2020?" "How will the euro affect you personally?" "Do you feel Europe will be a global player in the new century?" "What do you see as a potential major threat to Europe in the new century?" Here's what they had to say.

AUSTRIA

Peter Mitterbauer, president of the Austrian Federation of Industry and chief executive officer of an automotive parts firm, was interviewed by Robert J. Guttman.

What does it mean to be a European in the twenty-first century? To be a European in the twenty-first century means more to my children than to myself. I [grew] up in Austria, and have lived in the U.S., and have traveled [in] Europe extensively. For my children, who [were born] in Italy and in Brussels and have traveled and speak two to three languages, for them Europe is going to be more a home place than it will be for me. And Europe will be much more than something with lot of opportunities from the economic side.

I personally hope that Europe will find its own identity also as far as its position versus, so to say, the rest of the world. Which means that

213

we should come to a common foreign policy on certain matters, not on all of them—it will take a long time, also on the security matters. But Europe will be a much more thriving place than it is for the future, and with a unification process going on, it will be a much safer place in the future than it has been in the twentieth century. And the first part of the twentieth century for Europe [was] a horrible century.

What do you think Europe will look like politically in the year 2020? Well, in the year 2020 there will be the European Union of twenty-five or twenty-eight states. The enlargement process will have proceeded on. I don't think that it will have been completed. But politically, the big question will be: "What political system is governing Europe? What has the European Commission developed into, and who is leading that, and who is [making] the checks and the balances to that? What's the European Parliament going to be? Is it going to be something in [a] democratic state that controls the government or controls the Commission, supports it, helps it, checks it? Would it be a body which is governable for the thousand people? Could it be 500, [which is an] institutional question? Will we have a strong leader or more than one? Will the UK be in emotionally? What is the position of France then?" So, a lot of interesting questions coming in. My dream would be that we should be somehow on the way to a Commonwealth of Europe, not a United States. Historically, we cannot achieve that in twenty years' time.

What do you think Europe will look like economically under the euro? How will the euro be doing twenty years from now? Economically, I personally believe Europe will be a thriving economy because when the enlargement is . . . completed, it will be an additional hundred million people with all their aspirations, with all their ambitions, with all their drive. It will be a large market. It will still be a market of a lot of unfulfilled desires and wishes. Because the question we have economically is can we bring in the standardization and bring down the trade barriers, especially the hidden ones? Can we phase out nationalistic behaviors? Will the next generation be more European than our generation? I strongly believe it will.

And how do you think the euro will affect you personally? Very positively. The changeover from a national currency into the euro is a very emotional thing. You need, for a certain period of time, to adjust your calculation system. It will be especially hard for an Italian to have his espresso costing one euro, where up to now it cost 2,000 lira. It will take some time. But I think the euro will be definitely a very strong currency, equal to the dollar.

Do you think that Europe will be a global player in the next century? Europe is already a global player.

Do you think it will become more of a global player? I foresee that the economies between the U.S. and Europe will be much more intertwined. You see the concentration process going on. Look at the automotive industry, what's happening, and this will not be only Europeans coming to America; Americans will come to Europe. A large portion of the European automotive industry is also [becoming] American, or international, or global, and this will continue in other areas as well.

What do you see as a major threat to a unified Europe in the twenty-first century? One, economically, and two, politically. The biggest threat to Europe is the return of nationalism. And the return of nationalism has very much to do with consequences of a weak economy.

One of the biggest challenges we have for Europe in the coming years is to bring down the jobless rate or bring people more into the production process. And by production I mean productive work. And by productive work I mean being employed. And this is not only industry, this is [the] service industry, and this is also the third and fourth sectors.

The second big question in this respect would be, "How can we improve and adjust and fine-tune our educational system in a world where the knowledge base is exploding? How can we digest it and how can we work with the new tools, with the Internet, and with the computers and with all this technological electronic revolution?" The next generation is well prepared for that, but the main question is how the transfer of knowledge and the mobility of young people will foster that and will kind of spin that.

You said the twentieth century was a horrible century. What do you want people to say about the twenty-first century? That it was a peaceful century. It was a century [in which] a lot of people had, according to their ambition and according to their performance, good opportunities to make a decent and good living.

FRANCE

French minister of employment and solidarity Elisabeth Guigou was interviewed by Axel Krause in Paris.

What does it mean being a European today? I believe we have come to realize that one can be French, English, German, Italian, Spanish while being European as well. This goes contrary to the idea, expressed during the early days of building Europe, that national identities would be replaced by Europe. We no longer think this way. Yet we do not seek uniformity, but rather a Europe in which every member respects differences with regard to others. A Europe which takes on this role thus makes a rich asset out of diversity. This is what our citizens sense, constituting a genuine force.

More specifically, how would you define the European dimension of this role? First, we share common values, starting with the respect for differences, hardly a negligible factor. This encompasses the refusal to accept racism, anti-Semitism, xenophobia. Then, there is tolerance, which was also inherent in the values that inspired the building of Europe from the beginning. It helps explain the successful reconciliation of France and Germany after the war. Nobody was talking in these terms at the end of the 1940s. Nobody. Today this [set of common values] is not in evidence when we apply what we are talking about to Kosovo and the Balkans because there is an absence of respect for, and this tolerance of, others. And yet there is a lot to be accomplished together.

Are you referring to the emergence of some kind of new European dimension or identity based on common values? In a sense, there is a great deal which unites us. I have the feeling we share the same space, the same dimension. This is perhaps to a large degree psychological. The notion of a European space is particularly meaningful for younger people, those who will be in their thirties and forties in the next century. For them, it comes naturally. They travel. They seek to learn languages, to build personal contacts. They do not hesitate to marry, have children with others. This is being experienced as an enrichment of Europe, as an addition, not a subtraction. And it continues to evolve very quickly.

Yes, but aren't European young people now traveling, like their American counterparts, as globe-trotting, as opposed to European, citizens—without any particular message? They are traveling, but there is a sense of belonging to something being constructed, and this helps explain the solidarity among Europeans today. Why? Because there is a feeling that Europe does have a message to be transmitted to the rest of the world. And it is here where we find an answer to the inhumane aspects of economic globalization, to the fears of being swallowed by the supremacy of market forces. We say that yes, we are in a market economy—totally. We are not going back on liberalization, free circulation of capital. But for all of this, one needs rules. And Europe can provide an example. Emerging countries are incapable of doing it. Many are mired down in this world without rules. Just look at the multiplication of offshore financial centers in Asia and Latin America. It is frightening. The United States, which initially did not share the message, has started to change, in response to the problems posed by the pressures of criminality.

Has the introduction of identical, maroon-colored passports to EU citizens and of the euro changed attitudes? Yes. I believe that today when one is outside Europe, one says first of all that one is European, while inside, people identify themselves as French, German, whatever, and European. But I don't attach the same significance to the passport and the euro. For me, the passport is a true symbol, which little by little helps develop a sense of identity. The euro fulfills that role as well, but it is something completely different. It is an instrument of power.

As you look ahead over the next twenty years, what will Europe resemble—a large, free trade zone mainly, an influential, global political entity, or what? I have always believed in a political Europe, profoundly, from the beginning. Europe will not happen without political will, a political goal, and [a] purpose. I believe that can attract and inspire Europeans, and I include its leaders. When building Europe, as we saw with the euro, decisions have to be taken that can provoke impassioned and unpopular reactions everywhere. In the end, we are pleased when it works out. But Europe cannot come about without this engine of political will and determination.

At the same time . . . the juxtaposition of freedom of trade and a political Europe [is somewhat artificial]. The free flow of capital, trade, and people within Europe exists. But we are not suggesting we stop there, that we do just that. Thus, a free trade zone, yes. Suggesting the elimination of the Internet makes no sense. What we are saying is that political will also is needed to establish rules. This is what we tried to do and did with the euro, but it required gigantic political effort, moving mountains, considering what this represented for Germany, even for France. We are currently trying to move in a similar direction regarding a social Europe, with our Social Democratic partners, including Tony Blair of the United Kingdom.

But isn't something missing in all this institutional leadership? I believe we are necessarily moving toward an institution I support creating—a presidency of Europe. Will it be a man or a woman? How would he or she be designated? Would it be a triumvirate, functioning with the president of the European Commission, and the presiding president of the Council of Ministers? No one can provide answers today. What is clear is that in light of everything we are doing—the establishment of the euro, the plans for European defense, combating crime on a European level—we need an incarnation in the form of a presidency. It remains to be defined. However, I do not believe it can involve the president of the Commission only because the Commission has an absolutely key role to propose and to work for agreement. When it isn't given that role to play, among governments, the system doesn't work. So, the powers of this European executive, the presidency of Europe, should emanate simultaneously from the Commission and the Council, comprising heads of state and government, of course. This is what we should be trying to invent and to build.

Does the term federalism *bother you, as it does some French political leaders?* No. What does bother me is when it is applied to, or translated into, the notion of a [European] federal state. Because I do not believe that Europe can, or should, be one single state. Subsidiarity should be allowed to play out, fully, positively, and completely. This is to say that we should assume as much responsibility as possible at the national level and then focus on what we can do at the European level. Subsidiarity for me is not a matter of Europe leaving the crumbs to nation-states. No one summed it up better than Jacques Delors when he suggested that what we need in our approach, above all, is simplicity. Indeed, when things don't work, which is the case for the Council of Ministers of Justice, it is [because of a lack of] simplicity and an absence of visibility. So, we won't be one single European state. But a federation of nation-states should not pose a problem. This is most natural for the Germans, perhaps less so for the French and the English, yet I do not see much difference between them. The problem is getting them to agree. When we are sounding out member governments and suggest they might have to abandon the rule of unanimous voting—we saw this clearly at Amsterdam [1997 EU summit]—Chancellor [Helmut] Kohl did not abandon the unanimous vote. The United States of Europe? No!

To whom should a European president be accountable? Simultaneously, and necessarily, to the European Parliament and national parliaments. This stems from the basic idea of the trio mentioned earlier. The president of the Commission is accountable to the European Parliament. The president of the Council, whose role rotates every six months, perhaps this will go to one year, is the head of state or government and is accountable to his national parliament. If we have a European president designated by the Council for five years, subsequently serving amid the heads of state and government, he would inevitably be accountable to them and to the European Parliament. Perhaps this sounds complicated, but all the institutions are complicated.

Looking ahead, say twenty years, how many EU member states do you foresee? A Europe that is very integrated politically is not a Europe of thirty countries. I do not think that we can, or should, shun the countries of eastern Europe. To the contrary. I think we should welcome them. And one day, to include the Balkans. We should provide them [eastern European countries] that prospect. But to do what? The central question needs to be posed: To what do they want to adhere?

At the same time, we need to be careful and avoid Europe turning into a system which allows members to shop around, as if they were in a supermarket. There can be one or two forms of membership, maybe three, but not twenty. What we are moving toward, inevitably, is a central core of countries that want and are willing to undertake all their responsibilities at the same time—common defense, political integration, and the like. Around them, there would be a second circle of countries that would constitute a market, the common market, with shared rules to ensure fair competition in matters of taxation and labor relations.

Acknowledging that startup of the European monetary system is recent, and the euro has still to be introduced as a currency, what impact do you foresee for France? In our daily lives, the euro will change an enormous amount. We will have to become used to a new currency. But I am not unduly concerned. In contrast to the switch from old to new francs in the 1960s, we have handy calculators today. For young people this is no problem. Shopkeepers have adjusted. In [the southern city of] Avignon for three years now, bakers have priced their bread in euros as well as in francs. For businessmen and bankers it will simplify many things. Costs will be reduced, but above all, [the European monetary system] will provide participating European countries [with] margins of maneuver for economic strategy that do not exist today. And because this new currency also has a projected role as one of the world's reserve currencies, we will have a greater capacity to resist crises. We saw this during the Asian financial crisis. Domestically, we will have a margin for autonomous action—not enormous—to fix interest rates, for example, when it is decided at the political level to stimulate growth, without being unduly influenced by the central bankers.

Will the euro have any impact on the EU's political future? Yes. It should bring us closer to reinforcing political integration. But I am not among those who believe the euro—by itself—is enough to establish political Europe. Nevertheless, it is an instrument of world power, assuming that it is used in a well-balanced way. I think it can allow Europe to affirm itself, its originality.

And on you, personally? The day that I actually have euro bills and coins, I will certainly be very moved. I will always remember where they came from. Along with others, I plunged in to what became an extraordinary adventure. I observed [former French president François] Mitterrand, [former German chancellor Helmut] Kohl, and [former European Commission president Jacques] Delors carrying the project forward at the political level, the three of them, amid general skepticism. In the background, helping make it happen, were just a few others— [Delors's chief of staff] Pascal Lamy, [Kohl's key EU adviser] Joachim

Bitterlich, and me. Then I had to confront the campaign for [the ratification] of [the Treaty of] Maastricht, which was a campaign against the euro. I think we did well. Voilà, that's what the euro means to me. It is a formidable accomplishment.

Does this mean Europe is emerging as a global player and global power? Of course. If I didn't believe it, I would stop militating for Europe. Motivating my involvement is the conviction that someday Europe will exist in its own right. We are in a world where only continents count. And Europe, I believe, has things to say to the rest of the world.

GERMANY

Stefan Röver, chief executive officer of Brokat Infosystems AG, based in Stuttgart, Germany, was interviewed by Carola Kaps.

Stefan Röver, thirty-four, is one of four original founders and current CEO of Brokat Infosystems, a highly successful software company specializing in strong encryption software for electronic banking and electronic business solutions. Brokat is one of the world leaders in this field; its technology is used by more than 1,600 companies worldwide.

Röver founded the company with four partners in 1994. In the meantime, Brokat has merged with MeTechnology; with the recent takeover of TST the company has a staff of 495 in twelve countries. In fiscal year 1997–1998 the turnover was 30 million deutsche marks.

Röver, who is married and has two children, is one of the leading young, successful German entrepreneurs. Educated partly in California and partly in Germany at the University of Tübingen, where he majored in economics and business administration, he had started his computer technology company in 1986, working mainly in system development and branching out as a consultant for software and project management at the same time.

Röver believes that as an entrepreneur he has a political and social responsibility. Moreover, he holds the conviction that business needs to be politically involved in order to be able to influence political decisionmaking and help build a better society.

He considers a close linkage between information technology and the political process to be of special importance because the rapid progress of information technology is fundamentally changing the way society works. Therefore, he is actively engaged in the German Chapter of the International Chamber of Commerce (ICC), where he fights for a reasonable and effective encryption policy. He is a member of the

Global Business Dialogue (GBD) on e-commerce as well as a regular participant and sought-after expert in the Transatlantic Business Dialogue (TABD).

What does it mean to be European in the twenty-first century? Europe is at a critical juncture. It can become a slow-moving, monolithic, bureaucratic, and artificial structure no one will be able to identify with. It could also become a model of a decentralized, culturally diverse federation of regions, which are in healthy economic competition.

Being a European at the outset of the twenty-first century to me means helping achieve the second alternative and preventing the dreadful first.

On one side we have the centralist/socialists, who to me are the real conservatives, [and] on the other side the independent-minded, new generation that wants to move and change things and prepare Europe for its role in the global economy.

How do you think Europe will look economically and politically in the year 2020? That depends on the outcome of that conflict. Hopefully, Europe will become a service-oriented society, playing a major role in the digital economy. The cultural diversity in Europe is an enormous asset, which will continue to make Europe a great place to live if we solve the economic issues.

How will the euro affect you personally? If everything goes well, I will not feel affected at all. The benefits are real but subtle. Only if things go wrong [will] people notice the euro.

As long as we maintain the independence of the [European] Central Bank and continue a policy of reasonably controlled budgets, things should go well.

Do you feel Europe will be a global player in the new century? Yes, Europe has great economic potential. The economic union will allow companies to grow beyond their current limits and boundaries and become global players.

What do you see as a potential major threat to you/Europe in the new century? Traditional socialist responses to the transition pains of an economy moving from manufacturing to services.

Does an entrepreneur have a political responsibility? Should he or she get involved? It is in his or her own interest to get involved. The world is changing dramatically, [and] business can and should supply input to help address the regulatory issues [for example, in the TABD, GBD, and ICC].

Apart from that, entrepreneurs are often listened to and generally respected. They can and should use this influence to help build a better society.

GREECE

George A. Papandreou, Greek minister of foreign affairs, was interviewed by Robert J. Guttman.

What does it mean to you to be a European in the twenty-first century? To be "European" in the twenty-first century means to live by a fresh set of principles that are equally founded on the history of Europe and the contemporary reality now arising from the process of European unification.

At the same time, to be European is a great challenge. How can we maintain our common traditions such as democracy and humanism, equal rights for all, multicultural plurality, and a strong sense of social conscience in a new globalized world of technological advances in information and biotechnology? This challenge poses important political and ethical questions that will have a profound bearing on the future of political reforms in the European Union.

How do you think Europe will look economically and politically in the year 2020? Given that we are living in an age of remarkable fluidity in all fields of human activity, including international relations, it would be unwise to make predictions about the long-term economic and political future of Europe. However, purely as a theoretical exercise and taking into consideration the increasing trend toward globalization and regional unification (with the European Union a perfect case in point), I could imagine the following scenario for Europe in the year 2020: after successfully achieving monetary union and hopefully political union soon afterwards with a strong defense and common foreign policy component, it is logical to assume that Europe will emerge as one of the two or three most powerful economic and political forces in the world.

How will the euro change life in Europe in the twenty-first century? The euro and the accompanying public and legal reforms, together with the subsequent stabilization of prices and currencies, will create favorable conditions for the macroeconomic environment. Consequently, investments, development, and employment will intensify and thrive. Ultimately, the citizens of Europe will themselves benefit from these economic policies. At the same time, the abolition of costly exchange rates both for international business and/or individual transactions will simplify the related procedures to the benefit of all citizens. Deeper issues of cultural identity, common educational policies, and political unification will soon top our agendas.

Do you feel Europe will be a global player in the new century? As I already mentioned, the institution of the European [economic and] monetary union will lay the foundations for Europe to become a major player in the international political arena. Moreover, the imminent expansion of the European Union to include new members such as Cyprus and several other countries in central and eastern Europe, as well as the prospect of political union, will guarantee that Europe plays an even greater role on the world stage during the twenty-first century. The successful accomplishment of European unification will have a positive impact not only within Europe itself but also in global economics and international relations in general, since a unified Europe will inevitably improve international economic and political stability.

What do you see as the major threat in the new century? There are a number of problems that might concern citizens worldwide during the twenty-first century, from national security and illegal migration to unemployment, protection of consumers, and the environment.

In my opinion, one of the main problems we face is the absence or inadequacy of international organizations to deal with such issues and the weakness of our nations to efficiently deal with these issues on a national level. In today's increasingly global society, these issues go beyond national borders. They require concerted, international cooperation. And while the international community must set up the relevant mechanisms and institutions to arbitrate and intervene in such matters—this in itself poses a profound question of what our democratic institutions will look like in the future. What do "citizen participation" or "direct elections" or "plebiscites," "political parties," and "parliaments" mean in a globalized world and in the European Union structures? I therefore believe the issue of democracy will be a major issue in the forthcoming century.

Are the Balkans as much a part of Europe, as, say, France or Germany? The Balkans are, of course, part of the European continent, but until recently Europe was divided because of the Cold War. Apart from Greece, all the countries in the region were incorporated into the Eastern European communist bloc. As a result, they were condemned to remain largely undeveloped, with weak or nonexistent democratic institutions. Now, with plans for European expansion under way, two Balkan countries, Bulgaria and Romania, will soon be joining the European Union. Furthermore, in the aftermath of the Kosovo crisis, the European Union has already drawn up a proposal to forge closer ties with the so-called western Balkans through the conclusion of agreements that will further stability and affiliation. I believe that the incorporation of the entire Balkan region into the European Union will reduce the distance that currently separates it from Europe and thus restore unity to the whole European continent.

Can the Balkan nations join the European Union in the early part of the twenty-first century? We must create a clear and realistic road map for all Balkan countries toward accession into the European Union. As I mentioned above, two candidates, Bulgaria and Romania, are already in the process of negotiating their entry into the European Union, so they are at a more advanced stage that the rest of the Balkan nations.

The European Union has set down a series of political and economic criteria that each candidate state will fulfill. In other words, each country must comply with the *acquis communautaire*. All candidates must fully comply with these common objectives. Therefore, the entry of each country depends on its individual progress in meeting these criteria. Naturally, the European Union has a duty to support the efforts of every candidate state, thus ensuring that they all join the Union as swiftly as possible.

IRELAND

Mary Robinson, United Nations high commissioner for human rights and former president of Ireland, was interviewed by Mike Burns in Dublin.

Mary Robinson was the first woman president and certainly the best-loved holder of that office in the history of Ireland. During her presidency, she opened her official residence to the poor and marginalized from all parts of the country. She made historic friendship visits to Northern Ireland and had a groundbreaking meeting with Britain's Queen Elizabeth. She traveled to famine-stricken regions of Africa and was shaken to the core by the scenes she witnessed.

Earlier, as a young liberal reforming lawyer, she was responsible for a series of landmark legal cases, particularly in the area of women's rights. As a member of the Irish Senate, she showed a fearless commitment to human rights issues and legislative change.

After her term as president of Ireland, in 1997 she became the United Nations high commissioner for human rights. In Dublin she gave Mike Burns her views on human rights, the future for women in politics and government, and the role of small countries.

Given the tragic events in various parts of the world over the last couple of decades and more recently in the Balkans, is there any reason to be hopeful that there will be a greater recognition of human rights in the new century? There's a lot of discussion about it. It's very much on the agenda of governments, which creates a challenge: to see how to promote human rights and also to do the more difficult thing, which is to confront governments with the fact that they are denying or violating human rights. So, in a way, it requires a two-strand approach: on the promotional side, I see more and more the value of working through regional or subregional contexts.

Obviously, in Europe, there are great strengths: from the Council of Europe, the [Organization for Security and Cooperation in Europe or] OSCE, the European Union, to the union of Baltic States; I link with these and work with them. But in other areas, for example the Asia-Pacific region, there's no regional human rights body, so we've created a dynamic of an annual workshop in which we bring together the countries, the governments, the nongovernmental organizations, and increasingly, representatives of national human rights institutions. They have agreed on a framework in which they discuss annually the progress they've made on national plans of action for human rights education, institutions, and strategies for economic and social rights and the rights to development.

What I've noted—and this is why I'm using this as a model elsewhere—is that governments are prepared to work within a kind of peer pressure, to compare notes and to be encouraged to put in place plans of action or national institutions. More difficult is to address violations of human rights by governments. Sitting with a foreign minister and saying "your government is still perpetrating torture, you haven't ratified this or that convention, you are violating, your prison system is terrible" is the tough side, and you have to do that at national level. However, I think that we have an opportunity to promote a kind of global alliance for human rights, a global community which links governments [and] multinational organizations, uses the regional framework, and above all else, builds up civil society. It's really the civil society that makes sure that human rights are well protected in a country and can ensure that governments fulfill their obligations.

You have been at the forefront of the campaign, a champion of women's rights. How do you see women in key roles in politics, in governments, in the twenty-first century? Certainly I believe it has been very important that, in the last twenty years, women have been participating in government, in administration, in business, in the trades union movement, and in community life.

Two points occur: one, it has helped to balance the priorities because women bring a whole range of concerns that haven't been addressed sufficiently at the political level; secondly, and equally important, women bring an organizational skill and way of doing things. It's reflected, for example, in the network approach. It's nonhierarchical, and it tends to be practical and ready to adapt to the realities of a situation instead of being hedged in by institutional, hierarchical structures. It's partly that women didn't exercise power in the traditional sense and are therefore more likely to want to resolve problems and to adapt the structure to do that, to have an ease about who is getting the main credit. I think that has influenced international and national institutions to their great benefit.

But women have been in government: Golda Meir in Israel, Margaret Thatcher in Britain. But you're pointing to individual women. I'm talking about a critical mass of women rather than the individual exceptional person who happens to have exercised a particular role. It's only in the last twenty years that we began to see that—and we still haven't seen it in real terms except in countries like Sweden, where approximately 50 percent of the parliament is female. But that's still rare.

Will it be easier in the twenty-first century for women to run for and hold office? It's interesting to see the kind of barriers that continue and the lack of full sharing of responsibilities in the home [that] still present[s] a barrier. You've got child care certainly, but women have the main responsibilities in that area. Even in countries like Sweden, I've talked to a number of women parliamentarians for whom it is more difficult still. Women in the business world find it difficult to break through to the top levels in the boardroom and to exercise a comparable influence in decisions in the financial world.

Given what's happened over the last twenty years, will it no longer be a rarity to see women in power in the new century because women like yourself are already in politics and hold senior positions in other areas? There's still quite a distance to go. I hear constant reference to those glass ceilings and invisible ceilings. They're still there. It's by no means the case that we have resolved these problems. We are talking about a developed world and, if you like, a privileged context in contrast to women worldwide.

In most of the countries in which I would be addressing a human rights situation, women are far from achieving even respect and recognition. They are the burden carriers; they do most of the work, but they don't have status and, in some instances, don't have a vote. This is more evidence of the positive contribution that having a good balance of women at every level can make. I don't think that women, empirically, are any better than men. It's the balance that is better for a country or a system.

It's good to have those examples to promote more participation by women, and again, it's through the civil society, through nongovernmental organizations, that women are playing more of a role and gradually getting in to local government. In India, for example, they have now a quota of women at [the] local government level and that has made a huge difference as hundreds of thousands of women exercise local power in local elections and local authorities. That is the beginning of a real coming up through the system, which is much more impressive than just having a very striking woman as prime minister or foreign minister or whatever. It needs that whole working through the system.

What do you see as the key difference between women and men in politics, government, and business? There isn't a stark black-and-white difference. Women are less hierarchical and perhaps less macho in their approach in certain ways, more pragmatic in problem solving. That is reflected in their approach to the exercise of power. It's more a shared experience. That's partly because of the way in which women come to the exercise of power. They had more of a struggle; they are more motivated to achieve a result rather than exercise power because a father or a grandfather had done it, although I recognize that women do come in to politics because it has been "in the family." Being the widow, the daughter, is still an entry point for quite a lot of women, but the approach is different and I believe more forward-looking. The kind of flexible, more problem-solving, pragmatic approach that women adopt also commends itself to industry, for example, and to transnational cooperation.

What is the role of small nations like Ireland in an enlarged European Union? Can small countries keep their identities, or will they become submerged subsidiaries of a federal state? I have felt that within a structure like the European Union, small countries can play a disproportionately active and proactive role. Ireland has demonstrated this by its ability to place people well within the structures of the European Union, the Commission, the Parliament, [and] the Council of Ministers and then play an active role in relation to issues.

Take one that's close to my own heart because it's very close to human rights: development policy toward third countries or developing countries. Successive Irish ministers—and they've been ministers of state, not full members of the cabinet—have used their position to influence the foreign ministers. Ireland has played a very significant role in shaping how the European Union as a whole addresses developing countries. Someone like Garret FitzGerald as Irish foreign minister, for example, played a very significant role in that regard, and there have been a number of others in recent years.

Do you feel European or Irish or what? I have felt for a considerable time both Irish and European and, more importantly, watched the ease with which our three young children feel Irish and European. Now, perhaps, I have a broader perspective: I don't want to be bracketed because a lot of my concerns are far away from Europe, and indeed, I would give priority to them. It's the imbalance in the world that concerns me, and so, I both accept more invitations to go to and want to be more in, places elsewhere that don't have adequate attention. I identify very much with them and I think part of the identification comes from an Irishness—it comes from that sense of our own roots.

What do you see as the key issues facing both Europe and the world in the next twenty years? A whole range of issues. World security is a big issue. We have lost the artificial stability of the Cold War. We need to be very concerned about both nuclear and chemical weapons and the hands they are in and the control over them. That's a big concern.

Another is the increasing capacity to create even further destructive weapons. Environmental degradation, what we are doing to this world and to our climate—these are huge concerns.

And, on the positive side, the challenge of the possibility of having a genuine culture of human rights at [the] national level and, therefore, developing a strategy to embed that culture. I find this very challenging, because we have to address the extent of violations by governments and by powerful nonstate actors within countries, powerful drug barons, those who traffic in women, those engaged in the selling of arms and armaments. These are all very big challenges. I see increasingly—and it's not just because I am working within the UN system—the importance of having a multilateral system that works. Because it's not acceptable to a very significant number of countries and regions to have one superpower policing our complex world. It's just not acceptable.

Increasingly, we are going to see the fractious resentment of one dominant power if it seeks to overpolice rather than encourage a multilateral, strong, agreed authoritative body to address these issues.

* * *

Peter Sutherland is cochairman of BP Amoco Plc and chairman and managing director of Goldman Sachs International. The former attorney general of Ireland, former European commissioner, and former director-general of the WTO and GATT was interviewed by Mike Burns.

What does it mean to be European in the twenty-first century, and how do you think Europe will look economically and politically in the year 2020? I believe that with globalization the regional identity of Europe is going to become more and more important. This does not mean in any sense that one loses one's sense of national identity. I would always be an Irishman first and a European second, rather than the other way around, but I happen to believe that an integrated Europe, which will require us to share more sovereignty, and to be more involved as a region, is both inevitable and desirable.

With globalization, we have to be in a position to positively influence the development of the world, and you cannot simply opt out. If Europe were to remain a fractured series of individual nation-states, none of them—even the most powerful—would be able to influence positively the development of the world, and as an entity we will be able to do so. We are already doing it through trade policy, where the European Union speaks with one voice. Economically, Europe will be quite successful, galvanized by the integration which is taking place, which is forcing us to become competitive and to restructure our industries on a regional basis rather than on a national basis.

I do not have a negative vision about the future of Europe. Many people look at the United States, with a far lower unemployment figure, currently at the rate of 4.5 percent against the 10.6 percent unemployment in the European Union: I think that this is a reflection of a greater economic dynamism—for the time being—in the United States, but it should also be borne in mind that between 1985 and 1992 the European Union had a greater growth rate than the United States, and secondly, the European Union today has a favorable balance of trade with the rest of the world, whereas the United States has a massive deficit. So, looking at Europe economically as being a failed entity or a failing entity, a sort of tourist resort for visiting Oriental businessmen, is really quite ridiculous. There is an inherent dynamism which the euro, in particular, is going to help to develop in Europe.

With regard to the political face of Europe in the year 2020, we will be going through our constant debate about the extent [to] which this integration process should proceed, complicated by the need to enlarge the European Union, ultimately perhaps to a membership approaching thirty.

This will require leadership and foresight at a European level, which is not very evident today: but we have muddled through—and more than muddled through. We have been rather successful in developing the European Union over some decades, and I cannot believe that we are going to permit ourselves to lose what has been achieved.

So I hope and basically believe that we will continue in our faltering progress toward greater integration. For an example, in the area of foreign policy and defense as well as the economic areas, we will begin to do more together because we have to.

How will the euro affect you personally, and how will it change Europe? If I take the latter part—how will it change Europe, because that is how it will affect each of us, including me—the euro is going to create a greater dynamism in the European economy because it will become transparently obvious what each country is doing, what each individual member state is doing, in terms of developing its economy vis-à-vis others.

Let me take a couple of examples: when we have a single European stock market—as we inevitably will have—investors, institutions, pension funds will no longer be constrained in any way to invest solely in their own country. They will look at companies and investment opportunities on a global basis, but more particularly on a Europe-wide basis. [Because] they will have no exchange risks in investing in other countries, they will simply look at the return on equity that is being provided by countries across Europe and they will invest in the companies which are providing the greatest shareholder return.

This, inevitably, will mean [a] restructuring of European industry. It will mean mergers; it will mean acquisitions; it will mean changes—rapid changes—where companies formerly leading in size in Europe will be relegated and others will improve.

This dynamism is going to be very, very positive for the citizen[s] of Europe, and it is particularly important for a small country like mine—Ireland—to be part of this process because it provides us with an access to a regional economy rather than simply being confined to a very much smaller area.

Do you feel Europe will be a global player in the new century? I do feel Europe will be a global player in the new century. It is already a global player. Having been intimately concerned with the conclusion of the Uruguay Round and setting up the World Trade Organization, I can say without hesitation that if Europe had not negotiated the Uruguay Round with one voice, there would not have been a Europe, there would not have been a World Trade Organization, and the whole process of globalization would not be taking place as it is taking place.

We need a balance in the global economy and government structures. We cannot simply have one player—the United States—which is so dominant in debate, whether it be political, economic, foreign policy, or defense areas, that there is only one decisionmaker. That is not good either for the United States or for Europe, and it would ultimately lead to tensions and pressures even greater than those which already exist between the major economic players in the world, the United States, Europe, and Japan.

This is something which prominent thinkers on both sides of the Atlantic are saying—that we need a balance in global governments, and the only way that you can acquire that is by Europe speaking with one voice and playing a constructive role in developing relationships, particularly transatlantic relationships but [also] global relationships, as a single player.

What do you see as the major threat to Europe in the new century? There are a series of major threats to Europe in the new century. The first one is to retain our economic model, which requires a certain degree of social support, if you like a social welfare system, at the same time as competing in a global economy where competition could be argued to create a race to the bottom in terms of tax or social policies, labor policies, and so on. It's possible to marry both. In other words, it is possible to increase competitiveness and productivity whilst retaining a sense of balance in regard to social responsibility within the European Union as a whole and the member states individually in particular.

The real crises that we will face in the new century are going to be global crises. There is, therefore, clearly a need to coordinate responses to environmental threats globally, and Europe has to play a significant role in that. Equally, we cannot pretend or profess indifference to major political events that are taking place in other parts of the world, including in our own continent.

We cannot, therefore, ignore the fact that there will be political and human crises around the world [in which] we have to play a part, and I see this ultimately as the constant battle, in political terms, between nationalism and a sense of recognition that we live in an interdependent world and that interdependence demands that we act together.

It's not irrelevant to Europe, for an example, that the emissions coming from coal-fired power stations in Asia have a major effect on global warming, nor that the forests in Brazil and their destruction has environmental effects everywhere else.

The real threat to the future is the threat that we cannot globally combine in advancing policies which are of importance to the survival of the planet and the people on it.

Where do you see the boundaries of Europe in the twenty-first century? The question of the physical boundaries [of] an integrated Europe is largely a question of pragmatic analysis. Can we restructure the European Union, institutionally, to actually effectively deal with the larger size of this extended Europe without alienating the individual peoples of Europe because of the size of the structure that they are part of and the fact that they feel that they have a diminishing involvement in decisionmaking? And secondly, are the countries like Russia who might join, ultimately—and that is a very long way away—are they able to play a full part in the system and abide by the disciplines and have the same commitments that exist with the European Union?

Or is the membership of Country X just too big a bite to take, as a result of which the entire edifice will become unworkable? I don't think therefore there is any predefined point beyond which you cannot go. It all depends on what can effectively be achieved.

My own view is that we have to tread very cautiously in extending and growing the European Union, because there isn't much point to anybody joining an entity which, as a result of their joining, is going to collapse under the weight of its size and inadequate structures.

On the other hand, we have a moral obligation to not be an exclusive club that denies access to those who have the commitment to the type of society which fundamentally we believe is appropriate—a democratic society, a society that protects human rights, a society which economically has developed to a level that it can accept and respond to the disciplines within the EU which are required to make it function as a single place.

So it's a pragmatic question. Jean Monnet and the other founding fathers of the European Union never saw it as being an exclusive club. They saw it as part of a process that ultimately—and maybe this is utopia—would lead to a greater global governing structure.

So I don't put a boundary. I don't say that Russia could never join the European Union, but star-gazing as to when and how that will actually happen may not be appropriate because at the moment it's clear that we are a very, very long way away from that being conceivable.

Do you see unemployment being one of the snags or pitfalls lying ahead for the European Union? The problem of unemployment can only be solved by the creation of a much more entrepreneurial society in Europe than exists at the moment. Every year in the United States an incredible 900,000 new businesses are created: 800,000 of them are gone within a year. But they have created and are creating, for example, in new technology, Internet technology and so on, advances which Europe simply hasn't duplicated.

They have created the Microsofts, the Intels, the Amazon dot-coms, all of the new companies that are growing and expanding and creating new employment.

They have lost, in the last six years, 42 million jobs, but they have created 76 million jobs. That's why they have a very low unemployment rate, and contrary to some of the impressions here, these are not hamburger-flipper jobs. Eighty percent of the new jobs created in the last six years in the United States have been paying above the median level of pay.

So let's not disparage the United States model as being totally irrelevant to us. We may have different perceptions about some aspects of the welfare state and how it should develop, but we have to recognize that the United States is showing a dynamism in creating new entrepreneurs who are the ones who are going to create the jobs in the future, which we haven't done.

We pump all our money into old industries in Europe, and we have to change the culture of our young people to get them out of the fixation with security in jobs and into the attitude of creating new businesses.

I actually think we are already doing it in Ireland, although it's not very obvious yet. The real successes in Ireland, nobody reads about in the newspapers. The small software companies, which are incredibly dynamic, with young people who are living in a world which is very different from the one that you and I were brought up in, and we don't even know of their existence. They don't want us to know of their existence. I don't mean that in the sense that they are hiding it, but it's irrelevant to them. They are living in a different world.

We have to create this dynamism which Europe has lacked, and we have to create a more entrepreneurial society with people who are prepared to go out and start their own thing in a different way that links into education, which is the key to the whole business.

The catalytic effect of the euro, which is going to change attitudes in terms of shareholder values and so on, is going to have an immensely positive effect. We held ourselves back by having a whole lot of state monopolies in Europe which were not subject to competitive forces.

These are going to become dynamic—they have to become dynamic to survive, whether it's our telecom companies or air transport companies. They have to adapt to change. They have to adapt to the challenge of change, and by doing that, the overall economy of Europe is going to improve.

Where would we be in Ireland if we didn't have competition in air transport? It's good for Aer Lingus [the Irish State airline], and it's certainly good for Ireland. It's reducing costs; it's creating mobility; it's developing our capacity to relate to the outside world, and all [this is] a good thing.

There is another problem in Europe—the demographic one. It is really serious in terms of the pension time bomb that is going to exist in Europe, with a lot more old people, particularly in Italy and Spain, where we are not regenerating population.

Nor have we funded properly our pension schemes into the future. So we are leaving a huge burden across Europe. It's not an Irish problem to the same extent or a United Kingdom problem, but it's a European problem and it's a euro problem.

There has to be a rapid recognition that the funding of pensions into the future, particularly having regard to the demographic time bomb that we are facing, is creating a major problem and will create a major problem in the future unless the funding issue is addressed—which means taking more money from individuals or making individuals more responsible for their own pension scheme.

ITALY

Massimo Capuano, chief executive officer of Borsa Italiana Spa in Italy, was interviewed in Milan by Stephen Jewkes.

Born September 9, 1954, in Palermo, Italy, Capuano is married with two children. He has an honors degree in electrical engineering from the Universita degli Studi in Rome (1978). Capuano worked for Rank Xerox, IBM, and McKinsey and Co. before taking up his position in 1998 as president and CEO at Borsa Italiana Spa, the company that runs Milan's stock exchange.

Do you feel European? At the moment let's say I feel a "virtual" European. But I can see in all the various cultural, professional, and social stimuli the potential to become an actual European citizen.

What does it mean to you to be European in the twenty-first century? It means perhaps being able to transmit the idea of being European to the next generation, which, in my case, means to my children. I'm part of a generation that's seen Europe being created bit by bit, in stages. The good thing about being European in the twenty-first century will be that you're born with the concept already there.

How do you think Europe will look economically and politically in the year 2020? I think medium- to long-term economic success is closely tied to the feasibility of creating a political Europe. It seems to me 2020 is a bit premature for the political project to be seen through. Economically, however, Europe will have had the opportunity by then of putting in place the necessary infrastructure, such as tax systems and standardized transmission networks, which are the basis of all investment projects.

Politically, it's true there'll be a new generation in power with a stronger European identity than the present one. But there'll still be friction between local and supranational politics, even though the rules should be in place for tackling the problem, which I see as very troublesome. As CEO of the Italian bourse, I see European financial markets more integrated as well as more segmented. The trend is for markets to specialize so we'll have segments for high-growth companies, blue chip stocks, mid caps, [and] small caps.

How will the euro affect you personally? Coming from an international and multinational background, I don't see that much impact on my present mindset.

Do you think Europe will be a global player in the twenty-first century? I think so, providing it can build the proper common infrastructure regarding taxes, administration, transport, and information networks.

Do you think Italy will be able to adapt politically and economically to the new Europe in the age of globalization? Italy has always been pro-Europe, and almost all of Italy's political parties today are in favor of integration. Italians, too, as they showed recently when they stumped up the money to help get the country into monetary union through the so-called euro-tax, are pro-Europe.

That's a good starting point. Now it's up to those who take the decisions to come up with the plans. It's my opinion that on this score there's still some way to go. It's not just a question of applying European directives. There has to be active planning to make sure we stay in Europe.

And that means difficult decisions are needed on issues like labor market flexibility, welfare, and health. The problem of economic rigor associated with EMU is behind us now, though we will be feeling the repercussions of the tough measures taken to get Italy into the single currency for a while yet, as well as the effects of the country's mountain of debt.

* * *

Emma Marcegaglia, president of Italy's young businessperson's association and president of Young Entrepreneurs of Europe (YES), was interviewed by Stephen Jewkes in Milan.

Do you feel European? I certainly do. Both as a businesswoman and as a private individual. While in the past I tended to travel a lot to the United States and Southeast Asia, I now do a lot more of my traveling in Europe, both for business and for pleasure. Compared to, say, five years ago, I feel increasingly more European.

What does it mean to you to be European in the twenty-first century? With the advent of the euro, we will feel increasingly European. As time goes by, we will feel our European identity more and lose some of our attachment to our individual countries.

How do you think Europe will look economically and politically in the year 2020? Europe will have to become increasingly united from a political point of view. The euro was a first step, and we're now heading toward greater harmonization on fiscal measures and the labor market.

In about twenty to thirty years Europe will have to be much more politically united, with its national institutions steadily losing their powers. However, there should be more democracy than now. I would like to see, for example, the president of the Commission or of the EU Parliament elected directly by the European electorate.

I'm upbeat about the economic future for Europe and am confident it will be able to overcome certain hurdles such as overly high public spending, generous welfare states, [and] inefficient state systems. It will become an area where there will be less production [that is] low tech and more high-quality, value-added manufacturing. It's true that with monetary policy concentrated in Frankfurt, certain countries have one less weapon to defend their economies with, but that's not a bad thing. In Italy, devaluation helped us one year, but the next we had inflation. What I feel is that the greater rigor imposed by a centralized monetary policy should be offset by more flexible labor markets with greater mobility for workers.

How will the euro affect you personally? As a businesswoman, many payments are already made in euros. From a personal point of view, in eighteen months when we have the euro in our pocket it will make us feel more European. Money does inform identity to a certain extent.

Do you think Europe will be a global player in the twenty-first century? Absolutely yes. One of the main aims of the euro project was to make Europe a global player, something Italy or Germany by [itself] couldn't do.

Do you think Italy will be able to adapt politically and economically to the new Europe in the age of globalization? Yes, even though there are a few problems. It's very hard to carry out structural reform in Italy. But if you look at Italy ten years ago, there have already been a lot of important changes. The whole mentality of the Italians is undergoing change. The economic discipline imposed by Europe is doing us good. There's always been a lot of populism in Italian politics, but the voters are now starting to punish governments that don't carry out what they promised. Being part of Europe has also forced governments to do things like the liberalization of our markets. I also feel that the trade unions, which have enormous political clout in Italy, will have a less important role in the European future.

LUXEMBOURG

Prime Minister of Luxembourg Jean-Claude Juncker was interviewed by Alan Osborn in the capital city of Luxembourg.

Luxembourg, it's often said, punches above its weight diplomatically. Perhaps because it is so tiny and for centuries has had to deal with far more powerful neighbors, its leaders have become skilled in the arts of negotiation, of political cut and thrust, and of knowing when to compromise and when not to. If the dream of a federal Europe becomes a reality, it will owe much to Luxembourg's role as a fixer.

Few European leaders can out-box Luxembourg prime minister Jean-Claude Juncker in this area. At forty-four, he is already a veteran of top-level EU negotiations, having chaired the key council setting up the ground-breaking Maastricht Treaty in 1991 and subsequently playing a major role in brokering deals to get economic and monetary union off the ground. The key decisions on setting up the single European currency were taken under his presidency of the EU Council in 1997.

The son of a steel worker who was a committed trade unionist, Juncker grew up in a political environment and has been active in public life since graduating from Strasbourg University as a lawyer. He entered his country's government at the age of twenty-eight and became prime minister in 1995. In the June 1999 elections he led his Christian Social Party to victory and is now as secure politically as any government leader in Europe.

Juncker's shrewd political skills and relative youth suggest he could reasonably expect to be a major player on the European stage for another twenty-five years or more. He spoke of the European Union as it is today and how it could develop in the twenty-first century.

Do you feel European or Luxembourgish? Both things do not exclude each other; on the contrary, they are complementary. Being a Luxembourger means being a European by conviction through necessity. Luxembourg knows that it would never have developed as a politically independent, economically competitive, and socially stable country without its integration in the European Union.

Since Luxembourg owes its existence and prosperity to its membership in the European Union, Luxembourgers tend to consider the European Union as the most natural thing in the world and are thus Europeans as well as Luxembourgers.

What does it mean to be a European at the beginning of the twenty-first century? Probably more than it meant fifty years ago. One has to consider that the European integration process was born out of the ashes of the old European order, a nationalist order that was at the core of the two world wars that were fought on this continent. Ever since the 1950s the political will to create a European sphere of security, solidarity, and prosperity has taken shape and has brought us to the creation of the European Union.

Concepts like European citizenship lead to a higher degree of consciousness that being a European means as much as being English, French, German, or Luxembourgish. All these nationalities share centuries of common history that in its diversity has created a really unique European identity that is well worth preserving. I believe that the European integration process as well as the European social model, for instance, [set] examples for any part of the world to move toward more cooperation and less confrontation.

What will the position of Europe be in the world in the twenty-first century, economically, politically, and culturally? Will Europe be a global force in these areas? Europe, or the European Union at least, is already the biggest global player as far as its economic strengths and impact are concerned. The Amsterdam Treaty and the recent decisions taken at the Cologne summit [June 1999] will give the European Union an improved visibility in international and security politics. It should, however, be clear that the European Union has no ambitions whatsoever to become a competitor to anybody. What we want is to be a reliable partner, ready to assume responsibilities and act according to them.

What are the possible threats to Europe, both internally and externally? Europe, being the complicated continent it is, will always be in danger of being haunted by the ghosts that we thought to have banned forever after World War II. Nationalism and extremism still exist in Europe, and they still have enough destructive potential to destabilize parts of the continent. With the decisions to enlarge the European Union to central and eastern Europe, a first step has been made to contain this potential. Other steps will have to follow, necessarily. Geographical enlargement is one thing, further economic and political integration another.

How do you see your own personal future in terms of Europe? Will you continue to try and play a role in the European Union? Playing a role in the European Union is much more a question of necessity than of personal ambitions. I cannot imagine myself applying for any role in the European Union just for the sake of playing a particular role. Politics, especially European politics, is not a game. When problems arise— and they do arise very often—between member states, everyone has the duty to try and solve these problems. If I can be helpful in looking for or finding such solutions, I take it as a great honor to be asked to do so. The fact that I am a representative from Luxembourg, which is particularly well known for its commitment to the European integration process and its long experience in European affairs, tends to make life a little easier sometimes.

SWEDEN

Anna Lindh, foreign minister of Sweden, was interviewed by Robert J. Guttman.

What will Europe look like in 2020? We will see in the next century that we are more integrated in Europe. Enlargement will continue to lead to a more integrated Europe. I hope that in the year 2020, enlargement will have gone through. We will also see the Balkan countries as members of the European Union.

At the same time, we will have big regional differences, and that is important as well—not to take the cultural differences away in Europe—but we will have joined together in our efforts both for security and for jobs, for the environment, and all those questions which we can most easily solve together. When I'm talking about Europe in 2020, I'm talking about the European Union. It will be the dominant institution, absolutely.

How will the euro affect you personally and how will it affect Europe? The euro is part of the peace process. The euro might integrate Europe more, but at the same time one has to deal with the negative aspects of the euro; as for example, the democratic and political influence.

Do you think Europe's going to be a global power in the new century? Yes. It's very important that Europe has a more developed discussion on foreign policy. Europe is now starting on a more Common Foreign and Security Policy, and that is very important also to be a global player, but also to take care of Europe's own security; as for example, Kosovo, which shows this is necessary.

As a former environment minister, do you think Europe's going to continue to be a leader in the environment field in the next twenty years? I hope so because so far Europe has really been dominating the international scene concerning the environment, and Europe should continue in order to get other parts of the world to go along and to prove that it's possible to have economic growth at the same time as you have sustainable development.

Why is it that Europe seems to be more ahead of the other countries on the environment? We started to deal with the environmental problems before most other countries did.

Then another factor which is quite important is that you have also a very strong belief among the European citizens and a very strong concern about the environment. And so it's also very important for politicians to really deal with the environment.

And the third reason, and it is the same for European and U.S. enterprises, [is] that all businesses realize that the environment is important for having a more long-term perspective on business, and therefore also the business society, at least in some European countries, cares quite a lot about the environment and getting sustainable development and about production, for example.

Will Europe continue to be an environmental leader in the next twenty years, showing the way to the United States, Japan, and other countries? Yes, Europe will especially show the way for Asia and all the developing countries who are now growing very quick[ly] and building their infrastructure. It's very important that Europe shows that there are possibilities to have an infrastructure and a growing economy, but at the same time care for the environment. And there, both Europe and the U.S. have common interests. Otherwise, we will have problems with developing countries not taking care of the economy.

I hope Europe will provide a model for these developing nations on the environment. One thing more concerning Europe and developing countries I also feel is very important. Europe really can develop partnerships with the developing countries to show them that the European Union is for an open Europe. You won't have Europe looking only into its own problem, but the European Union will really be cooperating and developing a partnership with developing countries to prove that the European Union is open to the world outside Europe.

What are the major threats to Europe in the twenty-first century? Internally, as long as we can handle democracy and human rights in all European countries, security will be improved, and what we saw in Kosovo will just be part of history. Kosovo proves that it's very important that we are very concerned about human rights and democracy. We also need to have open frontiers not only toward developing countries, but also, for example, with Russia. Even if Russia won't be a member of the European Union, the European Union will have a very close cooperation and partnership with Russia.

UNITED KINGDOM

Robin Cook, foreign secretary of the United Kingdom, was interviewed by David Lennon in London.

Do you feel European? Yes. I am proud to be European, just as I am proud to be Scottish and proud to be British. I believe strongly that the days have gone when you had to define yourself in terms of a single nationality, ethnicity, or religion.

The modern Europe proves that a country is stronger for being diverse and for having citizens of varied ethnic and religious background[s]. Sadly, the conflict over Kosovo showed that it is a message not everyone has understood.

What does it mean to be European in the twenty-first century? It means being part of a common European home in which diversity is celebrated, national cultures are thriving, and pan-European cooperation comes naturally. It means accepting each other for how we are, rather than trying to create a homogeneous single whole. It means being as at home in Warsaw and Budapest as in Paris or Edinburgh. And it means traveling, working, living, and learning freely and happily across the continent.

How do you think Europe will look politically and economically in the year 2020? Following the conflict in Kosovo, Europe faces a major challenge—can we end, once and for all, the conflicts and divisions that have plagued our continent for so many centuries? Right now, Europe has the chance finally to put its past behind it and create a new Europe founded on peace and prosperity from Belfast to Belgrade.

If we meet that challenge, then Europe in 2020 will have—across the continent—democratic national governments, respect for human rights, and observance of the rule of law. Ours will be a continent of individual sovereign nations that freely come together to work together for their mutual benefit. We will have a European Union that embraces the whole of Europe, either as members or as close partners. And we will have a NATO [North Atlantic Treaty Organization] that still underpins the security of the continent.

Within the European Union, we will have an agenda genuinely set by the concerns of our peoples. We will be working together fighting the drug trade and protecting the environment. We will have a clear voice in the world and a respect among our partners in the international community, who will know that European solidarity is not a threat but [is] good for them as well.

We will have a powerful, information-based economy, in which our workers are well trained and have the skills they need to find and keep jobs. We will need to make sure that everyone is part of that economy and that no part of society gets left out. European companies will work across the continent and do business in each other's countries with ease. And Europe will be fully plugged into the global economy, as barriers to trade will have come down and the economic links between different regions of the world will have multiplied.

How will the euro change the EU? The single currency is a profound step for Europe. It will, of course, make business across the euro zone much easier and encourage our own and foreign companies to see the European market as a whole. Greater price transparency will intensify competition across the single market. The pressure for economic reform will be increased, and if the governments of Europe respond positively to that challenge, their economies will become more competitive as a result. Lower interest rates and inflation will help this process. But for those countries in Euroland, it will also foster a much stronger sense of European identity. It is a step that will have a direct impact on the lives of all our peoples.

Britain has not joined the first wave of countries in the euro zone. The economic conditions were not right at the time. But when those economic conditions do fall into place, we will want to offer the choice to our people in a referendum. And despite not being part of the single currency, we are keen to see it succeed—after all, we do more trade with the euro zone than with anyone else, so its prosperity is our prosperity as well.

Do you think Europe will be a global player in the twenty-first century? By speaking and acting with one voice, Europe should become an increasingly influential global player. The appointment of Javier Solana as the high representative for Europe's Common Foreign and Security Policy is an important step. I am personally delighted that Solana will be the first occupant of this new post. He will bring to it the right mix of authority, experience, and global perspective. The ongoing debate launched by Britain on European security and defense should give Europe the capability to act effectively. What we need to learn now is the habit of talking and acting together—not so we can dilute our countries' individual sovereignty, but the reverse. If we work together, then we all have more influence than if we worked individually.

What do you see as the major threats to Europe in the twenty-first century? Globalization is bringing us many benefits, but it also brings with it new threats and new dangers. The drug trade is now second only to the oil trade in value. International criminals lead the way in working effectively across borders. Weapons proliferators are learning how easy it can be to ship dangerous weapons around. And the global environment is in serious danger.

We will have to continue to be resolute in standing up for our values and defending our security. If we are, then despite all the threats we face, Europe will pull through.

Notes

CHAPTER 2

1. Robert Schuman Declaration, May 9, 1950.
2. Quoted from Les Entretiens Européens d'Epernay, "Quelle Union Après Amsterdam et les Elargissements?" January 23, 1999.
3. Ibid.
4. Karel van Miert, personal interview.
5. Quote from *Le Nouvel Observateur,* no. 1783, January 7, 1999.
6. The information in the Appendix is used with permission.

CHAPTER 3

1. *Politiken,* "Danish Vote 'No'," June 2, 1992.
2. Simon Serfaty, "Memories of Europe's Future: Farewell to Yesteryear," CSIS Press, Washington, D.C., 1999.
3. Strabo, *Geographika,* first century.
4. Euan Cameron, ed., *Early Modern Europe: An Oxford History* (Oxford University Press, 1999).
5. Jose Maria Aznar, quoted in *EUROPE Magazine,* October 1998.
6. U.S. Information Agency, pamphlet, 1998.
7. Gerhard Schröder, interview broadcast on BBC, March 1998.
8. Hugo Young, *This Blessed Plot: Britain and Europe from Churchill to Blair* (Overlook Press, October 1999).
9. *EUROPE Magazine,* April 1999.
10. "The New European Way" discussion document, introduced by Finance Minister Rudolf Edlinger of Austria and approved by socialist ministers of the EU Finance Council, November 1998.
11. Ibid.
12. Romano Prodi, *EUROPE Magazine,* June 1999.

13. Ulrich Beck, quoted in *New York Times,* April 9, 1999.
14. Leszek Balcerowicz, quoted in *EUROPE Magazine,* June 1999.

CHAPTER 4

1. The last survey was taken in 1996 (see *Eurobarometer,* no. 45, Spring 1996), but such perceptions change slowly.
2. See "The Global Union and the Nation State," *Foreign Affairs* (September 1997).
3. The Danish referendum on the euro was held on September 28, 2000, and the first months of the spring 2000 campaign were dominated by the political issue of the future of Denmark as a nation-state in an economic and monetary union.
4. Peter F. Drucker, *Management Challenges in the 21st Century* (HarperBusiness, 1999).

CHAPTER 5

1. Joschka Fischer, quoted in Ministers of European Parliament, January 15, 1999.
2. Romano Prodi, speaking before the Royal Political Science Academy, Madrid, May 1998.
3. Hans van den Broek, *EUROPE Magazine,* April 1998.
4. EU agriculture commissioner Franz Fischler, *EUROPE Magazine,* November 1999.

CHAPTER 6

1. Bill Clinton, quoted in *EUROPE Magazine,* October 1992.
2. Bill Clinton, quoted on White House website, May 15, 1999.
3. Jozeas van Aartsen, "European Security with the Americans If Possible, on Our Own When Necessary," (Ministry of Foreign Affairs, 1999).
4. Ibid.

CHAPTER 7

1. The ten countries are Bulgaria, the Czech Republic, Estonia, Hungary, Latvia, Lithuania, Poland, Romania, Slovakia, and Slovenia.

CHAPTER 8

1. The debate in President Bill Clinton's first term and remarks by Secretary of State Warren Christopher in April–May 1993 (Washington, D.C.: U.S. State Department).

2. Samuel Huntington, "The Lonely Superpower," *Foreign Affairs* 78, no. 2 (March–April 1999).

3. James Chace, *Acheson: The Secretary of State Who Created the American World* (Simon and Schuster, 1998).

4. James Schlesinger, *The National Interest,* January 1999.

5. Geoffrey Treverton, quoted in David C. Gompert and F. Stephen Larrabee, eds., *America and Europe: A Partnership for a New Era* (Cambridge University Press, 1997).

6. Sir Leon Brittan, *Diet of Brussels: The Changing Face of Europe* (Little, Brown, 2000).

7. "Towards Transatlantic Partnership," Part 3, a document presented to the European Parliament by the Transatlantic Policy Network, September 1998.

8. Javier Solana, *The Economist,* March 13, 1999.

9. Interview with a senior European diplomat, October 1996.

10. Gordon Adams, *Financial Times,* January 28, 1999.

11. Stuart Eizenstat, *The National Interest.* See also his "Farewell Remarks to EU Committee of the American Chamber of Commerce," Brussels, February 8, 1996.

12. Philippe de Schoutheete, *Une Europe pour tous* (Paris: Editions Odile Jacob, 1997). See also the English-language translation, *The Case for Europe: Unity, Diversity, and Democracy in the European Union* (Boulder, Colo.: Lynne Rienner, 2000).

13. Richard Holbrooke, "America: A European Power," *Foreign Affairs* (March–April 1995).

CHAPTER 9

1. Lionel Barber, "Seeking Closer Asian Ties," *EUROPE Magazine* (November 1997).

2. Terry Martin, unpublished report on ASEM, January 2000.

3. Ibid.

4. Personal interview with Etienne Reuter, head of the EU delegation to Hong Kong, July 7, 1999.

5. Ibid.

6. Pascal Lamy, May 19, 2000

7. European Union, *The European Union: A Guide for Americans* (European Union, 1999).

8. Ibid.

9. Interview with Etienne Reuter, July 7, 1999.

10. Ibid.

11. Ibid.

12. Personal interview with Ove Juul Jorgensen, head of the EU delegation to Japan, February 28, 2000.

13. Ibid.

14. Ibid.

15. *International Herald Tribune,* January 7, 1999.

16. *International Herald Tribune,* January 8, 1999.

17. Interview with Ove Juul Jorgensen.

18. Ibid.

CHAPTER 10

1. "Santer to Tour Middle East," MEMO/98/9, European Commission, Brussels, February 5, 1998.

2. Personal interview with Diego de Ojeda at the European Commission's directorate-general for external affairs, March 11, 1999.

3. Ibid.

4. Ibid.

5. "The Middle East: Role of the European Union in the Peace Process and Its Future Assistance," Communication 16/01/98, a proposal issued by the European Parliament, directorate-general for external affairs, legislative planning division, and adopted in committee on January 21, 1999.

CHAPTER 11

1. See A. Cohen, "The New IMF Credits to Russia and the Russian Economic Crisis," testimony to House Banking Committee, U.S. Congress, June 10, 1999. Cohen does not include the U.S.$35 billion special facility package paid by Germany to ensure Soviet troop withdrawals from the former DDR, which included direct aid and credits. See also J. Odding-Smee, "What Went Wrong in Russia?" *Central European Economic Review,* November 18, 1998; Janine R. Wedel, *Collision and Collusion: The Strange Case of Western Aid to Eastern Europe 1989–1998* (St. Martin's Press, 1998); and Wedel, "Tainted Transactions: Harvard, the Chubais Clan and Russia's Ruin," *The National Interest* (Spring 2000).

2. Kommersant, July 21, 1991. See also J. M. Waller, "The KGB and Its Successors," *Perspective* 4 (April–May 1994), Institute for the Study of Conflict, Ideology, and Policy, Boston University.

3. "Russia May Become Oil Importer—Minister," Reuters, November 20, 1998.

4. Martin Walker, "Assassination Puts Democracy in Peril," editorial, *Los Angeles Times*, November 29, 1998.

5. "Presidency Conclusions," European Council, December 7, 1998, Vienna.

6. Interview with the Paavo Lipponen, Helsinki, May 14, 1998.

7. "The Northern Dimension," Foreign Ministry of Finland, 1998.

8. Michael Emerson, *Redrawing the Map of Europe* (Macmillan, 1998); see also the website of the Center for European Policy Studies, www.ceps.be.

CHAPTER 12

1. See Adrian Cox and Antonique Koning, *Understanding European Community Aid* (Overseas Development Institute, London, and European Commission, Brussels, 1997); and "Communication from the Commission to the Council and the European Parliament on Complementarity Between Community and Member State Policies on Development Cooperation," draft, February 16, 1999.

2. Cox and Koning, *Understanding European Community Aid.*

3. OECD Development Assistance Committee, *Shaping the 21st Century: The Contribution of Development Cooperation,* May 1996; and Clare Short, UK secretary of state for international development, responding to criticism of aid policy in "Fifty Years of Failure," a booklet by the Center for Policy Studies, London 1999.

4. European Parliament Resolution of September 30, 1993, on the Commission's communication on development cooperation policy in the run-up to 2000.

5. *A European Community Strategy for Private Sector Development in ACP Countries,* a communication from the Commission to the Council and the European Parliament, Brussels, November 20, 1998; and "Development and the Private Sector: A Partnership for Change," a speech by Clare Short, UK secretary of state for international development, at the Institute of Directors, London, July 8, 1997.

6. Development Policy, European Commission directorate-general for development, Brussels, March 11, 1999.

7. *Feeding the World's Hungry: Is It the Greatest Humanitarian Challenge of All? Humanitarian Affairs Review* (Autumn 1998), based on statistics from OECD.

8. Emma Bonino, quoted in *EUROPE Magazine,* November 1995.

9. Statistics provided by the European Community Humanitarian Office (ECHO), Brussels, March 1999.

10. Commission of the European Communities, *Annual Report on Humanitarian Aid,* Brussels, September 3, 1997.

11. Information from the 1995 midterm review of the fourth Lomé convention, European Parliament directorate-general for research, January 1996; and from a personal interview with Phillipe Darmuzey, Lomé negotiator for the European Commission directorate-general for development, March 12, 1999.

12. Statistics from the PHARE and TACIS Information Center, Brussels, March 1999; and from a personal interview with Fidelma O'Shaughnessy of the PHARE Information Center, March 12, 1999.

13. From a personal interview with Mikael Barfod, head of unit, ECHO-4 Planning, Strategy, and Policy Analyses, March 11, 1999.

14. From a personal interview with Philip Lowe, European Commission director-general for development, March 12, 1999.

15. From a personal interview with Alaistair Fernie, UK Department for International Development, March 18, 1999.

16. Interview with Philip Lowe.

CHAPTER 13

1. Many of the opening thoughts in this chapter are drawn from my own published work in the *Financial Times* and *The Birth of the Euro: The Financial Guide to EMU* (Penguin Books, 1999).

2. Paper delivered to the Talleroies Seminar, June 1998.

3. For French and German traditions in economic policy, see Lionel Barber, *Britain and the European Agenda,* Center for European Reform, January 1998.

4. Interview with Wim Duisenberg, *Financial Times*, December 3, 1998.
5. *Financial Times*, May 5, 1998.
6. ECB, monthly bulletin, February 1999.
7. Dominique Strauss-Kahn, speech to French banker's association, December 1998.
8. On the attitude of UK trade unions toward EMU, reference various speeches and public remarks by John Monks, TUC general secretary.
9. David Smith, *Euro Futures, Five Scenarios for the Next Millennium* (Capstone Publishing, 1997).
10. "The Dollar and the Euro," *Foreign Affairs* 76, no. 4 (July–August 1997).
11. For a contrary view, see Martin Wolf, "Euro's World Test," *Financial Times*, July 7, 1998.
12. Interview with senior Federal Reserve official, November 1997.

CHAPTER 14

1. Economist Intelligence Unit, quoted in Business Briefs, *EUROPE Magazine*, November 1999.

CHAPTER 16

1. Philip J. O'Connell (with Vanessa Gash and Rory O'Donnell), *Country Employment Policy Reviews: Ireland* (Dublin: Government Publications, 1999).
2. Telephone interviews, April–May 1999.
3. Ibid.
4. Ibid.
5. Ibid.
6. Ibid.
7. Joop Hartog, *The Netherlands: So What's So Special About the Dutch Model?* Employment and Training Paper No. 54 (International Labour Organization, 1999).
8. OECD, *Employment Outlook*, June 1998.
9. Per Kongshoj Madsen, *Denmark: Flexibility, Security, and Labour Market Success*, Employment and Training Paper No. 53 (International Labour Organization, 1999).
10. Telephone interviews, April–May 1999.
11. Dirk Hudig, "Key Ingredients for Job Creation Recipe," *European Voice*, April 8–14, 1999.
12. Telephone interviews, April–May 1999.
13. Ibid.
14. Ibid.
15. Peter Auer, *Employment Revival in Europe: Labour Market Success in Austria, Denmark, Ireland, and the Netherlands* (International Labour Organization, 2000).

Further Reading

Armstrong, Kenneth A., and Simon J. Bulmer. *The Governance of the Single European Market*. Manchester University Press, 1998.

Blackwill, Robert D. *The Future of Transatlantic Relations*. Council on Foreign Relations, 1999.

Bretherton, Charlotte, and John Vogler. *The European Union as a Global Actor*. Routledge, 1999.

Buchan, David. *Europe: The Strange Superpower*. Dartmouth, 1993.

Chabot, Christian N. *Understanding the EURO: The Clear and Concise Guide to the New Trans-European Economy*. McGraw-Hill, 1998.

Corbett, Richard. *The Treaty of Maastricht: From Conception to Ratification: A Comprehensive Reference Guide*. Longman, 1993.

de Schoutheete, Philippe. *The Case for Europe: Unity, Diversity, and Democracy in the European Union*. Lynne Rienner Publishers, 2000.

Dinan, Desmond. *Ever Closer Union: An Introduction to European Integration*. 2nd ed. Lynne Rienner Publishers, 1999.

Dinan, Desmond, ed. *Encyclopedia of the European Union*. Updated ed. Lynne Rienner Publishers, 2000.

Duina, Francesco G. *Harmonizing Europe: Nation-States Within the Common Market*. State University of New York Press, 1999.

Edwards, Geoffrey, and David Spence, eds. *The European Commission*. Longman, 1994.

EUROPE Magazine, the official publication of the European Commission, published in the United States ten times per year.

Featherstone, Kevin, and Roy Ginsberg. *The United States and the EU in the 1990s: Partners in Transition*. St. Martin's Press, 1996.

Feld, Werner J. *The Integration of the European Union and Domestic Political Issues*. Praeger Publishers, 1998.

Frost, Gerald, and William E. Odom, eds. *The Congress of Prague*. AEI Press, 1997.

Grilli, Enzo. *European Community and Developing Countries.* Cambridge University Press, 1993.

Haass, Richard N., ed. *Transatlantic Tensions: The United States, Europe, and Problem Countries.* Brookings Institution Press, 1999.

Hocking, Brian, and Michael Smith. *Beyond Foreign Economic Policy: The United States, the Single European Market and the Changing World Economy.* Pinter Publishers, 1997.

Hunnings, Neville. *European Courts.* Cartermill, 1996.

Purcell, Susan Kaufman, and Françoise Simon, eds. *Europe and Latin America in the World Economy.* Lynne Rienner Publishers, 1995.

Kenen, Peter. *Economic and Monetary Union in Europe: Moving Beyond Maastricht.* Cambridge University Press, 1995.

Keohane, Robert, and Helen Milner, eds. *Internationalization and Domestic Politics.* Cambridge University Press, 1996.

Mannin, Mike, ed. *Pushing Back the Boundaries: The European Union and Central and Eastern Europe.* Manchester University Press, 1999.

McCormick, John Spencer. *The European Union: Politics and Policies.* Westview Press, 1999.

McNamara, Kathleen R. *The Currency of Ideas: Monetary Politics in the European Union.* Cornell University Press, 1999.

Miall, Hugh. *Shaping a New European Order.* Council on Foreign Relations Press, 1994.

Mortensen, Jorgen. *Improving Economic and Social Cohesion in the EC.* St. Martin's Press, 1994.

Nelsen, Brent, and Alexander Stubb. *The European Union: Readings on the Theory and Practice of European Integration.* 2nd ed. Lynne Rienner Publishers, 1998.

Newman, Michael. *Democracy, Sovereignty and the European Union.* St. Martin's Press, 1996.

Peterson, John. 1996. *Europe and America: The Prospects for Partnership.* Routledge, 1996.

Peterson, John, and Elizabeth E. Bomberg. *Decision-Making in the European Union.* St. Martin's Press, 1999.

Piening, Christopher. *Global Europe: The European Union in World Affairs.* Lynne Rienner Publishers, 1997.

Pinder, Jonathan. *European Community: The Building of a Union.* 2nd ed. Oxford University Press, 1995.

Pond, Elizabeth. *The Rebirth of Europe.* Brookings Institution Press, 1999.

Reinicke, Wolfgang H. *Deepening the Atlantic: Toward a New Transatlantic Marketplace.* Bertelsmann Foundation, 1999.

Rhodes, Carolyn, ed. *The European Union in the World Community.* Lynne Rienner Publishers, 1998.

Rodrik, Dani. *The Global Economy and Developing Countries: Making Openness Work.* Johns Hopkins University Press, 1999.

Sperling, J., and E. Kirchner. *Recasting the European Order: Security Architectures and Economic Cooperation.* Manchester University Press, 1997.

Springer, Beverly. *The European Union and Its Citizens: The Social Agenda.* Greenwood Press, 1994.

Story, Jonathan, and Ingo Walter. *Political Economy of Financial Integration in Europe: The Battle of the Systems.* MIT Press, 1997.

Usher, John. *General Principles of European Community Law.* Longman, 1996.

Wallace, Helen, and William Wallace, eds. *Policy-making in the European Union.* Oxford University Press, 1996.

Watson, Alison M. S. *Aspects of European Monetary Integration: The Politics of Convergence.* St. Martin's Press, 1998.

Westlake, M. *A Modern Guide to the European Parliament.* Pinter Publishers, 1994.

The Contributors

Lionel Barber has worked for the *Financial Times* since 1985, serving as Washington correspondent and chief European correspondent in Brussels and currently as news editor in London. He has lectured widely in the United States and Europe on transatlantic relations and on monetary union.

Bruce Barnard was the *Journal of Commerce*'s Brussels-based correspondent from 1987 to 1997, covering the European Commission and the European Parliament as well as business across Europe. He is currently a freelance journalist in London and is a regular contributor to *EUROPE Magazine* and *European Voice*. He cowrote "1992 and Beyond," a study of the European Union's single market.

Mike Burns worked on local and national newspapers in Ireland and Britain before joining Radio Telefís Éireann (RTÉ), the Irish national broadcasting service, as a news reporter and, subsequently, foreign correspondent covering Europe, the Middle East, India, North Africa, and North America. He later headed RTÉ's radio news division before becoming its London editor. He now runs a small media information company that operates in Ireland and Britain.

Reginald Dale is a syndicated columnist for the *International Herald Tribune* (IHT) and lives in Washington DC. He was previously the IHT's economic and financial editor in Paris. Before joining the IHT, he was a senior editor and foreign correspondent for the London

Financial Times, where his posts included bureau chief in Brussels and U.S. editor in Washington, and a visiting fellow at Harvard University.

Leif Beck Fallesen has been the editor-in-chief of *Borsen,* Denmark's business daily, since 1990, and chief executive officer of Greens, a public and business polling institute, since 1987. He lectured on international economics and finance in the DIS Program at the University of Copenhagen from 1983 to 1995 and was an economics correspondent for Radio Denmark in 1978.

Robert J. Guttman has been editor-in-chief of *EUROPE Magazine* since 1989. For *EUROPE,* the magazine of the European Union, Guttman regularly conducts interviews with leading political and business leaders in Europe. He has been an adjunct professor at American University and George Washington University in Washington, D.C. Guttman, who writes and lectures regularly on the euro and European affairs, helped establish the Russian edition of *EUROPE Magazine* in Moscow.

Stephen Jewkes worked at the Center for the History of Universities at the University of Bologna before becoming a consultant for Nomisma, Italy's Bologna-based economic think tank founded by European Commission president Romano Prodi. Since 1998 Jewkes has been working as a reporter for Dow Jones and Bridge News in Milan, reporting on Italy's financial markets.

Carola Kaps has been the Washington correspondent for the German daily newspaper *Frankfurter Allgemeine* for more than a decade.

Axel Krause, formerly corporate editor of and economics correspondent for the *International Herald Tribune* and bureau chief for *Business Week,* has served in Paris, Washington, and Moscow. He is the author of *Inside the New Europe* and for more than twenty years has been a regular contributor to *EUROPE Magazine.* From his Paris base, he contributes regularly to TV5, France's international television network, and is secretary-general of the Anglo-American Press Association. He is an adjunct professor at the Institute for Political Studies in Paris.

Susan Ladika is *EUROPE Magazine*'s Vienna contributor. She has lived in Austria since 1995 and has written about a wide range of political, economic, and social issues related to central and eastern Europe, and the Balkans. She works part-time for the Associated Press, and her freelance work has appeared in such publications as the *Wall Street*

Journal–Europe, U.S. News & World Report, The Economist, TWA Ambassador, the *Chicago Tribune,* and the *San Francisco Chronicle.*

David Lennon was based in the Middle East for fifteen years, reporting all the key developments in the region. More recently, he worked as a senior executive journalist with the *Financial Times* in London. The Dublin-born writer has actively covered European affairs for many years and has been a contributing editor for *EUROPE Magazine* for more than a decade.

Alan Osborn, Luxembourg editor and writer on the European Parliament and EU affairs for *EUROPE Magazine,* is a freelance journalist based in England. He worked for five years as a political correspondent in London for the *Daily Telegraph* until 1994 and before that spent sixteen years in Brussels as the *Telegraph*'s European Community correspondent. He has also worked for the World Bank and Reuters in Washington, D.C.

Christopher Patten is the European Commissioner for External Relations. From 1992–1997 he served as the last British governor of Hong Kong and from 1998–1999 he was chairman of the Independent Commission on Policing for Northern Ireland. A former member of Parliament in the United Kingdom, Patten also served for the British government in the late 1980s as Minister for Overseas Development and Secretary of State for the Environment. He is the author of *East and West: China, Power, and the Future of Asia.*

Solange Villes was an editor of European Report, a Brussels-based news agency, and also wrote for French newspapers such as *Le Monde* and *La Tribune.* Villes is currently working for *FRANCE Magazine* at the French Embassy in Washington, D.C.

Martin Walker formerly worked for the *Guardian,* serving as bureau chief in Moscow and Washington and as European editor in Brussels. A senior fellow for the World Policy Institute in New York, he is also a contributing editor to the *Los Angeles Times, EUROPE Magazine,* and the Internet op-ed service, Intellectualcapital.com. His books include *The Waking Giant: Gorbachev and Perestroika* (1986); *The Cold War: A History* (1993); *The President We Deserve: Bill Clinton's Rise, Fall, and Comebacks* (1996); and *America Reborn* (2000). A regular broadcaster and commentator for CNN, the BBC, and NPR, Walker is currently a public policy fellow of the Woodrow Wilson Institute in Washington, D.C.

Index

About the Book

Europe in the New Century is an intriguing look at the future, drawing on the experience and foresight of the leading journalists working in Europe today, as well as the visions of heads of state, government ministers, CEOs, entrepreneurs, and young people from each of the fifteen European Union member countries.

The contributors forecast what Europe might look like down the not-too-distant road. Their subjects range from domestic politics to foreign policy and from technology to international trade, with absorbing stops along the way. Entertaining and informative, *Europe in the New Century* is a must for anyone seeking insight into the trajectory of this new global superpower.

Robert J. Guttman is editor in chief of *EUROPE Magazine* and head of publications for the European Commission office in Washington, D.C. He has been an adjunct professor of political communications at George Washington University and of U.S. politics and communications at American University.